D0594481

Merriam-Webster's easy learning Spanish Verbs

Merriam-Webster, Incorporated
Springfield, Massachusetts, USA

DEVELOPED IN ASSOCIATION WITH Collins

HarperCollins Publishers
Westerhill Road
Bishopbriggs
Glasgow
G64 2QT
Great Britain

First Edition 2011

Reprint 10 9 8 7 6 5 4 3 2 1 0

© HarperCollins Publishers 2011

ISBN 978-0-87779-565-0

Collins® is a registered trademark of HarperCollins Publishers Limited

www.collinslanguage.com

Typeset by Davidson Pre-Press, Glasgow, UK

Printed in the USA by RR Donnelley

Acknowledgements
We would like to thank those authors and publishers who kindly gave permission for copyright material to be used in the Collins Word Web. We would also like to thank Times Newspapers Ltd for providing valuable data.

All rights reserved. No part of this publication may be reproduced, stored in a retrieval system or transmitted, in any form or by any means, electronic, mechanical, photocopying, recording or otherwise, without the prior permission of the publisher. This book is sold subject to the conditions that it shall not, by way of trade or otherwise, be lent, re-sold, hired out or otherwise circulated without the publisher's prior consent in any form of binding or cover other than that in which it is published and without a similar condition including this condition being imposed on the subsequent purchaser.

Entered words that we have reason to believe constitute trademarks have been designated as such. However, neither the presence nor absence of such designation should be regarded as affecting the legal status of any trademark.

SERIES EDITOR
Rob Scriven

MANAGING EDITOR
Gaëlle Amiot-Cadey

EDITORIAL COORDINATION
Susanne Reichert
Rachel Smith

CONTRIBUTORS
Cordelia Lilly
Victoria Romero Cerro
José María Luiz Vaca
Fernando León Solís
Jeremy Butterfield

Contents

Introduction **5**

Glossary of Verb Grammar Terms **6**

Introduction to Verb Formation **10**

The present simple tense 12

The present continuous tense 18

The imperative 19

Reflexive verbs 24

The future tense 26

The conditional 29

The preterite 32

The imperfect tense 37

The perfect tense 40

The pluperfect or past perfect tense 43

The passive 46

The gerund 48

The subjunctive 49

Accents 54

Verb Combinations **56**

Verbs followed by the preposition a and the infinitive 59

Verbs followed by the preposition de and the infinitive 61

Verbs followed by the preposition con and the infinitive 62

Verbs followed by the preposition en and the infinitive 62

Verbs followed by **a** and an object 63

Verbs followed by **de** and an object 65

Verbs followed by **con** and an object 67

Verbs followed by **en** and an object 68

Verbs followed by **por** and an object 69

Verbs taking a direct object in Spanish but not in English 70

Verbs followed by personal **a** 71

Verb Tables 1-241

Verb Index 242

Introduction

Merriam-Webster's Easy Learning Spanish Verbs is designed for both young and adult learners. Whether you are learning Spanish for the very first time, brushing up your language skills, or studying for exams, this book is here to help.

Because newcomers can sometimes struggle with the technical terms they come across when they start to explore the grammar of a new language, this book contains a glossary which explains verb grammar terms using simple language and cutting out jargon.

The text is divided into sections to help you become confident in using and understanding Spanish verbs. The first section looks at verb formation. Written in clear language, with numerous examples in real Spanish, this section helps you to understand the rules which are used to form verb tenses.

The next section of text looks at certain common prepositions which are used with a number of verbs. Each combination of verb plus preposition is shown with a simple example of real Spanish to show exactly how it is used.

The **Verb Tables** contain 120 important Spanish verbs (both regular and irregular), which are given in full for various tenses. Examples show how to use these verbs in your own work. If you are unsure how a verb functions in Spanish, you can look up the Verb Index at the back of the book to find either the conjugation of the verb itself or a cross-reference to a model verb, which will show you the patterns that the verb follows.

Glossary of Verb Grammar Terms

ACTIVE a form of the verb that is used when the subject of the verb is the person or thing doing the action, for example, *I wrote a letter*. Compare with **passive**.

AFFIRMATIVE an affirmative sentence or instruction is one that does not contain a negative word such as *not*. Compare with **negative**.

AGREE (with) in the case of verbs, to have the form which goes with the person or thing carrying out the action.

AUXILIARY VERB a verb such as *be*, *have* or *do* used with a main verb to form tenses.

BASE FORM the form of the verb without any endings added to it, for example, *walk, have, be, go*.

CLAUSE a group of words containing a verb.

CONDITIONAL a verb form used to talk about things that *would* happen or *would* be true under certain conditions, for example, *I would help you if I could*. It is also used to say what you *would* like or need, for example, *Could you give me the bill?*

CONJUGATE to give a verb different endings according to whether you are referring to *I, you, they* and so on, and according to whether you are referring to the present, past or future, for example, *I have, she had, they will have*.

CONJUGATION a group of verbs which have the same endings as each other or change according to the same pattern.

CONTINUOUS TENSE a verb tense formed using *to be* and the *-ing* form of the main verb, for example, *They're swimming* (present continuous); *He was eating* (past continuous).

DIRECT OBJECT a noun or pronoun used with verbs to show who or what is acted on by the verb. For example, in *He wrote a letter* and *He wrote me a letter*, *letter* is the direct object. Compare **indirect object**.

DIRECT OBJECT PRONOUN a word such as *me, him, us* and *them* which is used instead of a noun to stand in for the person or thing most directly affected by the action expressed by the verb. Compare with **indirect object pronoun**.

ENDING a form added to something such as a verb, for example, *go* > *goes*.

FUTURE a verb tense used to talk about something that *will* happen or *will* be true.

GERUND a verb form in English ending in *-ing*, for example, *eating, sleeping*.

IMPERATIVE the form of a verb used when giving orders and instructions, for example, *Shut the door!; Sit down!; Don't go!; Let's eat*.

IMPERFECT one of the verb tenses used to talk about the past in Spanish, especially in descriptions, and to say what *was happening* or *used to happen*, for example, *It was sunny during the weekend; We were living in Spain at the time; I used to walk to school*. Compare with preterite.

IMPERSONAL VERB a verb whose subject is *it*, but where the *it* does not refer to any specific thing, for example, *It's raining; It's 10 o'clock*.

INDICATIVE ordinary verb forms that aren't subjunctive, such as the present, preterite or future. Compare with subjunctive.

INDIRECT OBJECT a noun or pronoun used with verbs to show who benefits or is harmed by an action. For example, in *I gave the carrot to the rabbit*, *the rabbit* is the indirect object and *the carrot* is the direct object. Compare with direct object.

INDIRECT OBJECT PRONOUN a pronoun used with verbs to show who benefits or is harmed by an action. For example, in *I gave him the carrot* and *I gave it to him*, *him* is the indirect object pronoun and the *carrot* and *it* are the direct objects. Compare with direct object pronoun.

INDIRECT SPEECH the words you use to report what someone has said when you aren't using their actual words, for example, *He said that he was going out*. Also called reported speech.

INFINITIVE a form of the verb that hasn't any endings added to it and doesn't relate to any particular tense. In English the infinitive is usually shown with *to*, as in *to speak, to eat*.

INTRANSITIVE VERB a type of verb that does not take a direct object, for example, *to sleep, to rise, to laugh*. Compare with transitive verb.

IRREGULAR VERB a verb whose forms do not follow a general pattern. Compare with regular verb.

NEGATIVE a question or statement which contains a word such as *not, never* or *nothing*, and is used to say that something is not happening, is not true or is absent, for example, *I never eat meat; Don't you love me?* Compare with positive.

OBJECT a noun or pronoun which refers to a person or thing that is affected by the action described by the verb. Compare with direct object, indirect object and subject.

OBJECT PRONOUN one of the set of pronouns including *me, him* and *them*, which are used instead of the noun as the object of a verb or preposition. Compare with subject pronoun.

PASSIVE a form of the verb that is used when the subject of the verb is the person or thing that is affected by the action, for example, *We were told* or *It was sold*.

PAST PARTICIPLE a verb form which is used to form perfect and pluperfect tenses and passives, for example, *watched, swum*. Some past participles are also used as adjectives, for example, *a broken watch*.

PAST PERFECT see pluperfect.

PERFECT a verb form used to talk about what *has* or *hasn't* happened, for example, *I've broken my glasses; We haven't eaten yet*.

PERSON one of three classes: the first person (*I, we*), the second person (*you* singular and *you* plural), and the third person (*he, she, it* and *they*).

PERSONAL PRONOUN one of the group of words including *I, you* and *they* which are used to refer to you, the people you are talking to, or the people or things you are talking about.

PLUPERFECT one of the verb tenses used to describe something that *had* happened or *had* been true at a point in the past, for example, *I'd forgotten to finish my homework*. Also called past perfect.

PLURAL the form of a word which is used to refer to more than one person or thing. Compare with singular.

POSITIVE a positive sentence or instruction is one that does not contain a negative word such as *not*. Compare with negative.

PREPOSITION is a word such as *at, for, with, into* or *from*, which is usually followed by a noun, pronoun or, in English, a word ending in *-ing*. Prepositions show how people and things relate to the rest of the sentence, for example, *She's at home; a tool for cutting grass; It's from David*.

PRESENT a verb form used to talk about what is true at the moment, what happens regularly, and what is happening now, for example, *I'm a student; I travel to college by train; I'm studying Language*.

PRESENT CONTINUOUS see continuous tense.

PRESENT PARTICIPLE a verb form in English ending in *-ing*, for example, *eating, sleeping*.

PRESENT SIMPLE see simple tense.

PRETERITE a verb form used to talk about actions that were completedin the past in Spanish. It often corresponds to the ordinary past tense in English, for example, *I bought a new bike; Mary went to the store; I typed two reports yesterday*.

PRONOUN a word which you use instead of a noun, when you do not need or want to name someone or something directly, for example, *it, you, none*.

PROPER NOUN the name of a person, place, organization or thing. Proper nouns are always written with a capital letter, for example, *Kevin, Boston, Europe*.

RADICAL-CHANGING VERBS in Spanish, verbs which change their stem or root in certain tenses and in certain persons.

REFLEXIVE PRONOUN a word ending in *-self* or *-selves*, such as *myself* or *themselves*, which refers back to the subject, for example, *He hurt himself; Take care of yourself*.

REFLEXIVE VERB a verb where the subject and object are the same, and where the action "reflects back" on the subject. A reflexive verb is used with a reflexive pronoun such as *myself, yourself, herself*, for example, *I washed myself; He shaved himself*.

REGULAR VERB a verb whose forms follow a general pattern or the normal rules. Compare with irregular verb.

SIMPLE TENSE a verb tense in which the verb form is made up of one word, rather than being formed from *to have* and a past participle or *to be* and an *-ing* form; for example, *She plays tennis; He wrote a book*.

SINGULAR the form of a word which is used to refer to one person or thing. Compare with plural.

STEM the main part of a verb to which endings are added.

SUBJECT a noun or pronoun that refers to the person or thing doing the action or being in the state described by the verb, for example, *My cat doesn't drink milk*. Compare with object.

SUBJECT PRONOUN a word such as *I, he, she* and *they* which carries out the action described by the verb. Pronouns stand in for nouns when it is clear who is being talked about, for example, *My brother isn't here at the moment. He'll be back in an hour*. Compare with object pronoun.

SUBJUNCTIVE a verb form used in certain circumstances to indicate some sort of feeling, or to show doubt about whether something will happen or whether something is true. It is only used occasionally in modern English, for example, *If I were you, I wouldn't bother; So be it*.

TENSE the form of a verb which shows whether you are referring to the past, present or future.

TRANSITIVE VERB a type of verb that takes a direct object, for example, *to spend, to raise, to waste*. Compare with intransitive verb.

VERB a "doing" word which describes what someone or something does, is, or what happens to them, for example, *be, sing, live*.

Introduction to Verb Formation

Verbs are frequently used with a noun, with somebody's name or, particularly in English, with a pronoun such as *I*, *you* or *she*. They can relate to the present, the past and the future; this is called their tense.

Verbs are either:

regular; their forms follow the normal rules
irregular; their forms do not follow the normal rules

Almost all verbs have a form called the infinitive. This is a base form of the verb (for example, *walk*, *see*, *hear*) that hasn't had any endings added to it and doesn't relate to any particular tense.

In English, the infinitive is usually shown with *to*, as in *to speak*, *to eat*, *to live*. In Spanish, the infinitive is always made up of just one word (never two as in *to speak* in English) and ends in -ar, -er or -ir: for example, hablar (meaning *to speak*), comer (meaning *to eat*) and vivir (meaning *to live*). All Spanish verbs belong to one of these three types, which are called conjugations. We will look at each of these three conjugations in turn in the next few pages.

Regular English verbs have other forms besides the infinitive: a form ending in *-s* (*walks*), a form ending in *-ing* (*walking*), and a form ending in *-ed* (*walked*). Spanish verbs have many more forms than this, which are made up of endings added to a stem. The stem of a verb can usually be worked out from the infinitive.

Spanish verb endings change depending on who or what is doing the action and on when the action takes place. In fact, the ending is very often the only thing that shows you who is doing the action, as the Spanish equivalents of *I*, *you*, *he* and so on (yo, tú, él and so on) are not used very much. So, both hablo on its own and yo hablo mean *I speak*. Sometimes there is a name or a noun in the sentence to make it clear who is doing the action.

For further explanation of grammatical terms, please see pages 6-9.

José **habla español.** José speaks Spanish.
El profesor **habla español.** The teacher speaks Spanish.

Spanish verb forms also change depending on whether you are talking about the present, past or future, so **(yo) hablaré** means *I will speak* while **(yo) hablé** means *I spoke*.

Some verbs in Spanish do not follow the usual patterns. These irregular verbs include some very common and important verbs like **ir** (meaning *to go*), **ser** and **estar** (meaning *to be*) and **hacer** (meaning *to do* or *to make*). Other verbs are only slightly irregular, changing their stems in certain tenses.

The following sections give you all the help you need on how to form the different verb tenses used in Spanish.

The present simple tense

Forming the present simple tense of regular -ar verbs

If the infinitive of the Spanish verb ends in -ar, it means that the verb belongs to the first conjugation, for example, hablar, lavar, llamar.

To know which form of the verb to use in Spanish, you need to figure out what the stem of the verb is and then add the correct ending. The stem of regular -ar verbs in the present simple tense is formed by taking the infinitive and chopping off -ar.

Infinitive	Stem (without -ar)
hablar (*to speak*)	habl-
lavar (*to wash*)	lav-

Now you know how to find the stem of a verb, you can add the correct ending. The one you choose will depend on who or what is doing the action.

Here are the present simple endings for regular -ar verbs:

Present simple endings	Present simple of hablar	Meaning: *to speak*
-o	(yo) hablo	I speak
-as	(tú) hablas	you speak
-a	(él/ella) habla	he/she/it speaks
	(usted) habla	you speak
-amos	(nosotros/nosotras) hablamos	we speak
-áis	(vosotros/vosotras) habláis	you speak
-an	(ellos/ellas) hablan	they speak
	(ustedes) hablan	you speak

For further explanation of grammatical terms, please see pages 6-9.

Trabajo en un banco. I work in a bank.
No hablo alemán. I don't speak German.
¿Buscas algo? Are you looking for something?
Compra pan todos los días. He/She buys bread every day.
Lydia estudia medicina. Lydia studies *or* is studying medicine.
Funciona bien. It works well.
Viajamos mucho. We travel a lot.
¿Recuerdan aquella noche? Do you remember that night?
Ustedes fabrican ventanas, ¿no? You make windows, don't you?
Mis profesores me ayudan mucho. My teachers help me a lot.

Forming the present simple tense of regular -er verbs

If the infinitive of the Spanish verb ends in -er, it means that the verb belongs to the second conjugation, for example, comer, depender.

The stem of regular -er verbs in the present simple tense is formed by taking the infinitive and chopping off -er.

Infinitive	Stem (without -er)
comer (*to eat*)	com-
depender (*to depend*)	depend-

Now add the correct ending, depending on who or what is doing the action.

Here are the present simple endings for regular -er verbs:

Present simple endings	Present simple of comer	Meaning: *to eat*
-o	(yo) como	I eat
-es	(tú) comes	you eat
-e	(él/ella) come	he/she/it eats
	(usted) come	you eat
-emos	(nosotros/nosotras) comemos	we eat
-éis	(vosotros/vosotras) coméis	you eat
-en	(ellos/ellas) comen	they eat
	(ustedes) comen	you eat

Juan come demasiado. Juan eats too much.
Mis padres me deben 50 pesos. My parents owe me 50 pesos.
Depende. It depends.

For further explanation of grammatical terms, please see pages 6-9.

Forming the present simple tense of regular -ir verbs

If the infinitive of the Spanish verb ends in -ir, it means that the verb belongs to the third conjugation, for example, **vivir**, **recibir**.

The stem of regular -ir verbs in the present simple tense is formed by taking the infinitive and chopping off -ir.

Infinitive	Stem (without -ir)
vivir (*to live*)	viv-
recibir (*to receive*)	recib-

Now add the correct ending, depending on who or what is doing the action.

Here are the present simple endings for regular -ir verbs:

Present simple endings	Present simple of vivir	Meaning: *to live*
-o	(yo) vivo	I live
-es	(tú) vives	you live
-e	(él/ella) vive	he/she/it lives
	(usted) vive	you live
-imos	(nosotros/nosotras) vivimos	we live
-ís	(vosotros/vosotras) vivís	you live
-en	(ellos/ellas) viven	they live
	(ustedes) viven	you live

Mi padre recibe muchas cartas. My father gets a lot of letters.
Javier y Antonia viven aquí. Javier and Antonia live here.
Ocurre frecuentemente. It happens frequently.

Forming the present simple tense of less regular verbs

Many Spanish verbs do not follow the regular patterns shown above. There are lots of verbs that change their stem in the present tense when the stress is on the stem. This means that all forms are affected in the present simple EXCEPT FOR the nosotros and vosotros forms. Such verbs are often called radical-changing verbs, meaning root-changing verbs.

For example, some verbs containing an -o in the stem change it to -ue in the present simple for all forms EXCEPT FOR the nosotros/nosotras and vosotros/vosotras forms.

	encontrar *to find*	**recordar** *to remember*	**poder** *to be able*	**dormir** *to sleep*
(yo)	encuentro	recuerdo	puedo	duermo
(tú)	encuentras	recuerdas	puedes	duermes
(él/ella/usted)	encuentra	recuerda	puede	duerme
(nosotros/as)	encontramos	recordamos	podemos	dormimos
(vosotros/as)	encontráis	recordáis	podéis	dormís
(ellos/ellas/ustedes)	encuentran	recuerdan	pueden	duermen

Other verbs containing an -e in the stem change it to -ie for all forms EXCEPT FOR the nosotros/nosotras and vosotros/vosotras forms.

	cerrar *to close*	**pensar** *to think*	**entender** *to understand*	**perder** *to lose*	**preferir** *to prefer*
(yo)	cierro	pienso	entiendo	pierdo	prefiero
(tú)	cierras	piensas	entiendes	pierdes	prefieres
(él/ella/usted)	cierra	piensa	entiende	pierde	prefiere
(nosotros/as)	cerramos	pensamos	entendemos	perdemos	preferimos
(vosotros/as)	cerráis	pensáis	entendéis	perdéis	preferís
(ellos/ellas/ustedes)	cierran	piensan	entienden	pierden	prefieren

For further explanation of grammatical terms, please see pages 6-9.

A few -ir verbs containing -e in the stem change this to -i in the present simple for all forms APART FROM the nosotros/nosotras and vosotros/ vosotras forms.

	pedir	**servir**
	to ask (for)	***to serve***
(yo)	pido	sirvo
(tú)	pides	sirves
(él/ella/usted)	pide	sirve
(nosotros/as)	pedimos	servimos
(vosotros/as)	pedís	servís
(ellos/ellas/ustedes)	piden	sirven

The present continuous tense

The Spanish present continuous tense is formed from the present tense of estar and the gerund of the verb. The gerund is the form of the verb that ends in -ando (for -ar verbs) or -iendo (for -er and -ir verbs) and is the same as the *-ing* form of the verb in English (for example, *walking*, *swimming*).

Estoy trabajando. I'm working.
No estamos comiendo. We aren't eating.
¿Estás escribiendo? Are you writing?

To form the gerund of an -ar verb, take off the -ar ending of the infinitive and add -ando:

Infinitive	Meaning	Stem (without -ar)	Gerund	Meaning
hablar	to speak	habl-	hablando	speaking
trabajar	to work	trabaj-	trabajando	working

Levanta al niño, que está llorando. Pick the baby up; he's crying.
Está intentando perder peso. He's trying to lose weight.

To form the gerund of an -er or -ir verb, take off the -er or -ir ending of the infinitive and add -iendo:

Infinitive	Meaning	Stem (without -er/-ir)	Gerund	Meaning
comer	to eat	com-	comiendo	eating
escribir	to write	escrib-	escribiendo	writing

Estoy haciendo la tarea. I'm doing my homework.
¿Qué está ocurriendo? What's happening?

For further explanation of grammatical terms, please see pages 6-9.

The imperative

Forming the imperative: Instructions not to do something

In orders that tell you NOT to do something and that have no in front of them in Spanish, the imperative forms for tú, usted, nosotros/nosotras, vosotros/vosotras and ustedes are all taken from a verb form called the present subjunctive. It's easy to remember because the endings for -ar and -er verbs are the opposite of what they are in the ordinary present tense. Note that the imperative form for vosotros/vosotras is not used in Latin America.

In regular -ar verbs, you take off the -as, -a, -amos, -áis and -an endings of the present tense and replace them with: -es, -e, -emos, -éis and -en.

-ar verb	**trabajar**	***to work***
tú form	¡no trabajes!	Don't work!
usted form	¡no trabaje!	Don't work!
nosotros/as form	¡no trabajemos!	Let's not work!
vosotros/as form	¡no trabajéis!	Don't work!
ustedes form	¡no trabajen!	Don't work!

In regular -er verbs, you take off the -es, -e, -emos, -éis and -en endings of the present tense and replace them with -as, -a, -amos, -áis and -an.

-er verb	**comer**	***to eat***
tú form	¡no comas!	Don't eat!
usted form	¡no coma!	Don't eat!
nosotros/as form	¡no comamos!	Let's not eat!
vosotros/as form	¡no comáis!	Don't eat!
ustedes form	¡no coman!	Don't eat!

In regular -ir verbs, you take off the -es, -e, -imos, -ís and -en endings of the present tense and replace them with -as, -a, -amos, -áis and -an.

-ir verb	decidir	*to decide*
tú form	¡no decidas!	Don't decide!
usted form	¡no decida!	Don't decide!
nosotros/as form	¡no decidamos!	Let's not decide!
vosotros/as form	¡no decidáis!	Don't decide!
ustedes form	¡no decidan!	Don't decide!

A number of irregular verbs also have irregular imperative forms. These are shown in the table below.

	dar *to give*	decir *to say*	estar *to be*	hacer *to do/make*	ir *to go*
tú form	¡no des! don't give!	¡no digas! don't say!	¡no estés! don't be!	¡no hagas! don't do/make!	¡no vayas! don't go!
usted form	¡no dé! don't give!	¡no diga! don't say!	¡no esté! don't be!	¡no haga! don't do/make!	¡no vaya! don't go!
nosotros form	¡no demos! let's not give!	¡no digamos! let's not say!	¡no estemos! let's not be!	¡no hagamos! let's not do/make!	¡no vayamos! let's not go!
vosotros form	¡no deis! don't give!	¡no digáis! don't say!	¡no estéis! don't be!	¡no hagáis! don't do/make!	¡no vayáis! don't go!
ustedes form	¡no den! don't give!	¡no digan! don't say!	¡no estén! don't be!	¡no hagan! don't do/make!	¡no vayan! don't go!
	poner *to put*	**salir** *to leave*	**ser** *to be*	**tener** *to have*	**venir** *to come*
tú form	¡no pongas! don't put!	¡no salgas! don't leave!	¡no seas! don't be!	¡no tengas! don't have!	¡no vengas! don't come!
usted form	¡no ponga! don't put!	¡no salga! don't leave!	¡no sea! don't be!	¡no tenga! don't have!	¡no venga! don't come!
nosotros form	¡no pongamos! let's not put!	¡no salgamos! let's not leave!	¡no seamos! let's not be!	¡no tengamos! let's not have!	¡no vengamos! let's not come!
vosotros form	¡no pongáis! don't put!	¡no salgáis! don't leave!	¡no seáis! don't be!	¡no tengáis! don't have!	¡no vengáis! don't come!
ustedes form	¡no pongan! don't put!	¡no salgan! don't leave!	¡no sean! don't be!	¡no tengan! don't have!	¡no vengan! don't come!

For further explanation of grammatical terms, please see pages 6-9.

Note that if you take the yo form of the present tense, take off the -o and add the endings to this instead for instructions NOT TO DO something, some of these irregular forms will be more predictable.

digo	*I say*	>	negative imperative stem	>	dig-
hago	*I do*	>	negative imperative stem	>	hag-
pongo	*I put*	>	negative imperative stem	>	pong-
salgo	*I leave*	>	negative imperative stem	>	salg-
tengo	*I have*	>	negative imperative stem	>	teng-
vengo	*I come*	>	negative imperative stem	>	veng-

Forming the imperative: Instructions to do something

In instructions telling you TO DO something, the forms for usted, nosotros and ustedes are exactly the same as they are in negative instructions (instructions telling you not to do something) except that there isn't a no.

	trabajar ***to work***	**comer** ***to eat***	**decidir** ***to decide***
usted form	¡Trabaje!	¡Coma!	¡Decida!
nosotros/as form	¡Trabajemos!	¡Comamos!	¡Decidamos!
ustedes form	¡Trabajen!	¡Coman!	¡Decidan!

There are special forms of the imperative for tú and vosotros/vosotras in positive instructions (instructions telling you to do something). The tú form of the imperative is the same as the tú form of the ordinary present simple tense, but without the final -s.

trabajar	>	¡Trabaja!
to work		Work!
comer	>	¡Come!
to eat		Eat!
decidir	>	¡Decide!
to decide		Decide!

The vosotros/vosotras form of the imperative is the same as the infinitive, except that you take off the final -r and add -d instead.

trabajar	>	Trabajad!
to work		Work!
comer	>	Comed!
to eat		Eat!
decidir	>	Decidid!
to decide		Decide!

There are a number of imperative forms that are irregular in Spanish. The irregular imperative forms for **usted**, **nosotros/nosotras** and **ustedes** are the same as the irregular negative imperative forms without the **no**. The **tú** and vosotros/vosotras forms are different again.

	dar *to give*	**decir** *to say*	**estar** *to be*	**hacer** *to do/make*	**ir** *to go*
tú form	¡da! give!	¡di! say!	¡está! be!	¡haz! do/make!	¡ve! go!
usted form	¡dé! give!	¡diga! say!	¡esté! be!	¡haga! do/make!	¡vaya! go!
nosotros/as form	¡demos! let's give!	¡digamos! let's say!	¡estemos! let's be!	¡hagamos! let's do/make!	¡vamos! let's go!
vosotros/as form	¡dad! give!	¡decid! say!	¡estad! be!	¡haced! do/make!	¡id! go!
ustedes form	¡den! give!	¡digan! say!	¡estén! be!	¡hagan! do/make!	¡vayan! go!
	poner *to put*	**salir** *to leave*	**ser** *to be*	**tener** *to have*	**venir** *to come*
tú form	¡pon! put!	¡sal! leave!	¡sé! be!	¡ten! have!	¡ven! come!
usted form	¡ponga! put!	¡salga! leave!	¡sea! be!	¡tenga! have!	¡venga! come!
nosotros/as form	¡pongamos! let's put!	¡salgamos! let's leave!	¡seamos! let's be!	¡tengamos! let's have!	¡vengamos! let's come!
vosotros/as form	¡poned! put!	¡salid! leave!	¡sed! be!	¡tened! have!	¡venid! come!
ustedes form	¡pongan! put!	¡salgan! leave!	¡sean! be!	¡tengan! have!	¡vengan! come!

For further explanation of grammatical terms, please see pages 6-9.

Note that the nosotros/nosotras form for ir in instructions TO DO something is usually vamos; in instructions NOT TO DO something, it is no vayamos.

Position of object pronouns

If you are telling someone NOT TO DO something, any object pronouns go BEFORE the verb.

¡No me lo mandes! Don't send it to me!
¡No me molestes! Don't disturb me!
¡No los castigue! Don't punish them!
¡No se la devolvamos! Let's not give it back to him/her/them!
¡No las contesten! Don't answer them!

If you are telling someone TO DO something, any object pronouns are attached to the END of the verb. An accent is usually added to make sure that the stress in the imperative verb stays the same.

¡Explícamelo! Explain it to me!
¡Perdóneme! Excuse me!
¡Dígame! Tell me!
¡Esperémosla! Let's wait for her/it!

Reflexive verbs

Forming the present tense of reflexive verbs

The present tense of a reflexive verb is formed in the same way as that of a non-reflexive verb, except that reflexive pronouns are included before the verb.

The following table shows the reflexive verb lavarse in full.

Reflexive forms of lavarse	Meaning
(yo) me lavo	I wash (myself)
(tú) te lavas	you wash (yourself)
(él) se lava	he washes (himself)
(ella) se lava	she washes (herself)
(uno) se lava	one washes (oneself)
se lava	it washes (itself)
(usted) se lava	you wash (yourself)
(nosotros/nosotras) nos lavamos	we wash (ourselves)
(vosotros/vosotras) os laváis	you wash (yourselves)
(ellos) se lavan	they wash (themselves)
(ellas) se lavan	they wash (themselves)
(ustedes) se lavan	you wash (yourselves)

Position of reflexive pronouns

In ordinary tenses such as the present simple, the reflexive pronoun goes BEFORE the verb.

Me acuesto temprano. I go to bed early.
¿Cómo se llama usted? What's your name?

When telling someone NOT TO DO something, you also put the reflexive pronoun BEFORE the verb.

For further explanation of grammatical terms, please see pages 6-9.

No te levantes. Don't get up.
¡No se vayan! Don't go away!

When telling someone TO DO something, you attach the reflexive pronoun to the end of the verb.

¡Siéntense! Sit down!
¡Cállate! Be quiet!

When adding reflexive pronouns to the end of the imperative, you drop the final -s of the nosotros form and the final -d of the vosotros form before the pronoun.

¡Vámonos! Let's go!
¡Sentaos! Sit down!

You always attach the reflexive pronoun to the end of infinitives and gerunds (the -ando or -iendo forms of the verb), unless the infinitive or gerund follows another verb.

Hay que relajarse de vez en cuando. You have to relax from time to time.
Acostándose temprano, se descansa mejor.
You feel more rested if you go to bed early.

Where the infinitive or gerund follows another verb, you can put the reflexive pronoun either at the end of the infinitive or gerund or before the other verb.

Quiero bañarme *or* Me quiero bañar. I want to have a bath.
Tienes que vestirte *or* Te tienes que vestir. You must get dressed.
Está vistiéndose *or* Se está vistiendo. She's getting dressed.
¿Estás duchándote? *or* ¿Te estás duchando? Are you having a shower?

Note that, when adding pronouns to the ends of verb forms, you will often have to add a written accent to preserve the stress.

The future tense

Forming the future tense

To form the future tense of regular -ar, -er and -ir verbs, add the following endings to the infinitive of the verb: -é, -ás, -á, -emos, -éis, -án.

The following table shows the future tense of three regular verbs: hablar (meaning *to speak*), comer (meaning *to eat*) and vivir (meaning *to live*).

(yo)	hablaré	comeré	viviré	I'll speak/eat/live
(tú)	hablarás	comerás	vivirás	you'll speak/eat/live
(él, ella) (usted)	hablará	comerá	vivirá	he'll speak/eat/live she'll speak/eat/live it'll speak/eat/live you'll speak/eat/live
(nosotros/nosotras)	hablaremos	comeremos	viviremos	we'll speak/eat/live
(vosotros/vosotras)	hablaréis	comeréis	viviréis	you'll speak/eat/live
(ellos/ellas/ustedes)	hablarán	comerán	vivirán	they'll/you'll speak/eat/live

Hablaré con ella. I'll speak to her.
Comeremos en casa de José. We'll eat at José's.
No volverá. He won't come back.
¿Lo entenderás? Will you understand it?

Note that in the future tense only the nosotros/nosotras form doesn't have an accent.

For further explanation of grammatical terms, please see pages 6-9.

Verbs with irregular stems in the future tense

There are a few verbs that DO NOT use their infinitives as the stem for the future tense. Here are some of the most common.

Verb	Stem	(yo)	(tú)	(él) (ella) (usted)	(nosotros) (nosotras)	(vosotros) (vosotras)	(ellos) (ellas) (ustedes)
decir *to say*	dir-	diré	dirás	dirá	diremos	diréis	dirán
haber *to have*	habr-	habré	habrás	habrá	habremos	habréis	habrán
hacer *to do/make*	har-	haré	harás	hará	haremos	haréis	harán
poder *to be able*	podr-	podré	podrás	podrá	podremos	podréis	podrán
poner *to put*	pondr-	pondré	pondrás	pondrá	pondremos	pondréis	pondrán
querer *to want*	querr-	querré	querrás	querrá	querremos	querréis	querrán
saber *to know*	sabr-	sabré	sabrás	sabrá	sabremos	sabréis	sabrán
salir *to leave*	saldr-	saldré	saldrás	saldrá	saldremos	saldréis	saldrán
tener *to have*	tendr-	tendré	tendrás	tendrá	tendremos	tendréis	tendrán
venir *to come*	vendr-	vendré	vendrás	vendrá	vendremos	vendréis	vendrán

Lo haré mañana. I'll do it tomorrow.
No podremos hacerlo. We won't be able to do it.
Lo pondré aquí. I'll put it here.
Saldrán por la mañana. They'll leave in the morning.
¿A qué hora vendrás? What time will you come?

Reflexive verbs in the future tense

The future tense of reflexive verbs is formed in exactly the same way as for ordinary verbs, except that you have to remember to give the reflexive pronoun (me, te, se, nos, os, se).

Me levantaré temprano. I'll get up early.

For further explanation of grammatical terms, please see pages 6-9.

The conditional

Forming the conditional

To form the conditional of regular -ar, -er, and -ir verbs, add the following endings to the infinitive of the verb: -ía, -ías, -ía, -íamos, -íais, -ían.

The following table shows the conditional tense of three regular verbs: hablar (meaning *to speak*), comer (meaning *to eat*) and vivir (meaning *to live*).

(yo)	hablaría	comería	viviría	I would speak/eat/live
(tú)	hablarías	comerías	vivirías	you would speak/eat/live
(él, ella) (usted)	hablaría	comería	viviría	he would speak/eat/live she would speak/eat/live it would speak/eat/live you would speak/eat/live
(nosotros/nosotras)	hablaríamos	comeríamos	viviríamos	we would speak/eat/live
(vosotros/vosotras)	hablaríais	comeríais	viviríais	you would speak/eat/live
(ellos/ellas/ustedes)	hablarían	comerían	vivirían	they would/you would speak/eat/live

Me gustaría ir a China. I'd like to go to China.
Dije que hablaría con ella. I said that I would speak to her.
Debería llamar a mis padres. I should call my parents.

Don't forget to put an accent on the í in the conditional.

Note that the endings in the conditional tense are identical to those in the imperfect tense for -er and -ir verbs. The only difference is that they are added to a different stem.

Verbs with irregular stems in the conditional

To form the conditional of irregular verbs, use the same stem as for the future tense, then add the usual endings for the conditional. The same verbs that are irregular in the future tense are irregular in the conditional.

Verb	Stem	(yo)	(tú)	(él) (ella) (usted)	(nosotros) (nosotras)	(vosotros) (vosotras)	(ellos) (ellas) (ustedes)
decir *to say*	dir-	diría	dirías	diría	diríamos	diríais	dirían
haber *to have*	habr-	habría	habrías	habría	habríamos	habríais	habrían
hacer *to do/make*	har-	haría	harías	haría	haríamos	haríais	harían
poder *to be able*	podr-	podría	podrías	podría	podríamos	podríais	podrían
poner *to put*	pondr-	pondría	pondrías	pondría	pondríamos	pondríais	pondrían
querer *to want*	querr-	querría	querrías	querría	querríamos	querríais	querrían
saber *to know*	sabr-	sabría	sabrías	sabría	sabríamos	sabríais	sabrían
salir *to leave*	saldr-	saldría	saldrías	saldría	saldríamos	saldríais	saldrían
tener *to have*	tendr-	tendría	tendrías	tendría	tendríamos	tendríais	tendrían
venir *to come*	vendr-	vendría	vendrías	vendría	vendríamos	vendríais	vendrían

For further explanation of grammatical terms, please see pages 6-9.

¿Qué harías tú en mi lugar? What would you do if you were me?
¿Podrías ayudarme? Could you help me?
Yo lo pondría aquí. I would put it here.

Reflexive verbs in the conditional

The conditional of reflexive verbs is formed in exactly the same way as for ordinary verbs, except that you have to remember to give the reflexive pronoun (me, te, se, nos, os, se).

Le dije que me levantaría temprano. I told him I would get up early.

The preterite

Forming the preterite of regular verbs

To form the preterite of any regular -ar verb, you take off the -ar ending to form the stem, and add the endings: -é, -aste, -ó, -amos, -asteis, -aron.

To form the preterite of any regular -er or -ir verb, you also take off the -er or -ir ending to form the stem and add the endings: -í, -iste, -ió, -imos, -isteis, -ieron.

The following table shows the preterite of three regular verbs: hablar (meaning *to speak*), comer (meaning *to eat*) and vivir (meaning *to live*).

(yo)	hablé	comí	viví	I spoke/ate/lived
(tú)	hablaste	comiste	viviste	you spoke/ate/lived
(él, ella) (usted)	habló	comió	vivió	he spoke/ate/lived she spoke/ate/lived it spoke/ate/lived you spoke/ate/lived
(nosotros/nosotras)	hablamos	comimos	vivimos	we spoke/ate/lived
(vosotros/vosotras)	hablasteis	comisteis	vivisteis	you spoke/ate/lived
(ellos/ellas) (ustedes)	hablaron	comieron	vivieron	they spoke/ate/lived you spoke/ate/lived

Bailé con mi hermana. I danced with my sister.
No hablé con ella. I didn't speak to her.
Comimos demasiado. We ate too much.
¿Cerraste la ventana? Did you close the window?

For further explanation of grammatical terms, please see pages 6-9.

Irregular verbs in the preterite

A number of verbs have very irregular forms in the preterite. The table shows some of the most common.

Verb	(yo)	(tú)	(él) (ella) (usted)	(nosotros) (nosotras)	(vosotros) (vosotras)	(ellos) (ellas) (ustedes)
andar *to walk*	anduve	anduviste	anduvo	anduvimos	anduvisteis	anduvieron
conducir *to drive*	conduje	condujiste	condujo	condujimos	condujisteis	condujeron
dar *to give*	di	diste	dio	dimos	disteis	dieron
decir *to say*	dije	dijiste	dijo	dijimos	dijisteis	dijeron
estar *to be*	estuve	estuviste	estuvo	estuvimos	estuvisteis	estuvieron
hacer *to do, to make*	hice	hiciste	hizo	hicimos	hicisteis	hicieron
ir *to go*	fui	fuiste	fue	fuimos	fuisteis	fueron
poder *to be able*	pude	pudiste	pudo	pudimos	pudisteis	pudieron
poner *to put*	puse	pusiste	puso	pusimos	pusisteis	pusieron
querer *to want*	quise	quisiste	quiso	quisimos	quisisteis	quisieron
saber *to know*	supe	supiste	supo	supimos	supisteis	supieron
ser *to be*	fui	fuiste	fue	fuimos	fuisteis	fueron
tener *to have*	tuve	tuviste	tuvo	tuvimos	tuvisteis	tuvieron
traer *to bring*	traje	trajiste	trajo	trajimos	trajisteis	trajeron
venir *to come*	vine	viniste	vino	vinimos	vinisteis	vinieron
ver *to see*	vi	viste	vio	vimos	visteis	vieron

Note that hizo (the él/ella/usted form of hacer) is spelled with a z.

Fue a Madrid. He went to Madrid.
Te vi en el parque. I saw you in the park.
No vinieron. They didn't come.
¿Qué hizo? What did she do?
Se lo di a Teresa. I gave it to Teresa.
Fue en 1999. It was in 1999.

The preterite forms of ser (meaning *to be*) are the same as the preterite forms of ir (meaning *to go*).

Some other verbs are regular EXCEPT FOR the él/ella/usted and ellos/ellas/ustedes forms (*third persons singular and plural*). In these forms the stem vowel changes.

Verb	(yo)	(tú)	(él) (ella) (usted)	(nosotros) (nosotras)	(vosotros) (vosotras)	(ellos) (ellas) (ustedes)
dormir *to sleep*	dormí	dormiste	durmió	dormimos	dormisteis	durmieron
morir *to die*	morí	moriste	murió	morimos	moristeis	murieron
pedir *to ask for*	pedí	pediste	pidió	pedimos	pedisteis	pidieron
reír *to laugh*	reí	reíste	rió	reímos	reísteis	rieron
seguir *to follow*	seguí	seguiste	siguió	seguimos	seguisteis	siguieron
sentir *to feel*	sentí	sentiste	sintió	sentimos	sentisteis	sintieron

For further explanation of grammatical terms, please see pages 6-9.

Note that reír also has an accent in all persons EXCEPT FOR the ellos/ellas/ustedes forms.

Antonio durmió diez horas. Antonio slept for ten hours.
Murió en 1066. He died in 1066.
Pidió paella. He ordered paella.
¿Los siguió? Did she follow them?
Sintió un dolor en la pierna. He felt a pain in his leg.
Nos reímos mucho. We laughed a lot.
Juan no se rió. Juan didn't laugh.

caer (meaning *to fall*) and leer (meaning *to read*) have an accent in all persons EXCEPT FOR the ellos/ellas/ustedes form (*third person plural*). In addition, the vowel changes to y in the él/ella/usted and ellos/ellas/ustedes forms (*third persons singular and plural*).

Verb	**(yo)**	**(tú)**	**(él)** **(ella)** **(usted)**	**(nosotros)** **(nosotras)**	**(vosotros)** **(vosotras)**	**(ellos)** **(ellas)** **(ustedes)**
caer ***to fall***	caí	caíste	cayó	caímos	caísteis	cayeron
construir ***to build***	construí	construiste	construyó	construimos	construisteis	construyeron
leer ***to read***	leí	leíste	leyó	leímos	leísteis	leyeron

Note that construir also changes to y in the él/ella/usted and ellos/ellas/ustedes forms (*third persons singular and plural*), but only has accents in the yo and él/ella/usted forms.

Se cayó por la ventana. He fell out the window.
Ayer leí un artículo muy interesante.
I read a very interesting article yesterday.
Construyeron una nueva autopista. They built a new highway.

Other spelling changes in the preterite

Spanish verbs that end in -zar, -gar and -car in the infinitive change the z to c, the g to gu and the c to qu in the yo form (*first person singular*).

Verb	(yo)	(tú)	(él) (ella) (usted)	(nosotros) (nosotras)	(vosotros) (vosotras)	(ellos) (ellas) (ustedes)
cruzar *to cross*	crucé	cruzaste	cruzó	cruzamos	cruzasteis	cruzaron
empezar *to begin*	empecé	empezaste	empezó	empezamos	empezasteis	empezaron
pagar *to pay for*	pagué	pagaste	pagó	pagamos	pagasteis	pagaron
sacar *to follow*	saqué	sacaste	sacó	sacamos	sacasteis	sacaron

Crucé el río. I crossed the river.
Empecé a llorar. I started crying.
No pagué la cuenta. I didn't pay the bill.
Saqué las llaves del bolsillo. I took the keys out of my pocket.

Note that the change from g to gu and c to qu before e is to keep the sound hard.

Reflexive verbs in the preterite

The preterite of reflexive verbs is formed in exactly the same way as for ordinary verbs, except that you have to remember to give the reflexive pronoun (me, te, se, nos, os, se).

Me levanté a las siete. I got up at seven.

For further explanation of grammatical terms, please see pages 6-9.

The imperfect tense

Forming the imperfect tense

To form the imperfect of any regular -ar verb, you take off the -ar ending of the infinitive to form the stem and add the endings: -aba, -abas, -aba,-ábamos, -abais, -aban.

The following table shows the imperfect tense of one regular -ar verb: hablar (meaning *to speak*).

(yo)	hablaba	I spoke
		I was speaking
		I used to speak
(tú)	hablabas	you spoke
		you were speaking
		you used to speak
(él/ella/usted)	hablaba	he/she/it/you spoke
		he/she/it was speaking, you were speaking
		he/she/it/you used to speak
(nosotros/nosotras)	hablábamos	we spoke
		we were speaking
		we used to speak
(vosotros/vosotras)	hablabais	you spoke
		you were speaking
		you used to speak
(ellos/ellas/ustedes)	hablaban	they/you spoke
		they/you were speaking
		they/you used to speak

Note that in the imperfect tense of -ar verbs, the only accent is on the nosotros/nosotras form.

Hablaba francés e italiano. He spoke French and Italian.
Antes viajábamos mucho. We used to travel a lot.
Estudiábamos matemáticas e inglés. We were studying Math and English.

To form the imperfect of any regular **-er** or **-ir** verb, you take off the **-er** or **-ir** ending of the infinitive to form the stem and add the endings: **-ía**, **-ías**, **-ía**, **-íamos**, **-íais**, **-ían**.

The following table shows the imperfect of two regular verbs: **comer** (meaning *to eat*) and **vivir** (meaning *to live*).

(yo)	comía	vivía	I ate/lived I was eating/living I used to eat/live
(tú)	comías	vivías	you ate/lived you were eating/living you used to eat/live
(él/ella/usted)	comía	vivía	he/she/it/you ate/lived he/she/it was eating/living, you were eating/living he/she/it was eating/living, you were eating/living
(nosotros/nosotras)	comíamos	vivíamos	we ate/lived we were eating/living we used to eat/live
(vosotros/vosotras)	comíais	vivíais	you ate/lived you were eating/living you used to eat/live
(ellos/ellas/ustedes)	comían	vivían	they/you ate/lived they/you were eating/living they/you used to eat/live

For further explanation of grammatical terms, please see pages 6-9.

Note that in the imperfect tense of -er and -ir verbs, there's an accent on all the endings.

A veces, comíamos en casa de Pepe. We sometimes used to eat at Pepe's.
Vivía en un apartamento muy grande.
She lived in a very large apartment.
Cuando llegó el médico, ya se sentían mejor.
They were already feeling better when the doctor arrived.

The imperfect endings for -er and -ir verbs are the same as the endings used to form the conditional for all verbs. The only difference is that, in the conditional, the endings are added to the future stem.

Reflexive verbs in the imperfect tense

The imperfect of reflexive verbs is formed in exactly the same way as for ordinary verbs, except that you have to remember to give the reflexive pronoun (me, te, se, nos, os, se).

Antes se levantaba temprano. He used to get up early.

The perfect tense

Forming the perfect tense

As in English, the perfect tense in Spanish has two parts to it. These are:

- the present tense of the verb haber (meaning *to have*)
- a part of the main verb called the past participle.

Forming the past participle

To form the past participle of regular -ar verbs, take off the -ar ending of the infinitive and add -ado.

hablar (*to speak*) > hablado (*spoken*)

To form the past participle of regular -er or -ir verbs, take off the -er or -ir ending of the infinitive and add -ido.

comer (*to eat*) > comido (*eaten*)
vivir (*to live*) > vivido (*lived*)

The perfect tense of some regular verbs

The following table shows how you can combine the present tense of haber with the past participle of any verb to form the perfect tense.
In this case, the past participles are taken from the following regular verbs:

hablar (meaning *to speak*); trabajar (meaning *to work*); comer (meaning *to eat*); vender (meaning *to sell*); vivir (meaning *to live*); decidir (meaning *to decide*).

For further explanation of grammatical terms, please see pages 6-9.

	Present of haber	Past participle	Meaning
(yo)	he	hablado	I have spoken
(tú)	has	trabajado	you have worked
(él/ella/usted)	ha	comido	he/she/it has eaten, you have eaten
(nosotros/nosotras)	hemos	vendido	we have sold
(vosotros/vosotras)	habéis	vivido	you have lived
(ellos/ellas/ustedes)	han	decidido	they/you have decided

Has trabajado mucho. You've worked hard.
No he comido nada. I haven't eaten anything.

Verbs with irregular past participles

Some past participles are irregular. There aren't too many, so try to learn them.

abrir (*to open*) > abierto (*opened*)
cubrir (*to cover*) > cubierto (*covered*)
decir (*to say*) > dicho (*said*)
escribir (*to write*) > escrito (*written*)
freír (*to fry*) > frito (*fried*)
hacer (*to do, to make*) > hecho (*done, made*)
morir (*to die*) > muerto (*died*)
oír (*to hear*) > oído (*heard*)
poner (*to put*) > puesto (*put*)
romper (*to break*) > roto (*broken*)
ver (*to see*) > visto (*seen*)
volver (*to return*) > vuelto (*returned*)

No ha dicho nada. He hasn't said anything.
Hoy he hecho muchas cosas. I've done a lot today.
Han muerto tres personas. Three people have died.
Carlos ha roto el espejo. Carlos has broken the mirror.
Jamás he visto una cosa parecida. I've never seen anything like it.

he/has/ha and so on must NEVER be separated from the past participle. Any object pronouns go before the form of haber being used, and NOT between the form of haber and the past participle.

No lo he visto. I haven't seen it.
¿Lo has hecho ya? Have you done it yet?

Reflexive verbs in the perfect tense

The perfect tense of reflexive verbs is formed in the same way as for ordinary verbs. The reflexive pronouns (me, te, se, nos, os, se) come before he, has, ha, and so on. The table below shows the perfect tense of lavarse in full.

(Subject pronoun)	Reflexive pronoun	Present tense of haber	Past Participle	Meaning
(yo)	me	he	lavado	I have washed
(tú)	te	has	lavado	you have washed
(él, ella, uno) (usted)	se	ha	lavado	he has washed she has washed one has washed it has washed you have washed
(nosotros) (nosotras)	nos	hemos	lavado	we have washed we have washed
(vosotros) (vosotras)	os	habéis	lavado	you have washed you have washed
(ellos) (ellas) (ustedes)	se	han	lavado	they have washed they have washed you have washed

For further explanation of grammatical terms, please see pages 6-9.

The pluperfect or past perfect tense

Forming the pluperfect tense

Like the perfect tense, the pluperfect tense in Spanish has two parts to it:

- the imperfect tense of the verb **haber** (meaning *to have*)
- the past participle.

The table below shows how you can combine the imperfect tense of **haber** with the past participle of any verb to form the pluperfect tense. Here, the past participles are taken from the following regular verbs: **hablar** (meaning *to speak*); **trabajar** (meaning *to work*); **comer** (meaning *to eat*); **vender** (meaning *to sell*); **vivir** (meaning *to live*); **decidir** (meaning *to decide*).

(Subject pronoun)	Imperfect of haber	Past Participle	Meaning
(yo)	había	hablado	I had spoken
(tú)	habías	trabajado	you had worked
(él/ella/usted)	había	comido	he/she/it/you had eaten
(nosotros/nosotras)	habíamos	vendido	we had sold
(vosotros/vosotras)	habíais	vivido	you had lived
(ellos/ellas/ustedes)	habían	decidido	they/you had decided

Había decidido escribirle. I had decided to write to her.
No había trabajado antes. He hadn't worked before.
Había vendido su caballo. She had sold her horse.
Ya habíamos comido. We had already eaten.
Habían hablado con el médico. They had spoken to the doctor.

Remember that some very common verbs have irregular past participles.

abrir (*to open*)	>	abierto (*opened*)
cubrir (*to cover*)	>	cubierto (*covered*)
decir (*to say*)	>	dicho (*said*)
escribir (*to write*)	>	escrito (*written*)
freír (*to fry*)	>	frito (*fried*)
hacer (*to do, to make*)	>	hecho (*done, made*)
morir (*to die*)	>	muerto (*died*)
oír (*to hear*)	>	oído (*heard*)
poner (*to put*)	>	puesto (*put*)
romper (*to break*)	>	roto (*broken*)
ver (*to see*)	>	visto (*seen*)
volver (*to return*)	>	vuelto (*returned*)

No había dicho nada. He hadn't said anything.
Tres personas habían muerto. Three people had died.

había/habías/habían and so on must NEVER be separated from the past participle. Any object pronouns go before the form of haber being used, and NOT between the form of haber and the past participle.

No lo había visto. I hadn't seen it.

Reflexive verbs in the pluperfect tense

The pluperfect tense of reflexive verbs is formed in the same way as for ordinary verbs. The reflexive pronouns (me, te, se, nos, os, se) come before había, habías, había, and so on. The table on the next page shows the pluperfect tense of lavarse in full.

For further explanation of grammatical terms, please see pages 6-9.

(Subject pronoun)	Reflexive pronoun	Imperfect tense of haber	Past Participle	Meaning
(yo)	me	había	lavado	I had washed
(tú)	te	habías	lavado	you had washed
(él, ella, uno) (usted)	se	había	lavado	he had washed she had washed one had washed it had washed you had washed
(nosotros) (nosotras)	nos	habíamos	lavado	we had washed we had washed
(vosotros) (vosotras)	os	habíais	lavado	you had washed you had washed
(ellos) (ellas) (ustedes)	se	habían	lavado	they had washed they had washed you had washed

The passive

Forming the passive

In English, we use the verb *to be* with a past participle (*was painted, were seen, are made*) to form the passive. In Spanish, the passive is formed in exactly the same way, using the verb ser (meaning *to be*) and a past participle. When you say who the action is or was done by, you use the preposition por (meaning *by*).

Son fabricados en España. They're made in Spain.
Fue escrito por JK Rowling. It was written by JK Rowling.
La casa fue construida en 1956. The house was built in 1956.
El cuadro fue pintado por mi padre. The picture was painted by my father.
El colegio va a ser modernizado. The school is going to be modernized.

Note that the ending of the past participle agrees with the subject of the verb ser in exactly the same way as an adjective would.

Here is the preterite of the -ar verb enviar (meaning *to send*) in its passive form.

(Subject pronoun)	Preterite of ser	Past Participle	Meaning
(yo)	fui	enviado (masculine) enviada (feminine)	I was sent
(tú)	fuiste	enviado (masculine) enviada (feminine)	you were sent
(él)	fue	enviado	he was sent
(ella)		enviada	she was sent
(usted)		enviado (masculine) enviada (feminine)	you were sent

For further explanation of grammatical terms, please see pages 6-9.

(Subject pronoun)	Preterite of ser	Past Participle	Meaning
(nosotros)	fuimos	enviados	we were sent
(nosotras)		enviadas	we were sent
(vosotros)	fuisteis	enviados	you were sent
(vosotras)		enviadas	you were sent
(ellos)	fueron	enviados	they were sent
(ellas)		enviadas	they were sent
(ustedes)		enviados (masculine)	you were sent
		enviadas (feminine)	you were sent

You can form other tenses in the passive by changing the tense of the verb ser.

Future: serán enviados they will be sent
Perfect: han sido enviados they have been sent

Irregular past participles are the same as they are in the perfect tense. These are shown for many common verbs in the **Verb Tables** at the back of the book.

The gerund

Forming the gerund of regular verbs

To form the gerund of regular -ar verbs, take off the -ar ending of the infinitive to form the stem, and add -ando.

Infinitive	Stem	Gerund
hablar	habl-	hablando
trabajar	trabaj-	trabajando

To form the gerund of regular -er and -ir verbs, take off the -er and -ir ending of the infinitive to form the stem, and add -iendo.

Infinitive	Stem	Gerund
comer	com-	comiendo
vivir	viv-	viviendo

Position of pronouns with the gerund

Object pronouns and reflexive pronouns are attached to the end of the gerund or alternatively put before estar in continuous tenses.

Estoy hablándote or Te estoy hablando. I'm talking to you.
Está vistiéndose or Se está vistiendo. He's getting dressed.
Estaban mostrándoselo *or* Se lo estaban mostrando.
They were showing it to him/her/them/you.

Note that you will always have to add an accent to keep the stress in the same place when adding pronouns to the end of a gerund.

For further explanation of grammatical terms, please see pages 6-9.

The subjunctive

Forming the present subjunctive

To form the present subjunctive of most verbs, take off the -o ending of the yo form of the present simple, and add a fixed set of endings.

For -ar verbs, the endings are: -e, -es, -e, -emos, -éis, -en.

For both -er and -ir verbs, the endings are: -a, -as, -a, -amos, -áis, -an.

The following table shows the present subjunctive of three regular verbs: hablar (meaning *to speak*), comer (meaning *to eat*) and vivir (meaning *to live*).

Infinitive	**(yo)**	**(tú)**	**(él)** **(ella)** **(usted)**	**(nosotros)** **(nosotras)**	**(vosotros)** **(vosotras)**	**(ellos)** **(ellas)** **(ustedes)**
hablar ***to speak***	hable	hables	hable	hablemos	habléis	hablen
comer ***to eat***	coma	comas	coma	comamos	comáis	coman
vivir ***to live***	viva	vivas	viva	vivamos	viváis	vivan

Quiero que comas algo. I want you to eat something.
Me sorprende que no hable inglés. I'm surprised he doesn't speak English.
No es verdad que trabajen aquí. It isn't true that they work here.

Some verbs have very irregular yo forms in the ordinary present tense and these irregular forms are reflected in the stem for the present subjunctive.

Infinitive	(yo)	(tú)	(él) (ella) (usted)	(nosotros) (nosotras)	(vosotros) (vosotras)	(ellos) (ellas) (ustedes)
decir *to say*	diga	digas	diga	digamos	digáis	digan
hacer *to do/make*	haga	hagas	haga	hagamos	hagáis	hagan
poner *to put*	ponga	pongas	ponga	pongamos	pongáis	pongan
salir *to leave*	salga	salgas	salga	salgamos	salgáis	salgan
tener *to have*	tenga	tengas	tenga	tengamos	tengáis	tengan
venir *to come*	venga	vengas	venga	vengamos	vengáis	vengan

Voy a limpiar la casa antes de que vengan.
I'm going to clean the house before they come.

Note that only the vosotros form has an accent.

The present subjunctive endings are the opposite of what you'd expect, as -ar verbs have endings starting with -e, and -er and -ir verbs have endings starting with -a.

Forming the present subjunctive of radical-changing verbs

Verbs that change their stems (radical-changing verbs) in the ordinary present usually change them in the same way in the present subjunctive.

For further explanation of grammatical terms, please see pages 6-9.

Infinitive	(yo)	(tú)	(él) (ella) (usted)	(nosotros) (nosotras)	(vosotros) (vosotras)	(ellos) (ellas) (ustedes)
pensar *to think*	piense	pienses	piense	pensemos	penséis	piensen
entender *to understand*	entienda	entiendas	entienda	entendamos	entendáis	entiendan
poder *to be able*	pueda	puedas	pueda	podamos	podáis	puedan
querer *to want*	quiera	quieras	quiera	queramos	queráis	quieran
volver *to return*	vuelva	vuelvas	vuelva	volvamos	volváis	vuelvan

No hace falta que vuelvas. There's no need for you to come back.
Me alegro de que puedas venir. I'm pleased you can come.

Sometimes the stem of the nosotros and vosotros forms isn't the same as it is in the ordinary present tense.

Infinitive	(yo)	(tú)	(él) (ella) (usted)	(nosotros) (nosotras)	(vosotros) (vosotras)	(ellos) (ellas) (ustedes)
dormir *to sleep*	duerma	duermas	duerma	durmamos	durmáis	duerman
morir *to die*	muera	mueras	muera	muramos	muráis	mueran
pedir *to ask for*	pida	pidas	pida	pidamos	pidáis	pidan
seguir *to follow*	siga	sigas	siga	sigamos	sigáis	sigan
sentir *to feel*	sienta	sientas	sienta	sintamos	sintáis	sientan

Lo hace sin que se lo pidamos.
She does it without our asking her.
Vendré a veros cuando os sintáis mejor.
I'll come and see you when you feel better.

Forming the imperfect subjunctive

For all verbs, there are two imperfect subjunctive forms that are exactly the same in meaning.

The stem for both imperfect subjunctive forms is the same: you take off the -aron *or* -ieron ending of the ellos form of the preterite and add a fixed set of endings to what is left.

For -ar verbs, the endings are: -ara, -aras, -ara, -áramos, -arais, -aran *or* -ase, -ases, -ase, -ásemos, -aseis, -asen. The first form is more common.

For -er and -ir verbs, the endings are: -iera, -ieras, -iera, -iéramos, -ierais, -ieran *or* -iese, -ieses, -iese, -iésemos, -ieseis, -iesen. The first form is more common.

The following table shows the subjunctive of three regular verbs: hablar (meaning *to speak*), comer (meaning *to eat*) and vivir (meaning *to live*).

Infinitive	**(yo)**	**(tú)**	**(él)** **(ella)** **(usted)**	**(nosotros)** **(nosotras)**	**(vosotros)** **(vosotras)**	**(ellos)** **(ellas)** **(ustedes)**
hablar	hablara	hablaras	hablara	habláramos	hablarais	hablaran
to speak	hablase	hablases	hablase	hablásemos	hablaseis	hablasen
comer	comiera	comieras	comiera	comiéramos	comierais	comieran
to eat	comiese	comieses	comiese	comiésemos	comieseis	comiesen
vivir	viviera	vivieras	viviera	viviéramos	vivierais	vivieran
to live	viviese	vivieses	viviese	viviésemos	vivieseis	viviesen

For further explanation of grammatical terms, please see pages 6-9.

Many verbs have irregular preterite forms which are reflected in the stem for the imperfect subjunctive. For example:

Infinitive	(yo)	(tú)	(él) (ella) (usted)	(nosotros) (nosotras)	(vosotros) (vosotras)	(ellos) (ellas) (ustedes)
dar	diera	dieras	diera	diéramos	dierais	dieran
to give	diese	dieses	diese	diésemos	dieseis	diesen
estar	estuviera	estuvieras	estuviera	estuviéramos	estuvierais	estuvieran
to be	estuviese	estuvieses	estuviese	estuviésemos	estuvieseis	estuviesen
hacer	hiciera	hicieras	hiciera	hiciéramos	hicierais	hicieran
to do/make	hiciese	hicieses	hiciese	hiciésemos	hicieseis	hiciesen
poner	pusiera	pusieras	pusiera	pusiéramos	pusierais	pusieran
to put	pusiese	pusieses	pusiese	pusiésemos	pusieseis	pusiesen
tener	tuviera	tuvieras	tuviera	tuviéramos	tuvierais	tuvieran
to have	tuviese	tuvieses	tuviese	tuviésemos	tuvieseis	tuviesen
venir	viniera	vinieras	viniera	viniéramos	vinierais	vinieran
to come	viniese	vinieses	viniese	viniésemos	vinieseis	viniesen

Forming the imperfect subjunctive of some irregular -ir verbs

In some irregular -ir verbs – the ones that don't have an i in the ellos form of the preterite – -era, -eras, -era, -éramos, -erais, -eran *or* -ese, -eses, -ese, -ésemos, -eseis, -esen are added to the preterite stem instead of -iera, -iese and so on.

Infinitive	(yo)	(tú)	(él) (ella) (usted)	(nosotros) (nosotras)	(vosotros) (vosotras)	(ellos) (ellas) (ustedes)
decir	dijera	dijeras	dijera	dijéramos	dijerais	dijeran
to say	dijese	dijeses	dijese	dijésemos	dijeseis	dijesen
ir	fuera	fueras	fuera	fuéramos	fuerais	fueran
to go	fuese	fueses	fuese	fuésemos	fueseis	fuesen
ser	fuera	fueras	fuera	fuéramos	fuerais	fueran
to be	fuese	fueses	fuese	fuésemos	fueseis	fuesen

Accents

When pronouns are added to the end of gerunds (the **-ando/-iendo** form of the verb), infinitives (the form of the verb ending in **-ar**, **-er** or **-ir**) or positive imperatives (instructions to do something), you often have to add an accent to show that the stress remains the same.

You should always add an accent to a gerund when attaching one or more pronouns:

> **Estoy bañándome.** I'm taking a bath.
> **Está limpiándotelo.** He's cleaning it for you.
> **Estaba diciéndoselo.** I was telling her.

You should only add an accent to an infinitive when adding two pronouns:

> **Quiero limpiártelo.** I want to clean it for you.
> **¿Podrías hacérmelo?** Could you do it for me?
> **Habría que decírselo.** Somebody should tell her.

Don't add an accent when adding only one pronoun to an infinitive:

> **Tengo que peinarme.** I must comb my hair.
> **Debo conseguirlo.** I must get it.

In positive imperatives (instructions to do something) an accent is usually required when attaching one or more pronouns:

> **Tómalo.** Take it.
> **Dígame la verdad.** Tell me the truth.
> **Cárguelo a mi cuenta.** Put it on my account.
> **¡Levantémonos!** Let's get up!
> **¡Digámoselo!** Let's tell him!

For further explanation of grammatical terms, please see pages 6-9.

Súbanmelo a casa. Bring it up to my house.
Díganmelo claro. Tell me clearly.
Confírmenmelo en cuanto puedan. Confirm it as soon as you can.
¡Arrepiéntanse! Repent!

However, you don't add an accent when adding just one pronoun to a one-syllable imperative or a vosotros imperative in -ar or -er verbs:

Acompañadle. Go with him.
Dame uno. Give me one.
Hazlo lo más pronto possible. Do it as soon as possible.

Verb Combinations

Verbs followed by the infinitive with no preposition

Some Spanish verbs and groups of verbs can be followed by an infinitive with no preposition:

- poder (meaning *to be able to, can, may*), saber (meaning *to know how to, can*), querer (meaning *to want*) and deber (meaning *to have to, must*)

  No puede venir. He can't come.
  ¿Sabes esquiar? Can you ski?
  Quiere estudiar medicina. He wants to study medicine.
  Debes hacerlo. You must do it.

- verbs like gustar, encantar and apetecer, where the infinitive is the subject of the verb

  Me gusta estudiar. I like studying.
  Nos encanta bailar. We love dancing.
  ¿Te apetece ir al cine? Would you like to go to the movies?

- verbs that relate to seeing or hearing, such as ver (meaning *to see*) and oír (meaning *to hear*)

  Nos vio llegar. He saw us arrive.
  Te oí cantar. I heard you singing.

- the verbs hacer (meaning *to make*) and dejar (meaning *to let*)

  ¡No me hagas reír! Don't make me laugh!
  Mis padres no me dejan salir por la noche.
  My parents don't let me go out at night.

For further explanation of grammatical terms, please see pages 6-9.

- the following common verbs

  decidir to decide
  Han decidido comprarse una casa. They've decided to buy a house.

  desear to wish, want
  No desea tener más hijos. She doesn't want to have any more children.

  esperar to hope
  Espero poder ir. I hope to be able to go.

  evitar to avoid
  Evita gastar demasiado dinero. Avoid spending too much money.

  necesitar to need
  Necesito salir un momento. I need to go out for a moment.

  olvidar to forget
  Olvidó dejar su dirección. She forgot to leave her address.

  pensar to think, to intend
  Pienso volver pronto. I intend to come back soon.

  preferir to prefer
  Prefiero ir mañana. I'd prefer to go tomorrow.

  recordar to remember
  Recuerdo haberlo visto. I remember having seen it.

  sentir to be sorry, to regret
  Siento molestarte. I'm sorry to bother you.

58 Verb Combinations

Some of these verbs combine with infinitives to make set phrases with a special meaning:

querer decir to mean
¿Qué quiere decir eso? What does that mean?

dejar caer to drop
Dejó caer las llaves. She dropped the keys.

For further explanation of grammatical terms, please see pages 6-9.

Verbs followed by the preposition a and the infinitive

The following verbs are the most common ones that can be followed by a and the infinitive:

- verbs relating to movement such as **ir** (meaning *to go*) and **venir** (meaning *to come*)

  Se va a comprar un caballo. He's going to buy a horse.
  Viene a vernos. He's coming to see us.

- the following common verbs

  aprender a hacer algo to learn to do something
  Me gustaría aprender a nadar. I'd like to learn to swim.

  comenzar a hacer algo to begin to do something
  Comenzó a llover. It began to rain.

  decidirse a hacer algo to decide to do something
  Ojalá se decida a visitarnos I hope she decides to visit us.

  empezar a hacer algo to begin to do something
  Ha empezado a nevar. It's started snowing.

  llegar a hacer algo to manage to do something
  No llegó a terminarlo. She didn't manage to finish it.

  llegar a ser algo to become something
  Llegó a ser primer ministro. He became prime minister.

  probar a hacer algo to try doing something
  Prueba a hacerlo más lentamente.
  Try doing it more slowly.

volver a hacer algo to do something again
No vuelvas a hacerlo nunca más. Don't ever do it again.

The following verbs can be followed by a and a person's name or else by a and a noun or pronoun referring to a person, and then by another a and an infinitive.

ayudar a alguien a hacer algo to help someone to do something
¿Le podrías ayudar a Antonia a poner la mesa?
Could you help Antonia set the table?

enseñar a alguien a hacer algo to teach someone to do something
Le enseñó a su hermano a nadar. He taught his brother to swim.

invitar a alguien a hacer algo to invite someone to do something
Los invité a tomar unas copas en casa.
I invited them over for drinks.

For further explanation of grammatical terms, please see pages 6-9.

Verbs followed by the preposition de and the infinitive

The following verbs are the most common ones that can be followed by de and the infinitive:

aburrirse de hacer algo to get bored with doing something
Me aburro de hacer siempro lo mismo.
I get bored with doing the same thing all the time.

acabar de hacer algo to have just done something
Acabo de comprar un celular. I've just bought a cell phone.
Acababan de llegar cuando... They had just arrived when...

acordarse de haber hecho algo/de hacer algo
to remember having done something/to do something
Acuérdate de cerrar la puerta con llave. Remember to lock the door.
Me acuerdo de haberle dado el dinero. I remember giving her the money.

alegrarse de hacer algo to be glad to do something
Me alegro de verte. I'm glad to see you.

dejar de hacer algo to stop doing something
¿Quieres dejar de hablar? Will you stop talking?

tener ganas de hacer algo to want to do something
Tengo ganas de volver a España. I want to go back to Spain.

tratar de hacer algo to try to do something
Traté de no pensar en ella. I tried not to think about her.

Verbs followed by the preposition con and the infinitive

The following verbs are the most common ones that can be followed by con and the infinitive:

amenazar con hacer algo to threaten to do something
Amenazó con denunciarlos. He threatened to report them.

soñar con hacer algo to dream about doing something
Sueño con vivir en Europa. I dream about living in Europe.

Verbs followed by the preposition en and the infinitive

The verb quedar is the most common one that can be followed by en and the infinitive:

quedar en hacer algo to agree to do something
Habíamos quedado en encontrarnos a las ocho.
We had agreed to meet at eight.

For further explanation of grammatical terms, please see pages 6-9.

Verbs followed by a and an object

a is often the equivalent of the English word *to* when it is used with an indirect object after verbs like mandar (meaning *to send*), dar (meaning *to give*), and decir (meaning *to say*).

darle algo a alguien to give something to someone
Se lo di a Teresa. I gave it to Teresa.

decirle algo a alguien to say something to someone
¿A quién se lo dijo? Who did she tell?

Mandarle algo a alguien to send something to someone
Tendrías que enviárselo a mi padre. You should send it to my father.

escribirle a alguien to write something to someone
¿Le has escrito a tu tía? Have you written to your aunt?

mostrarle algo a alguien to show something to someone
Quería mostrárselo al médico. I wanted to show it to the doctor.

Here are some verbs taking a in Spanish that have a different construction in English.

asistir a algo to attend something, to be at something
No asistieron a la ceremonia. They didn't go to the ceremony.

dirigirse a (un lugar) to head for (a place)
Se dirigió a la terminal del aeropuerto. He headed for the airport terminal.

dirigirse a alguien to address somebody
El Presidente se dirigió a la nación. The President addressed the nation.

jugar (a) algo to play something (sports/games)
Están jugando (al) ajedrez. They're playing chess.

llegar a (un lugar) to arrive at (a place)
¿A qué hora llegaste a casa? What time did you get home?

oler a algo to smell of something
Este perfume huele a jazmín. This perfume smells of jasmine.

parecerse a alguien/algo to look like somebody/something
Te pareces mucho a tu madre. You look very much like your mother.

subir(se) a un tren/un coche to get on a train/into a car
Nos subimos al taxi. We got into the cab.
No (se) subió al tren. He didn't get on the train.

subir(se) a un árbol to climb a tree
Se cayó al subirse a un árbol. He fell while climbing a tree.

tenerle miedo a alguien to be afraid of somebody
Le tenían miedo a su padre. They were afraid of their father.

For further explanation of grammatical terms, please see pages 6-9.

Verbs followed by de and an object

Here are some verbs taking de in Spanish that have a different construction in English:

acordarse de algo/alguien to remember something/somebody
¿Te acuerdas de mí? Do you remember me?

alegrarse de algo to be glad about something
Me alegro de tu ascenso. I'm glad about your promotion.

bajarse de un avión/un coche to get off a plane/out of a car
Se bajó del taxi. He got out of the cab.

darse cuenta de algo to realize something
Me di cuenta de que ya no lo quería.
I realized I no longer loved him.

depender de algo/alguien to depend on something/somebody
No depende de mí. It doesn't depend on me.

despedirse de alguien to say goodbye to somebody
Se fue sin despedirse de nosotros. He left without saying goodbye to us.

quejarse de algo to complain about something
Se quejaba de la falta de información.
He was complaining about the lack of information.

reírse de algo/alguien to laugh at something/somebody
¿De qué te ríes? What are you laughing at?

salir de (un cuarto/un edificio) to leave (a room/a building)
¿A qué hora sales de la oficina? What time do you leave the office?

tener miedo de algo to be afraid of something
Tiene miedo de la oscuridad. He's afraid of the dark.

trabajar de (enfermero/secretario) to work as (a nurse/secretary)
Trabajo de guía turística. I work as a tour guide.

tratarse de algo/alguien
to be a question of something/to be about somebody
Se trata de tu padre. It's about your father.

For further explanation of grammatical terms, please see pages 6-9.

Verbs followed by con and an object

Here are some verbs taking con in Spanish that sometimes have a different construction in English:

comparar algo/a alguien con algo/alguien
to compare something/somebody with something/somebody
Siempre me comparan con mi hermana.
I'm always being compared to my sister.

contar con alguien/algo to rely on somebody/something
Cuento contigo. I'm relying on you.

encontrarse con alguien to meet somebody (by chance)
Me encontré con ella al salir del banco.
I met her as I was coming out of the bank.

enojarse con alguien to get annoyed with somebody
No te enojes con él, lo hizo sin querer.
Don't be annoyed with him, he didn't mean to do it.

estar de acuerdo con alguien/algo to agree with somebody/something
Estoy totalmente de acuerdo contigo. I totally agree with you.

hablar con alguien to talk to somebody
¿Puedo hablar con usted un momento? May I talk to you for a moment?

soñar con alguien/algo to dream about somebody/something
Ayer soñé con él. I dreamed about him yesterday.

Verbs followed by en and an object

Here are some verbs taking en in Spanish that sometimes have a different construction in English:

entrar en (un edificio/un cuarto) to enter, go into (a building/a room)
Entré en la casa. I went into the house.

pensar en algo/alguien to think about something/somebody
No quiero pensar en eso. I don't want to think about that.

trabajar en (una oficina/una fábrica) to work in (an office/a factory)
Trabaja en un banco. She works in a bank.

For further explanation of grammatical terms, please see pages 6-9.

Verbs followed by por and an object

Here are some verbs taking por in Spanish that have a different construction in English:

interesarse por algo/alguien to be interested in something/somebody or to ask about something/somebody
Me interesaba mucho por la arqueología.
I was very interested in archaeology.
Llamó para interesarse por su salud. He called to ask about her health.

preguntar por alguien to ask for/about somebody
Si preguntan por mí, diles que no estoy.
If they ask about me, say I'm not in here.

preocuparse por algo/alguien to worry about something/somebody
Se preocupa mucho por su apariencia.
He worries a lot about his appearance.

Verbs taking a direct object in Spanish but not in English

In English there are a few verbs that are followed by *at*, *for* or *to* which, in Spanish, are not followed by any preposition other than the personal a where required.

mirar algo/a alguien to look at something/somebody
Mira esta foto. Look at this photo.
Mira a aquella mujer. Look at that woman.

escuchar algo/a alguien to listen to something/somebody
Me gusta escuchar música. I like listening to music.

buscar algo/a alguien to look for something/somebody
Estoy buscando mis guantes. I'm looking for my gloves.

pedir algo to ask for something
Pidió más tiempo. He asked for more time.

esperar algo/a alguien to wait for something/somebody
Estamos esperando el tren. We're waiting for the train.
Espera a tu hermana. Wait for your sister.

pagar algo to pay for something
¿Quién pagó la cena? Who paid for dinner?

For further explanation of grammatical terms, please see pages 6-9.

Verbs followed by personal a

Spanish speakers use a in a way that has no equivalent in English. They use it before nouns referring to specific people and pets when these are the direct object of a verb:

¿Conoces a Maite? Do you know Maite?
Quiere a Pablo. She loves Pablo.
No vi a Juan. I didn't see Juan.
Quiero invitar a Teresa a cenar. I want to invite Teresa to supper.
Llama a un médico. Call a doctor.

Personal a is also used before certain pronouns referring to people (but NOT object pronouns):

No conozco a nadie. I don't know anybody.
¿Viste a alguien? Did you see anyone?
¿A quién llamaste? Who did you call?

Personal a is NOT normally used after tener (meaning *to have*):

Tengo dos hermanas. I've got two sisters.
Tiene un perro. He's got a dog.

VERB TABLES

Introduction

The **Verb Tables** in the following section contain 120 tables of Spanish verbs (some regular and some irregular) in alphabetical order. Each table shows you the following forms: **Present, Present Perfect, Preterite, Imperfect, Future, Conditional, Present Subjunctive, Imperfect Subjunctive, Imperative,** and the **Past Participle** and **Gerund**. For more information on these tenses and how they are formed you should look at the section on Verb Formation in the main text on pages 10–55.

In order to help you use the verbs shown in the **Verb Tables** correctly, there are also a number of example phrases at the bottom of each page to show the verb as it is used in context.

In Spanish there are both **regular** verbs (their forms follow the normal rules) and **irregular** verbs (their forms do not follow the normal rules). The regular verbs in these tables that you can use as models for other regular verbs are:

hablar (regular **-ar** verb, Verb Table 118–119)
comer (regular **-er** verb, Verb Table 48–49)
vivir (regular **-ir** verb, Verb Table 234–235)

The irregular verbs are shown in full.

The **Verb Index** at the end of this section contains over 1,200 verbs, each of which is cross-referred to one of the verbs given in the Verb Tables. The table shows the patterns that the verb listed in the index follows.

abolir (to abolish)

	PRESENT	PRESENT PERFECT
(yo)		he abolido
(tú)		has abolido
(él/ella/usted)		ha abolido
(nosotros/as)	abolimos	hemos abolido
(vosotros/as)	abolís	habéis abolido
(ellos/ellas/ ustedes)		han abolido

Present tense only used in persons shown

	PRETERITE	IMPERFECT
(yo)	abolí	abolía
(tú)	aboliste	abolías
(él/ella/usted)	abolió	abolía
(nosotros/as)	abolimos	abolíamos
(vosotros/as)	abolisteis	abolíais
(ellos/ellas/ ustedes)	abolieron	abolían

GERUND	PAST PARTICIPLE
aboliendo	abolido

EXAMPLE PHRASES

Hay que **abolir** esta ley. This law should be abolished.

Habían abolido la pena de muerte. They had abolished the death penalty.

Abolieron la esclavitud. They abolished slavery.

abolir

	FUTURE	CONDITIONAL
(yo)	**aboliré**	**aboliría**
(tú)	**abolirás**	**abolirías**
(él/ella/usted)	**abolirá**	**aboliría**
(nosotros/as)	**aboliremos**	**aboliríamos**
(vosotros/as)	**aboliréis**	**aboliríais**
(ellos/ellas/ ustedes)	**abolirán**	**abolirían**

	PRESENT SUBJUNCTIVE	IMPERFECT SUBJUNCTIVE
(yo)	*not used*	**aboliera** *or* **aboliese**
(tú)		**abolieras** *or* **abolieses**
(él/ella/usted)		**aboliera** *or* **aboliese**
(nosotros/as)		**aboliéramos** *or* **aboliésemos**
(vosotros/as)		**abolierais** *or* **abolieseis**
(ellos/ellas/ ustedes)		**abolieran** *or* **aboliesen**

IMPERATIVE

abolid

EXAMPLE PHRASES

Prometieron que **abolirían** la censura. They promised they'd abolish censorship.

Remember that subject pronouns are not used very often in Spanish.

abrir (to open)

	PRESENT	PRESENT PERFECT
(yo)	abro	he abierto
(tú)	abres	has abierto
(él/ella/usted)	abre	ha abierto
(nosotros/as)	abrimos	hemos abierto
(vosotros/as)	abrís	habéis abierto
(ellos/ellas/ ustedes)	abren	han abierto

	PRETERITE	IMPERFECT
(yo)	abrí	abría
(tú)	abriste	abrías
(él/ella/usted)	abrió	abría
(nosotros/as)	abrimos	abríamos
(vosotros/as)	abristeis	abríais
(ellos/ellas/ ustedes)	abrieron	abrían

GERUND	PAST PARTICIPLE
abriendo	abierto

EXAMPLE PHRASES

Hoy **se abre** el periodo de inscripciones. Registration begins today.

Han abierto un nuevo restaurante cerca de aquí. They've opened a new restaurant near here.

¿Quién **abrió** la ventana? Who opened the window?

La llave **abría** el armario. The key opened the closet.

Remember that subject pronouns are not used very often in Spanish.

abrir

	FUTURE	CONDITIONAL
(yo)	**abriré**	**abriría**
(tú)	**abrirás**	**abrirías**
(él/ella/usted)	**abrirá**	**abriría**
(nosotros/as)	**abriremos**	**abriríamos**
(vosotros/as)	**abriréis**	**abriríais**
(ellos/ellas/ ustedes)	**abrirán**	**abrirían**

	PRESENT SUBJUNCTIVE	IMPERFECT SUBJUNCTIVE
(yo)	**abra**	**abriera** *or* **abriese**
(tú)	**abras**	**abrieras** *or* **abrieses**
(él/ella/usted)	**abra**	**abriera** *or* **abriese**
(nosotros/as)	**abramos**	**abriéramos** *or* **abriésemos**
(vosotros/as)	**abráis**	**abrierais** *or* **abrieseis**
(ellos/ellas/ ustedes)	**abran**	**abrieran** *or* **abriesen**

IMPERATIVE

abre / abrid

Use the present subjunctive in all cases other than these tú and vosotros affirmative forms.

EXAMPLE PHRASES

Abrirán todas las puertas de la catedral. They'll open all the doors of the cathedral.

Me dijo que hoy **abrirían** sólo por la tarde. He told me that they'd only be open in the evening today.

No creo que **abran** un nuevo supermercado por aquí. I don't think they'll open a new supermarket here.

No **abras** esa llave. Don't turn on that faucet.

Remember that subject pronouns are not used very often in Spanish.

actuar (to act)

	PRESENT	PRESENT PERFECT
(yo)	actúo	he actuado
(tú)	actúas	has actuado
(él/ella/usted)	actúa	ha actuado
(nosotros/as)	actuamos	hemos actuado
(vosotros/as)	actuáis	habéis actuado
(ellos/ellas/ ustedes)	actúan	han actuado

	PRETERITE	IMPERFECT
(yo)	actué	actuaba
(tú)	actuaste	actuabas
(él/ella/usted)	actuó	actuaba
(nosotros/as)	actuamos	actuábamos
(vosotros/as)	actuasteis	actuabais
(ellos/ellas/ ustedes)	actuaron	actuaban

GERUND	PAST PARTICIPLE
actuando	actuado

EXAMPLE PHRASES

Actúa de una forma muy rara. He's acting very strangely.

Actuó siguiendo un impulso. He acted on impulse.

Ha actuado en varias películas. He has been in several movies.

Actuaba como si no supiera nada. She was behaving as if she didn't know anything about it.

Remember that subject pronouns are not used very often in Spanish.

actuar

	FUTURE	CONDITIONAL
(yo)	**actuaré**	**actuaría**
(tú)	**actuarás**	**actuarías**
(él/ella/usted)	**actuará**	**actuaría**
(nosotros/as)	**actuaremos**	**actuaríamos**
(vosotros/as)	**actuaréis**	**actuaríais**
(ellos/ellas/ ustedes)	**actuarán**	**actuarían**

	PRESENT SUBJUNCTIVE	IMPERFECT SUBJUNCTIVE
(yo)	**actúe**	**actuara** *or* **actuase**
(tú)	**actúes**	**actuaras** *or* **actuases**
(él/ella/usted)	**actúe**	**actuara** *or* **actuase**
(nosotros/as)	**actuemos**	**actuáramos** *or* **actuásemos**
(vosotros/as)	**actuéis**	**actuarais** *or* **actuaseis**
(ellos/ellas/ ustedes)	**actúen**	**actuaran** *or* **actuasen**

IMPERATIVE

actúa / actuad

Use the present subjunctive in all cases other than these **tú** *and* **vosotros** *affirmative forms.*

EXAMPLE PHRASES

¿Quién **actuará** en su próxima película? Who will be in his next movie?

Yo nunca **actuaría** así. I'd never behave like that.

Si **actuara** de forma más lógica, sería más fácil atraparlo. It would be easier to catch him if he behaved in a more logical way.

Actúa como mejor te parezca. Do as you think best.

Remember that subject pronouns are not used very often in Spanish.

adquirir (to acquire; to obtain; to purchase)

	PRESENT	PRESENT PERFECT
(yo)	**adquiero**	**he adquirido**
(tú)	**adquieres**	**has adquirido**
(él/ella/usted)	**adquiere**	**ha adquirido**
(nosotros/as)	**adquirimos**	**hemos adquirido**
(vosotros/as)	**adquirís**	**habéis adquirido**
(ellos/ellas/ ustedes)	**adquieren**	**han adquirido**

	PRETERITE	IMPERFECT
(yo)	**adquirí**	**adquiría**
(tú)	**adquiriste**	**adquirías**
(él/ella/usted)	**adquirió**	**adquiría**
(nosotros/as)	**adquirimos**	**adquiríamos**
(vosotros/as)	**adquiristeis**	**adquiríais**
(ellos/ellas/ ustedes)	**adquirieron**	**adquirían**

GERUND	PAST PARTICIPLE
adquiriendo	**adquirido**

EXAMPLE PHRASES

Adquiere cada vez mayor importancia. It's becoming more and more important.

Está adquiriendo una reputación que no merece. It's getting a reputation it doesn't deserve.

Han adquirido más acciones. They've purchased more stock.

Con el tiempo **adquirió** madurez. Over the years he gained maturity.

Remember that subject pronouns are not used very often in Spanish.

adquirir

	FUTURE	CONDITIONAL
(yo)	**adquiriré**	**adquiriría**
(tú)	**adquirirás**	**adquiriría**
(él/ella/usted)	**adquirirá**	**adquiriría**
(nosotros/as)	**adquiriremos**	**adquiriríamos**
(vosotros/as)	**adquiriréis**	**adquiriríais**
(ellos/ellas/ ustedes)	**adquirirán**	**adquirirían**

	PRESENT SUBJUNCTIVE	IMPERFECT SUBJUNCTIVE
(yo)	**adquiera**	**adquiriera** *or* **adquiriese**
(tú)	**adquieras**	**adquirieras** *or* **adquirieses**
(él/ella/usted)	**adquiera**	**adquiriera** *or* **adquiriese**
(nosotros/as)	**adquiramos**	**adquiriéramos** *or* **adquiriésemos**
(vosotros/as)	**adquiráis**	**adquirierais** *or* **adquirieseis**
(ellos/ellas/ ustedes)	**adquieran**	**adquirieran** *or* **adquiriesen**

IMPERATIVE

adquiere / adquirid

Use the present subjunctive in all cases other than these tú and vosotros affirmative forms.

EXAMPLE PHRASES

Al final **adquirirán** los derechos de publicación. They will get the publishing rights in the end.

Adquiera o no la nacionalidad, podrá permanecer en el país. She'll be able to stay in the country whether she gets citizenship or not.

Tenía gran interés en que **adquiriera** el cuadro. He was eager that she should purchase the picture.

Remember that subject pronouns are not used very often in Spanish.

advertir (to warn; to notice)

	PRESENT	PRESENT PERFECT
(yo)	advierto	he advertido
(tú)	adviertes	has advertido
(él/ella/usted)	advierte	ha advertido
(nosotros/as)	advertimos	hemos advertido
(vosotros/as)	advertís	habéis advertido
(ellos/ellas/ ustedes)	advierten	han advertido

	PRETERITE	IMPERFECT
(yo)	advertí	advertía
(tú)	advertiste	advertías
(él/ella/usted)	advirtió	advertía
(nosotros/as)	advertimos	advertíamos
(vosotros/as)	advertisteis	advertíais
(ellos/ellas/ ustedes)	advirtieron	advertían

GERUND
advirtiendo

PAST PARTICIPLE
advertido

EXAMPLE PHRASES

Te **advierto** que no va a ser nada fácil. I must warn you that it won't be at all easy.

No **había advertido** nada extraño en su comportamiento. I hadn't noticed anything strange about his behavior.

Ya te **advertí** que no intervinieras. I warned you not to get involved.

Las señales **advertían** del peligro. The signs warned of danger.

Remember that subject pronouns are not used very often in Spanish.

advertir

	FUTURE	CONDITIONAL
(yo)	**advertiré**	**advertiría**
(tú)	**advertirás**	**advertirías**
(él/ella/usted)	**advertirá**	**advertiría**
(nosotros/as)	**advertiremos**	**advertiríamos**
(vosotros/as)	**advertiréis**	**advertiríais**
(ellos/ellas/ ustedes)	**advertirán**	**advertirían**

	PRESENT SUBJUNCTIVE	IMPERFECT SUBJUNCTIVE
(yo)	**advierta**	**advirtiera** *or* **advirtiese**
(tú)	**adviertas**	**advirtieras** *or* **advirtieses**
(él/ella/usted)	**advierta**	**advirtiera** *or* **advirtiese**
(nosotros/as)	**advirtamos**	**advirtiéramos** *or* **advirtiésemos**
(vosotros/as)	**advirtáis**	**advirtierais** *or* **advirtieseis**
(ellos/ellas/ ustedes)	**adviertan**	**advirtieran** *or* **advirtiesen**

IMPERATIVE

advierte / advertid

Use the present subjunctive in all cases other than these tú and vosotros affirmative forms.

EXAMPLE PHRASES

Si **advirtiera** algún cambio, llámenos. If you should notice any change, call us.

Adviértele del riesgo que entraña. Warn him about the risk involved.

amanecer (to get light; to wake up)

	PRESENT	PRESENT PERFECT
(yo)	amanezco	he amanecido
(tú)	amaneces	has amanecido
(él/ella/usted)	amanece	ha amanecido
(nosotros/as)	amanecemos	hemos amanecido
(vosotros/as)	amanecéis	habéis amanecido
(ellos/ellas/ ustedes)	amanecen	han amanecido

	PRETERITE	IMPERFECT
(yo)	amanecí	amanecía
(tú)	amaneciste	amanecías
(él/ella/usted)	amaneció	amanecía
(nosotros/as)	amanecimos	amanecíamos
(vosotros/as)	amanecisteis	amanecíais
(ellos/ellas/ ustedes)	amanecieron	amanecían

GERUND	PAST PARTICIPLE
amaneciendo	amanecido

EXAMPLE PHRASES

Siempre **amanece** nublado. The day always starts off cloudy.

Estaba amaneciendo. Dawn was breaking.

La ciudad **amaneció** desierta. In the morning, the town was deserted.

Amanecía de un humor de perros. She would wake up in a really bad mood.

Remember that subject pronouns are not used very often in Spanish.

amanecer

	FUTURE	CONDITIONAL
(yo)	**amaneceré**	**amanecería**
(tŭ)	**amanecerás**	**amanecerías**
(él/ella/usted)	**amanecerá**	**amanecería**
(nosotros/as)	**amaneceremos**	**amaneceríamos**
(vosotros/as)	**amaneceréis**	**amaneceríais**
(ellos/ellas/ ustedes)	**amanecerán**	**amanecerían**

	PRESENT SUBJUNCTIVE	IMPERFECT SUBJUNCTIVE
(yo)	**amanezca**	**amaneciera** *or* **amaneciese**
(tú)	**amanezcas**	**amanecieras** *or* **amanecieses**
(él/ella/usted)	**amanezca**	**amaneciera** *or* **amaneciese**
(nosotros/as)	**amanezcamos**	**amaneciéramos** *or* **amaneciésemos**
(vosotros/as)	**amanezcáis**	**amanecierais** *or* **amanecieseis**
(ellos/ellas/ ustedes)	**amanezcan**	**amanecieran** *or* **amaneciesen**

IMPERATIVE

amanece / amaneced

Use the present subjunctive in all cases other than these **tú** *and* **vosotros** *affirmative forms.*

EXAMPLE PHRASES

Pronto **amanecerá**. It will soon be daylight.

Saldremos en cuanto **amanezca**. We'll get going as soon as it gets light.

Si **amanecieras** con fiebre, toma una de estas pastillas. If you should wake up with a fever, take one of these pills.

Remember that subject pronouns are not used very often in Spanish.

andar (to be; to work; to ride; to walk)

	PRESENT	PRESENT PERFECT
(yo)	**ando**	**he andado**
(tú)	**andas**	**has andado**
(él/ella/usted)	**anda**	**ha andado**
(nosotros/as)	**andamos**	**hemos andado**
(vosotros/as)	**andáis**	**habéis andado**
(ellos/ellas/ ustedes)	**andan**	**han andado**

	PRETERITE	IMPERFECT
(yo)	**anduve**	**andaba**
(tú)	**anduviste**	**andabas**
(él/ella/usted)	**anduvo**	**andaba**
(nosotros/as)	**anduvimos**	**andábamos**
(vosotros/as)	**anduvisteis**	**andabais**
(ellos/ellas/ ustedes)	**anduvieron**	**andaban**

GERUND	PAST PARTICIPLE
andando	**andado**

EXAMPLE PHRASES

¿Cómo **andas**? How are you?

La lavadora no **andaba** bien. The washing machine wasn't working properly.

Andaban mal de dinero. They were short of money.

No sabe **andar** en bicicleta. She doesn't know how to ride a bike.

Remember that subject pronouns are not used very often in Spanish.

andar

	FUTURE	CONDITIONAL
(yo)	andaré	andaría
(tú)	andarás	andarías
(él/ella/usted)	andará	andaría
(nosotros/as)	andaremos	andaríamos
(vosotros/as)	andaréis	andaríais
(ellos/ellas/ ustedes)	andarán	andarían

	PRESENT SUBJUNCTIVE	IMPERFECT SUBJUNCTIVE
(yo)	ande	anduviera *or* anduviese
(tú)	andes	anduvieras *or* anduvieses
(él/ella/usted)	ande	anduviera *or* anduviese
(nosotros/as)	andemos	anduviéramos *or* anduviésemos
(vosotros/as)	andéis	anduvierais *or* anduvieseis
(ellos/ellas/ ustedes)	anden	anduvieran *or* anduviesen

IMPERATIVE

anda / andad

Use the present subjunctive in all cases other than these tú and vosotros affirmative forms.

EXAMPLE PHRASES

Andará por los cuarenta. He must be about forty.

Yo **me andaría** con pies de plomo. I'd tread very carefully.

Si **anduvieras** con más cuidado, no te pasarían esas cosas. If you were more careful, this sort of thing wouldn't happen to you.

Remember that subject pronouns are not used very often in Spanish.

apoderarse de (to take control of)

	PRESENT	PRESENT PERFECT
(yo)	me apodero	me he apoderado
(tú)	te apoderas	te has apoderado
(él/ella/usted)	se apodera	se ha apoderado
(nosotros/as)	nos apoderamos	nos hemos apoderado
(vosotros/as)	os apoderáis	os habéis apoderado
(ellos/ellas/ ustedes)	se apoderan	se han apoderado

	PRETERITE	IMPERFECT
(yo)	me apoderé	me apoderaba
(tú)	te apoderaste	te apoderabas
(él/ella/usted)	se apoderó	se apoderaba
(nosotros/as)	nos apoderamos	nos apoderábamos
(vosotros/as)	os apoderasteis	os apoderabais
(ellos/ellas/ ustedes)	se apoderaron	se apoderaban

GERUND	PAST PARTICIPLE
apoderando	apoderado

EXAMPLE PHRASES

En esas situaciones, el miedo **se apodera** de mí. In situations like that, I find myself gripped by fear.

Poco a poco **se han ido apoderando** de las riquezas del país. Little by little, they've taken control of the country's riches.

Se apoderaron de las joyas y huyeron. They took the jewels and ran off.

Remember that subject pronouns are not used very often in Spanish.

apoderarse de

	FUTURE	CONDITIONAL
(yo)	me apoderaré	me apoderaría
(tú)	te apoderarás	te apoderarías
(él/ella/usted)	se apoderará	se apoderaría
(nosotros/as)	nos apoderaremos	nos apoderaríamos
(vosotros/as)	os apoderaréis	os apoderaríais
(ellos/ellas/ ustedes)	se apoderarán	se apoderarían

	PRESENT SUBJUNCTIVE	IMPERFECT SUBJUNCTIVE
(yo)	me apodere	me apoderara *or* apoderase
(tú)	te apoderes	te apoderaras *or* apoderases
(él/ella/usted)	se apodere	se apoderara *or* apoderase
(nosotros/as)	nos apoderemos	nos apoderáramos *or* apoderásemos
(vosotros/as)	os apoderéis	os apoderarais *or* apoderaseis
(ellos/ellas/ ustedes)	se apoderen	se apoderaran *or* apoderasen

IMPERATIVE

apodérate / apoderaos

Use the present subjunctive in all cases other than these tú *and* vosotros *affirmative forms.*

EXAMPLE PHRASES

No dejes que la curiosidad **se apodere** de ti. Don't let curiosity get the better of you.

Remember that subject pronouns are not used very often in Spanish.

aprobar (to pass; to approve of)

	PRESENT	PRESENT PERFECT
(yo)	**apruebo**	**he aprobado**
(tú)	**apruebas**	**has aprobado**
(él/ella/usted)	**aprueba**	**ha aprobado**
(nosotros/as)	**aprobamos**	**hemos aprobado**
(vosotros/as)	**aprobáis**	**habéis aprobado**
(ellos/ellas/ ustedes)	**aprueban**	**han aprobado**

	PRETERITE	IMPERFECT
(yo)	**aprobé**	**aprobaba**
(tú)	**aprobaste**	**aprobabas**
(él/ella/usted)	**aprobó**	**aprobaba**
(nosotros/as)	**aprobamos**	**aprobábamos**
(vosotros/as)	**aprobasteis**	**aprobabais**
(ellos/ellas/ ustedes)	**aprobaron**	**aprobaban**

GERUND	PAST PARTICIPLE
aprobando	**aprobado**

EXAMPLE PHRASES

No **apruebo** esa conducta. I don't approve of that sort of behavior.

Este año lo **estoy aprobando** todo. So far this year I've passed everything.

Han aprobado una ley antitabaco. They've passed an anti-smoking law.

¿**Aprobaste** el examen? Did you pass the test?

La decisión **fue aprobada** por mayoría. The decision was approved by a majority.

Remember that subject pronouns are not used very often in Spanish.

aprobar

	FUTURE	CONDITIONAL
(yo)	aprobaré	aprobaría
(tú)	aprobarás	aprobarías
(él/ella/usted)	aprobará	aprobaría
(nosotros/as)	aprobaremos	aprobaríamos
(vosotros/as)	aprobaréis	aprobaríais
(ellos/ellas/ ustedes)	aprobarán	aprobarían

	PRESENT SUBJUNCTIVE	IMPERFECT SUBJUNCTIVE
(yo)	apruebe	aprobara *or* aprobase
(tú)	apruebes	aprobaras *or* aprobases
(él/ella/usted)	apruebe	aprobara *or* aprobase
(nosotros/as)	aprobemos	aprobáramos *or* aprobásemos
(vosotros/as)	aprobéis	aprobarais *or* aprobaseis
(ellos/ellas/ ustedes)	aprueben	aprobaran *or* aprobasen

IMPERATIVE

aprueba / aprobad

Use the present subjunctive in all cases other than these tú and vosotros affirmative forms.

Remember that subject pronouns are not used very often in Spanish.

arrancar (to pull up; to start)

	PRESENT	PRESENT PERFECT
(yo)	**arranco**	**he arrancado**
(tú)	**arrancas**	**has arrancado**
(él/ella/usted)	**arranca**	**ha arrancado**
(nosotros/as)	**arrancamos**	**hemos arrancado**
(vosotros/as)	**arrancáis**	**habéis arrancado**
(ellos/ellas/ ustedes)	**arrancan**	**han arrancado**

	PRETERITE	IMPERFECT
(yo)	**arranqué**	**arrancaba**
(tú)	**arrancaste**	**arrancabas**
(él/ella/usted)	**arrancó**	**arrancaba**
(nosotros/as)	**arrancamos**	**arrancábamos**
(vosotros/as)	**arrancasteis**	**arrancabais**
(ellos/ellas/ ustedes)	**arrancaron**	**arrancaban**

GERUND	PAST PARTICIPLE
arrancando	**arrancado**

EXAMPLE PHRASES

Lo tienes que **arrancar** de raíz. You must pull it up by its roots.

Estaba arrancando malas hierbas. I was pulling up weeds.

El viento **arrancó** varios árboles. Several trees were uprooted in the wind.

La moto no **arranca**. The motorcycle won't start.

Remember that subject pronouns are not used very often in Spanish.

arrancar

	FUTURE	CONDITIONAL
(yo)	arrancaré	arrancaría
(tú)	arrancarás	arrancarías
(él/ella/usted)	arrancará	arrancaría
(nosotros/as)	arrancaremos	arrancaríamos
(vosotros/as)	arrancaréis	arrancaríais
(ellos/ellas/ ustedes)	arrancarán	arrancarían

	PRESENT SUBJUNCTIVE	IMPERFECT SUBJUNCTIVE
(yo)	arranque	arrancara *or* arrancase
(tú)	arranques	arrancaras *or* arrancases
(él/ella/usted)	arranque	arrancara *or* arrancase
(nosotros/as)	arranquemos	arrancáramos *or* arrancásemos
(vosotros/as)	arranquéis	arrancarais *or* arrancaseis
(ellos/ellas/ ustedes)	arranquen	arrancaran *or* arrancasen

IMPERATIVE

arranca / arrancad

Use the present subjunctive in all cases other than these tú and vosotros affirmative forms.

EXAMPLE PHRASES

No **arranques** hojas del cuaderno. Don't tear pages out of the notebook.

Arranca y vámonos. Start the engine and let's get going.

arrepentirse (to be sorry; to change your mind)

	PRESENT	PRESENT PERFECT
(yo)	me arrepiento	me he arrepentido
(tú)	te arrepientes	te has arrepentido
(él/ella/usted)	se arrepiente	se ha arrepentido
(nosotros/as)	nos arrepentimos	nos hemos arrepentido
(vosotros/as)	os arrepentís	os habéis arrepentido
(ellos/ellas/ ustedes)	se arrepienten	se han arrepentido

	PRETERITE	IMPERFECT
(yo)	me arrepentí	me arrepentía
(tú)	te arrepentiste	te arrepentías
(él/ella/usted)	se arrepintió	se arrepentía
(nosotros/as)	nos arrepentimos	nos arrepentíamos
(vosotros/as)	os arrepentisteis	os arrepentíais
(ellos/ellas/ ustedes)	se arrepintieron	se arrepentían

GERUND
arrepintiéndose, etc

PAST PARTICIPLE
arrepentido

EXAMPLE PHRASES

¡**Te** vas a **arrepentir** de esto! You'll be sorry for this!

No **me arrepiento** de nada. I don't regret anything.

Se arrepintieron y decidieron no vender la casa. They changed their minds and decided not to sell the house.

Arrepintiéndote en serio, seguro que te perdonarán. If you're truly sorry, I'm sure they'll forgive you.

Remember that subject pronouns are not used very often in Spanish.

arrepentirse

	FUTURE	CONDITIONAL
(yo)	me arrepentiré	me arrepentiría
(tú)	te arrepentirás	te arrepentirías
(él/ella/usted)	se arrepentirá	se arrepentiría
(nosotros/as)	nos arrepentiremos	nos arrepentiríamos
(vosotros/as)	os arrepentiréis	os arrepentiríais
(ellos/ellas/ ustedes)	se arrepentirán	se arrepentirían

	PRESENT SUBJUNCTIVE	IMPERFECT SUBJUNCTIVE
(yo)	me arrepienta	me arrepintiera *or* arrepintiese
(tú)	te arrepientas	te arrepintieras *or* arrepintieses
(él/ella/usted)	se arrepienta	se arrepintiera *or* arrepintiese
(nosotros/as)	nos arrepintamos	nos arrepintiéramos *or* arrepintiésemos
(vosotros/as)	os arrepintáis	os arrepintierais *or* arrepintieseis
(ellos/ellas/ ustedes)	se arrepientan	se arrepintieran *or* arrepintiesen

IMPERATIVE

arrepiéntete / arrepentíos

Use the present subjunctive in all cases other than these tú and vosotros affirmative forms.

EXAMPLE PHRASES

Algún día **se arrepentirá** de no haber estudiado una carrera. One day he'll be sorry he didn't go to college.

No **te arrepientas** nunca de haber dicho la verdad. Don't ever regret having told the truth.

Remember that subject pronouns are not used very often in Spanish.

atravesar (to cross; to go through)

	PRESENT	PRESENT PERFECT
(yo)	**atravieso**	**he atravesado**
(tú)	**atraviesas**	**has atravesado**
(él/ella/usted)	**atraviesa**	**ha atravesado**
(nosotros/as)	**atravesamos**	**hemos atravesado**
(vosotros/as)	**atravesáis**	**habéis atravesado**
(ellos/ellas/ ustedes)	**atraviesan**	**han atravesado**

	PRETERITE	IMPERFECT
(yo)	**atravesé**	**atravesaba**
(tú)	**atravesaste**	**atravesabas**
(él/ella/usted)	**atravesó**	**atravesaba**
(nosotros/as)	**atravesamos**	**atravesábamos**
(vosotros/as)	**atravesasteis**	**atravesabais**
(ellos/ellas/ ustedes)	**atravesaron**	**atravesaban**

GERUND	PAST PARTICIPLE
atravesando	**atravesado**

EXAMPLE PHRASES

Estamos atravesando un mal momento. We're going through a bad patch.

Atravesamos el río a nado. We swam across the river.

La bala le **atravesó** el cráneo. The bullet went through his skull.

Un camión **se** nos **atravesó** en la carretera. A truck pulled out in front of us on the road.

Remember that subject pronouns are not used very often in Spanish.

atravesar

	FUTURE	CONDITIONAL
(yo)	**atravesaré**	**atravesaría**
(tú)	**atravesarás**	**atravesarías**
(él/ella/usted)	**atravesará**	**atravesaría**
(nosotros/as)	**atravesaremos**	**atravesaríamos**
(vosotros/as)	**atravesaréis**	**atravesaríais**
(ellos/ellas/ ustedes)	**atravesarán**	**atravesarían**

	PRESENT SUBJUNCTIVE	IMPERFECT SUBJUNCTIVE
(yo)	**atraviese**	**atravesara** *or* **atravesase**
(tú)	**atravieses**	**atravesaras** *or* **atravesases**
(él/ella/usted)	**atraviese**	**atravesara** *or* **atravesase**
(nosotros/as)	**atravesemos**	**atravesáramos** *or* **atravesásemos**
(vosotros/as)	**atraveséis**	**atravesarais** *or* **atravesaseis**
(ellos/ellas/ ustedes)	**atraviesen**	**atravesaran** *or* **atravesasen**

IMPERATIVE

atraviesa / atravesad

Use the present subjunctive in all cases other than these tú and vosotros affirmative forms.

EXAMPLE PHRASES

El túnel **atravesará** la montaña. The tunnel will go through the mountain.

Remember that subject pronouns are not used very often in Spanish.

aunar (to join together)

	PRESENT	PRESENT PERFECT
(yo)	**aúno**	**he aunado**
(tú)	**aúnas**	**has aunado**
(él/ella/usted)	**aúna**	**ha aunado**
(nosotros/as)	**aunamos**	**hemos aunado**
(vosotros/as)	**aunáis**	**habéis aunado**
(ellos/ellas/ustedes)	**aúnan**	**han aunado**

	PRETERITE	IMPERFECT
(yo)	**auné**	**aunaba**
(tú)	**aunaste**	**aunabas**
(él/ella/usted)	**aunó**	**aunaba**
(nosotros/as)	**aunamos**	**aunábamos**
(vosotros/as)	**aunasteis**	**aunabais**
(ellos/ellas/ustedes)	**aunaron**	**aunaban**

GERUND	PAST PARTICIPLE
aunando	**aunado**

EXAMPLE PHRASES

En esta obra **se aúnan** imaginación y técnica. This play combines imagination and technique.

Aunaron esfuerzos. They joined forces.

aunar

	FUTURE	CONDITIONAL
(yo)	aunaré	aunaría
(tú)	aunarás	aunarías
(él/ella/usted)	aunará	aunaría
(nosotros/as)	aunaremos	aunaríamos
(vosotros/as)	aunaréis	aunaríais
(ellos/ellas/ ustedes)	aunarán	aunarían

	PRESENT SUBJUNCTIVE	IMPERFECT SUBJUNCTIVE
(yo)	aúne	aunara *or* aunase
(tú)	aúnes	aunaras *or* aunases
(él/ella/usted)	aúne	aunara *or* aunase
(nosotros/as)	aunemos	aunáramos *or* aunásemos
(vosotros/as)	aunéis	aunarais *or* aunaseis
(ellos/ellas/ ustedes)	aúnen	aunaran *or* aunasen

IMPERATIVE

aúna / aunad

Use the present subjunctive in all cases other than these tú *and* vosotros *affirmative forms.*

Remember that subject pronouns are not used very often in Spanish.

avergonzar (to shame)

	PRESENT	PRESENT PERFECT
(yo)	**avergüenzo**	**he avergonzado**
(tú)	**avergüenzas**	**has avergonzado**
(él/ella/usted)	**avergüenza**	**ha avergonzado**
(nosotros/as)	**avergonzamos**	**hemos avergonzado**
(vosotros/as)	**avergonzáis**	**habéis avergonzado**
(ellos/ellas/ ustedes)	**avergüenzan**	**han avergonzado**

	PRETERITE	IMPERFECT
(yo)	**avergoncé**	**avergonzaba**
(tú)	**avergonzaste**	**avergonzabas**
(él/ella/usted)	**avergonzó**	**avergonzaba**
(nosotros/as)	**avergonzamos**	**avergonzábamos**
(vosotros/as)	**avergonzasteis**	**avergonzabais**
(ellos/ellas/ ustedes)	**avergonzaron**	**avergonzaban**

GERUND	PAST PARTICIPLE
avergonzando	**avergonzado**

EXAMPLE PHRASES

Tendrías que **avergonzarte**. You should be ashamed of yourself.

La **avergüenza** no tener dinero. She's ashamed of having no money.

Cuando me lo dijo **me avergoncé**. I was embarrassed when he told me.

Se avergonzaba de su familia. He was ashamed of his family.

Remember that subject pronouns are not used very often in Spanish.

avergonzar

	FUTURE	CONDITIONAL
(yo)	avergonzaré	avergonzaría
(tú)	avergonzarás	avergonzarías
(él/ella/usted)	avergonzará	avergonzaría
(nosotros/as)	avergonzaremos	avergonzaríamos
(vosotros/as)	avegonzaréis	avergonzaríais
(ellos/ellas/ ustedes)	avergonzarán	avergonzarían

	PRESENT SUBJUNCTIVE	IMPERFECT SUBJUNCTIVE
(yo)	avergüence	avergonzara *or* avergonzase
(tú)	avergüences	avergonzaras *or* avergonzases
(él/ella/usted)	avergüence	avergonzara *or* avergonzase
(nosotros/as)	avergoncemos	avergonzáramos *or* avergonzásemos
(vosotros/as)	avergoncéis	avergonzarais *or* avergonzaseis
(ellos/ellas/ ustedes)	avergüencen	avergonzaran *or* avergonzasen

IMPERATIVE

avergüenza / avergonzad

Use the present subjunctive in all cases other than these tú and vosotros affirmative forms.

EXAMPLE PHRASES

Si de verdad **se avergonzaran**, no se comportarían así. They wouldn't behave like that if they were really ashamed.

Remember that subject pronouns are not used very often in Spanish.

averiguar (to find out)

	PRESENT	PRESENT PERFECT
(yo)	averiguo	he averiguado
(tú)	averiguas	has averiguado
(él/ella/usted)	averigua	ha averiguado
(nosotros/as)	averiguamos	hemos averiguado
(vosotros/as)	averiguáis	habéis averiguado
(ellos/ellas/ ustedes)	averiguan	han averiguado

	PRETERITE	IMPERFECT
(yo)	averigüé	averiguaba
(tú)	averiguaste	averiguabas
(él/ella/usted)	averiguó	averiguaba
(nosotros/as)	averiguamos	averiguábamos
(vosotros/as)	averiguasteis	averiguabais
(ellos/ellas/ ustedes)	averiguaron	averiguaban

GERUND	PAST PARTICIPLE
averiguando	averiguado

EXAMPLE PHRASES

Trataron de **averiguar** su paradero. They tried to find out his whereabouts.

Poco a poco **van averiguando** más cosas sobre su vida. They're gradually finding out more about his life.

¿Cómo **averiguaste** dónde vivo? How did you find out where I live?

¿Cuándo lo **averiguaron**? When did they find out?

Remember that subject pronouns are not used very often in Spanish.

averiguar

	FUTURE	CONDITIONAL
(yo)	**averiguaré**	**averiguaría**
(tú)	**averiguarás**	**averiguarías**
(él/ella/usted)	**averiguará**	**averiguaría**
(nosotros/as)	**averiguaremos**	**averiguaríamos**
(vosotros/as)	**averiguaréis**	**averiguaríais**
(ellos/ellas/ ustedes)	**averiguarán**	**averiguarían**

	PRESENT SUBJUNCTIVE	IMPERFECT SUBJUNCTIVE
(yo)	**averigüe**	**averiguara** *or* **averiguase**
(tú)	**averigües**	**averiguaras** *or* **averiguases**
(él/ella/usted)	**averigüe**	**averiguara** *or* **averiguase**
(nosotros/as)	**averigüemos**	**averiguáramos** *or* **averiguásemos**
(vosotros/as)	**averigüéis**	**averiguarais** *or* **averiguaseis**
(ellos/ellas/ ustedes)	**averigüen**	**averiguaran** *or* **averiguasen**

IMPERATIVE

averigua / averiguad

Use the present subjunctive in all cases other than these tú *and* vosotros *affirmative forms.*

EXAMPLE PHRASES

Lo **averiguaré** pronto. I'll find out soon.

Dijo que si le dábamos tiempo lo **averiguaría**. She said that she'd find out if we gave her time.

En cuanto lo **averigüe** te lo digo. I'll tell you as soon as I find out.

¡**Averígualo** inmediatamente! Check it out immediately!

Remember that subject pronouns are not used very often in Spanish.

bendecir (to bless)

	PRESENT	PRESENT PERFECT
(yo)	**bendigo**	**he bendecido**
(tú)	**bendices**	**has bendecido**
(él/ella/usted)	**bendice**	**ha bendecido**
(nosotros/as)	**bendecimos**	**hemos bendecido**
(vosotros/as)	**bendecís**	**habéis bendecido**
(ellos/ellas/ ustedes)	**bendicen**	**han bendecido**

	PRETERITE	IMPERFECT
(yo)	**bendije**	**bendecía**
(tú)	**bendijiste**	**bendecías**
(él/ella/usted)	**bendijo**	**bendecía**
(nosotros/as)	**bendijimos**	**bendecíamos**
(vosotros/as)	**bendijisteis**	**bendecíais**
(ellos/ellas/ ustedes)	**bendijeron**	**bendecían**

GERUND	PAST PARTICIPLE
bendiciendo	**bendecido**

EXAMPLE PHRASES

La vida me **ha bendecido** con unos hijos maravillosos. I've been blessed with wonderful children.

Jesús **bendijo** los panes y los peces. Jesus blessed the loaves and the fishes.

Bendecía el día en que lo conoció. She blessed the day she met him.

Remember that subject pronouns are not used very often in Spanish.

bendecir

	FUTURE	CONDITIONAL
(yo)	**bendeciré**	**bendeciría**
(tú)	**bendecirás**	**bendecirías**
(él/ella/usted)	**bendecirá**	**bendeciría**
(nosotros/as)	**bendeciremos**	**bendeciríamos**
(vosotros/as)	**bendeciréis**	**bendeciríais**
(ellos/ellas/ ustedes)	**bendecirán**	**bendecirían**

	PRESENT SUBJUNCTIVE	IMPERFECT SUBJUNCTIVE
(yo)	**bendiga**	**bendijera** *or* **bendijese**
(tú)	**bendigas**	**bendijeras** *or* **bendijeses**
(él/ella/usted)	**bendiga**	**bendijera** *or* **bendijese**
(nosotros/as)	**bendigamos**	**bendijéramos** *or* **bendijésemos**
(vosotros/as)	**bendigáis**	**bendijerais** *or* **bendijeseis**
(ellos/ellas/ ustedes)	**bendigan**	**bendijeran** *or* **bendijesen**

IMPERATIVE

bendice / bendecid

Use the present subjunctive in all cases other than these tú and vosotros affirmative forms.

EXAMPLE PHRASES

El Papa **bendecirá** a los fieles desde el balcón. The Pope will bless the faithful from the balcony.

Quieren que sea él quien **bendiga** su unión. They want him to marry them.

Pidieron a un sacerdote que **bendijera** su nueva casa. They asked a priest to bless their new house.

Remember that subject pronouns are not used very often in Spanish.

caber (to fit)

	PRESENT	PRESENT PERFECT
(yo)	**quepo**	**he cabido**
(tú)	**cabes**	**has cabido**
(él/ella/usted)	**cabe**	**ha cabido**
(nosotros/as)	**cabemos**	**hemos cabido**
(vosotros/as)	**cabéis**	**habéis cabido**
(ellos/ellas/ ustedes)	**caben**	**han cabido**

	PRETERITE	IMPERFECT
(yo)	**cupe**	**cabía**
(tú)	**cupiste**	**cabías**
(él/ella/usted)	**cupo**	**cabía**
(nosotros/as)	**cupimos**	**cabíamos**
(vosotros/as)	**cupisteis**	**cabíais**
(ellos/ellas/ ustedes)	**cupieron**	**cabían**

GERUND	PAST PARTICIPLE
cabiendo	**cabido**

EXAMPLE PHRASES

No te preocupes, que va a **caber**. Don't worry, it will fit.
Aquí no **cabe**. There isn't enough room for it here.
Al final **cupo** todo. In the end everything went in.
No le **cupo** la menor duda. She wasn't in any doubt.
No **cabía** en sí de dicha. She was beside herself with joy.

Remember that subject pronouns are not used very often in Spanish.

caber

	FUTURE	CONDITIONAL
(yo)	**cabré**	**cabría**
(tú)	**cabrás**	**cabrías**
(él/ella/usted)	**cabrá**	**cabría**
(nosotros/as)	**cabremos**	**cabríamos**
(vosotros/as)	**cabréis**	**cabríais**
(ellos/ellas/ ustedes)	**cabrán**	**cabrían**

	PRESENT SUBJUNCTIVE	IMPERFECT SUBJUNCTIVE
(yo)	**quepa**	**cupiera** *or* **cupiese**
(tú)	**quepas**	**cupieras** *or* **cupieses**
(él/ella/usted)	**quepa**	**cupiera** *or* **cupiese**
(nosotros/as)	**quepamos**	**cupiéramos** *or* **cupiésemos**
(vosotros/as)	**quepáis**	**cupierais** *or* **cupieseis**
(ellos/ellas/ ustedes)	**quepan**	**cupieran** *or* **cupiesen**

IMPERATIVE

cabe / cabed

Use the present subjunctive in all cases other than these tú and vosotros affirmative forms.

EXAMPLE PHRASES

¿Crees que **cabrá**? Do you think there will be enough room for it?

Cabría cuestionarse si es la mejor solución. We should ask ourselves whether it's the best solution.

Hizo lo imposible para que le **cupiera** la redacción en una página. He did everything he could to fit the essay onto one page.

Remember that subject pronouns are not used very often in Spanish.

caer (to fall)

	PRESENT	PRESENT PERFECT
(yo)	**caigo**	**he caído**
(tú)	**caes**	**has caído**
(él/ella/usted)	**cae**	**ha caído**
(nosotros/as)	**caemos**	**hemos caído**
(vosotros/as)	**caéis**	**habéis caído**
(ellos/ellas/ ustedes)	**caen**	**han caído**

	PRETERITE	IMPERFECT
(yo)	**caí**	**caía**
(tú)	**caíste**	**caías**
(él/ella/usted)	**cayó**	**caía**
(nosotros/as)	**caímos**	**caíamos**
(vosotros/as)	**caísteis**	**caíais**
(ellos/ellas/ ustedes)	**cayeron**	**caían**

GERUND	PAST PARTICIPLE
cayendo	**caído**

EXAMPLE PHRASES

Su cumpleaños **cae** en viernes. Her birthday falls on a Friday.

Ese edificio **se está cayendo**. That building's falling down.

Se me **cayó** un guante. I dropped one of my gloves.

Me caí por las escaleras. I fell down the stairs.

Me caía muy bien. I really liked him.

Remember that subject pronouns are not used very often in Spanish.

caer

	FUTURE	CONDITIONAL
(yo)	caeré	caería
(tú)	caerás	caerías
(él/ella/usted)	caerá	caería
(nosotros/as)	caeremos	caeríamos
(vosotros/as)	caeréis	caeríais
(ellos/ellas/ ustedes)	caerán	caerían

	PRESENT SUBJUNCTIVE	IMPERFECT SUBJUNCTIVE
(yo)	caiga	cayera *or* cayese
(tú)	caigas	cayeras *or* cayeses
(él/ella/usted)	caiga	cayera *or* cayese
(nosotros/as)	caigamos	cayéramos *or* cayésemos
(vosotros/as)	caigáis	cayerais *or* cayeseis
(ellos/ellas/ ustedes)	caigan	cayeran *or* cayesen

IMPERATIVE

cae / caed

Use the present subjunctive in all cases other than these tú and vosotros affirmative forms.

EXAMPLE PHRASES

Tarde o temprano, **caerá** en manos del enemigo. Sooner or later, it will fall into enemy hands.

Yo **me caería** con esos tacones. I'd fall over if I wore heels like those.

Seguirá adelante **caiga** quien **caiga**. She'll go ahead no matter how many heads have to roll.

No **caigas** tan bajo. Don't stoop so low.

Remember that subject pronouns are not used very often in Spanish.

cambiar (to change)

	PRESENT	PRESENT PERFECT
(yo)	cambio	he cambiado
(tú)	cambias	has cambiado
(él/ella/usted)	cambia	ha cambiado
(nosotros/as)	cambiamos	hemos cambiado
(vosotros/as)	cambiáis	habéis cambiado
(ellos/ellas/ ustedes)	cambian	han cambiado

	PRETERITE	IMPERFECT
(yo)	cambié	cambiaba
(tú)	cambiaste	cambiabas
(él/ella/usted)	cambió	cambiaba
(nosotros/as)	cambiamos	cambiábamos
(vosotros/as)	cambiasteis	cambiabais
(ellos/ellas/ ustedes)	cambiaron	cambiaban

GERUND	PAST PARTICIPLE
cambiando	cambiado

EXAMPLE PHRASES

Necesito **cambiar** de ambiente. I need a change of scenery.

Te **cambio** mi bolígrafo por tu goma. I'll swap my pen for your eraser.

Cambié varias veces de trabajo. I changed jobs several times.

Cambiaban de idea a cada rato. They kept changing their minds.

Remember that subject pronouns are not used very often in Spanish.

cambiar

	FUTURE	CONDITIONAL
(yo)	cambiaré	cambiaría
(tú)	cambiarás	cambiarías
(él/ella/usted)	cambiará	cambiaría
(nosotros/as)	cambiaremos	cambiaríamos
(vosotros/as)	cambiaréis	cambiaríais
(ellos/ellas/ ustedes)	cambiarán	cambiarían

	PRESENT SUBJUNCTIVE	IMPERFECT SUBJUNCTIVE
(yo)	cambie	cambiara *or* cambiase
(tú)	cambies	cambiaras *or* cambiases
(él/ella/usted)	cambie	cambiara *or* cambiase
(nosotros/as)	cambiemos	cambiáramos *or* cambiásemos
(vosotros/as)	cambiéis	cambiarais *or* cambiaseis
(ellos/ellas/ ustedes)	cambien	cambiaran *or* cambiasen

IMPERATIVE

cambia / cambiad

Use the present subjunctive in all cases other than these tú and vosotros affirmative forms.

EXAMPLE PHRASES

Cuando la conozcas, **cambiarás** de idea. You'll change your mind when you meet her.

Si pudiéramos, **nos cambiaríamos** de casa. If we could, we'd move.

No quiero que **cambies**. I don't want you to change.

Cámbiate, que se nos hace tarde. Get changed, it's getting late.

Remember that subject pronouns are not used very often in Spanish.

cazar (to hunt; to shoot)

	PRESENT	PRESENT PERFECT
(yo)	cazo	he cazado
(tú)	cazas	has cazado
(él/ella/usted)	caza	ha cazado
(nosotros/as)	cazamos	hemos cazado
(vosotros/as)	cazáis	habéis cazado
(ellos/ellas/ustedes)	cazan	han cazado

	PRETERITE	IMPERFECT
(yo)	cacé	cazaba
(tú)	cazaste	cazabas
(él/ella/usted)	cazó	cazaba
(nosotros/as)	cazamos	cazábamos
(vosotros/as)	cazasteis	cazabais
(ellos/ellas/ustedes)	cazaron	cazaban

GERUND	PAST PARTICIPLE
cazando	cazado

EXAMPLE PHRASES

Salieron a **cazar** ciervos. They went deer-hunting.

Caza las cosas al vuelo. She's very quick on the uptake.

Los **cacé** robando. I caught them stealing.

Cazaban con lanza. They hunted with spears.

Remember that subject pronouns are not used very often in Spanish.

cazar

	FUTURE	CONDITIONAL
(yo)	**cazaré**	**cazaría**
(tú)	**cazarás**	**cazarías**
(él/ella/usted)	**cazará**	**cazaría**
(nosotros/as)	**cazaremos**	**cazaríamos**
(vosotros/as)	**cazaréis**	**cazaríais**
(ellos/ellas/ ustedes)	**cazarán**	**cazarían**

	PRESENT SUBJUNCTIVE	IMPERFECT SUBJUNCTIVE
(yo)	**cace**	**cazara** *or* **cazase**
(tú)	**caces**	**cazaras** *or* **cazases**
(él/ella/usted)	**cace**	**cazara** *or* **cazase**
(nosotros/as)	**cacemos**	**cazáramos** *or* **cazásemos**
(vosotros/as)	**cacéis**	**cazarais** *or* **cazaseis**
(ellos/ellas/ ustedes)	**cacen**	**cazaran** *or* **cazasen**

IMPERATIVE

caza / cazad

Use the present subjunctive in all cases other than these **tú** *and* **vosotros** *affirmative forms.*

EXAMPLE PHRASES

¡Quién **cazara** a un millonario! I wish I could land myself a millionaire!

Remember that subject pronouns are not used very often in Spanish.

cerrar (to close; to shut)

	PRESENT	PRESENT PERFECT
(yo)	cierro	he cerrado
(tú)	cierras	has cerrado
(él/ella/usted)	cierra	ha cerrado
(nosotros/as)	cerramos	hemos cerrado
(vosotros/as)	cerráis	habéis cerrado
(ellos/ellas/ ustedes)	cierran	han cerrado

	PRETERITE	IMPERFECT
(yo)	cerré	cerraba
(tú)	cerraste	cerrabas
(él/ella/usted)	cerró	cerraba
(nosotros/as)	cerramos	cerrábamos
(vosotros/as)	cerrasteis	cerrabais
(ellos/ellas/ ustedes)	cerraron	cerraban

GERUND	PAST PARTICIPLE
cerrando	cerrado

EXAMPLE PHRASES

No puedo **cerrar** la maleta. I can't close my suitcase.

No **cierran** al mediodía. They don't close at noon.

Había cerrado la puerta con llave. She'd locked the door.

Cerró el libro. He closed the book.

Se le **cerraban** los ojos. She couldn't keep her eyes open.

Remember that subject pronouns are not used very often in Spanish.

cerrar

	FUTURE	CONDITIONAL
(yo)	**cerraré**	**cerraría**
(tú)	**cerrarás**	**cerrarías**
(él/ella/usted)	**cerrará**	**cerraría**
(nosotros/as)	**cerraremos**	**cerraríamos**
(vosotros/as)	**cerraréis**	**cerraríais**
(ellos/ellas/ ustedes)	**cerrrarán**	**cerrarían**

	PRESENT SUBJUNCTIVE	IMPERFECT SUBJUNCTIVE
(yo)	**cierre**	**cerrara** *or* **cerrase**
(tú)	**cierres**	**cerraras** *or* **cerrases**
(él/ella/usted)	**cierre**	**cerrara** *or* **cerrase**
(nosotros/as)	**cerremos**	**cerráramos** *or* **cerrásemos**
(vosotros/as)	**cerréis**	**cerrarais** *or* **cerraseis**
(ellos/ellas/ ustedes)	**cierren**	**cerraran** *or* **cerrasen**

IMPERATIVE

cierra / cerrad

Use the present subjunctive in all cases other than these tú and vosotros affirmative forms.

EXAMPLE PHRASES

No dejes que **se cierre** la puerta de golpe. Don't let the door slam shut.

No **cierres** la ventana. Don't close the window.

Cierra la llave. Turn off the faucet.

cocer (to boil; to cook)

	PRESENT	PRESENT PERFECT
(yo)	cuezo	he cocido
(tú)	cueces	has cocido
(él/ella/usted)	cuece	ha cocido
(nosotros/as)	cocemos	hemos cocido
(vosotros/as)	cocéis	habéis cocido
(ellos/ellas/ustedes)	cuecen	han cocido

	PRETERITE	IMPERFECT
(yo)	cocí	cocía
(tú)	cociste	cocías
(él/ella/usted)	coció	cocía
(nosotros/as)	cocimos	cocíamos
(vosotros/as)	cocisteis	cocíais
(ellos/ellas/ustedes)	cocieron	cocían

GERUND	PAST PARTICIPLE
cociendo	cocido

EXAMPLE PHRASES

El pescado **se cuece** en un momento. Fish takes no time to cook.

Aquí nos **estamos cociendo**. It's boiling in here.

Coció el pan en el horno. He baked the bread in the oven.

cocer

	FUTURE	CONDITIONAL
(yo)	**coceré**	**cocería**
(tú)	**cocerás**	**cocerías**
(él/ella/usted)	**cocerá**	**cocería**
(nosotros/as)	**coceremos**	**coceríamos**
(vosotros/as)	**coceréis**	**coceríais**
(ellos/ellas/ ustedes)	**cocerán**	**cocerían**

	PRESENT SUBJUNCTIVE	IMPERFECT SUBJUNCTIVE
(yo)	**cueza**	**cociera** *or* **cociese**
(tú)	**cuezas**	**cocieras** *or* **cocieses**
(él/ella/usted)	**cueza**	**cociera** *or* **cociese**
(nosotros/as)	**cozamos**	**cociéramos** *or* **cociésemos**
(vosotros/as)	**cozáis**	**cocierais** *or* **cocieseis**
(ellos/ellas/ ustedes)	**cuezan**	**cocieran** *or* **cociesen**

IMPERATIVE

cuece / coced

Use the present subjunctive in all cases other than these **tú** *and* **vosotros** *affirmative forms.*

EXAMPLE PHRASES

Te dije que lo **cocieras** tapado. I told you to cook it covered.

No lo **cuezas** demasiado. Don't overcook it.

Cuécelo a fuego lento. Cook it over a low heat.

Remember that subject pronouns are not used very often in Spanish.

colgar (to hang)

	PRESENT	PRESENT PERFECT
(yo)	**cuelgo**	**he colgado**
(tú)	**cuelgas**	**has colgado**
(él/ella/usted)	**cuelga**	**ha colgado**
(nosotros/as)	**colgamos**	**hemos colgado**
(vosotros/as)	**colgáis**	**habéis colgado**
(ellos/ellas/ ustedes)	**cuelgan**	**han colgado**

	PRETERITE	IMPERFECT
(yo)	**colgué**	**colgaba**
(tú)	**colgaste**	**colgabas**
(él/ella/usted)	**colgó**	**colgaba**
(nosotros/as)	**colgamos**	**colgábamos**
(vosotros/as)	**colgasteis**	**colgabais**
(ellos/ellas/ ustedes)	**colgaron**	**colgaban**

GERUND	PAST PARTICIPLE
colgando	**colgado**

EXAMPLE PHRASES

Hay telarañas **colgando** del techo. There are cobwebs hanging from the ceiling.

Te **colgué** la chaqueta en el clóset. I hung your jacket in the closet.

Me **colgó** el teléfono. He hung up on me.

De la pared **colgaba** un espejo. There was a mirror hanging on the wall.

Remember that subject pronouns are not used very often in Spanish.

colgar

	FUTURE	CONDITIONAL
(yo)	**colgaré**	**colgaría**
(tú)	**colgarás**	**colgarías**
(él/ella/usted)	**colgará**	**colgaría**
(nosotros/as)	**colgaremos**	**colgaríamos**
(vosotros/as)	**colgaréis**	**colgaríais**
(ellos/ellas/ ustedes)	**colgarán**	**colgarían**

	PRESENT SUBJUNCTIVE	IMPERFECT SUBJUNCTIVE
(yo)	**cuelgue**	**colgara** *or* **colgase**
(tú)	**cuelgues**	**colgaras** *or* **colgases**
(él/ella/usted)	**cuelgue**	**colgara** *or* **colgase**
(nosotros/as)	**colguemos**	**colgáramos** *or* **colgásemos**
(vosotros/as)	**colguéis**	**colgarais** *or* **colgaseis**
(ellos/ellas/ ustedes)	**cuelguen**	**colgaran** *or* **colgasen**

IMPERATIVE

cuelga / colgad

Use the present subjunctive in all cases other than these tú and vosotros affirmative forms.

EXAMPLE PHRASES

Colgaremos el cuadro en esa pared. We'll hang the picture on that wall.

No **cuelgue**, por favor. Please don't hang up.

comer (to eat)

	PRESENT	PRESENT PERFECT
(yo)	como	he comido
(tú)	comes	has comido
(él/ella/usted)	come	ha comido
(nosotros/as)	comemos	hemos comido
(vosotros/as)	coméis	habéis comido
(ellos/ellas/ ustedes)	comen	han comido

	PRETERITE	IMPERFECT
(yo)	comí	comía
(tú)	comiste	comías
(él/ella/usted)	comió	comía
(nosotros/as)	comimos	comíamos
(vosotros/as)	comisteis	comíais
(ellos/ellas/ ustedes)	comieron	comían

GERUND	PAST PARTICIPLE
comiendo	comido

EXAMPLE PHRASES

No **come** carne. He doesn't eat meat.

Se lo **comió** todo. He ate it all.

Comimos en un restaurante. We had lunch in a restaurant.

Siempre **comían** demasiado. They always ate too much.

Remember that subject pronouns are not used very often in Spanish.

comer

	FUTURE	CONDITIONAL
(yo)	**comeré**	**comería**
(tú)	**comerás**	**comerías**
(él/ella/usted)	**comerá**	**comería**
(nosotros/as)	**comeremos**	**comeríamos**
(vosotros/as)	**comeréis**	**comeríais**
(ellos/ellas/ ustedes)	**comerán**	**comerían**

	PRESENT SUBJUNCTIVE	IMPERFECT SUBJUNCTIVE
(yo)	**coma**	**comiera** *or* **comiese**
(tú)	**comas**	**comieras** *or* **comieses**
(él/ella/usted)	**coma**	**comiera** *or* **comiese**
(nosotros/as)	**comamos**	**comiéramos** *or* **comiésemos**
(vosotros/as)	**comáis**	**comierais** *or* **comieseis**
(ellos/ellas/ ustedes)	**coman**	**comieran** *or* **comiesen**

IMPERATIVE

come / comed

Use the present subjunctive in all cases other than these tú and vosotros affirmative forms.

EXAMPLE PHRASES

Me lo **comeré** yo. I'll eat it.

Si no fuera por mí, no **comeríamos**. We wouldn't eat if it weren't for me.

No **comas** tan deprisa. Don't eat so fast.

Remember that subject pronouns are not used very often in Spanish.

conducir (to lead; to drive; to take)

	PRESENT	PRESENT PERFECT
(yo)	conduzco	he conducido
(tú)	conduces	has conducido
(él/ella/usted)	conduce	ha conducido
(nosotros/as)	conducimos	hemos conducido
(vosotros/as)	conducís	habéis conducido
(ellos/ellas/ustedes)	conducen	han conducido

	PRETERITE	IMPERFECT
(yo)	conduje	conducía
(tú)	condujiste	conducías
(él/ella/usted)	condujo	conducía
(nosotros/as)	condujimos	conducíamos
(vosotros/as)	condujisteis	conducíais
(ellos/ellas/ustedes)	condujeron	conducían

GERUND
conduciendo

PAST PARTICIPLE
conducido

EXAMPLE PHRASES

Nos **condujo** a su habitación. He took us to his room.

Enojarte no **conduce** a nada. Getting angry doesn't get you anywhere.

La pista nos **condujo** hasta él. The clue led us to him.

Remember that subject pronouns are not used very often in Spanish.

conducir

	FUTURE	CONDITIONAL
(yo)	**conduciré**	**conduciría**
(tú)	**conducirás**	**conducirías**
(él/ella/usted)	**conducirá**	**conduciría**
(nosotros/as)	**conduciremos**	**conduciríamos**
(vosotros/as)	**conduciréis**	**conduciríais**
(ellos/ellas/ ustedes)	**conducirán**	**conducirían**

	PRESENT SUBJUNCTIVE	IMPERFECT SUBJUNCTIVE
(yo)	**conduzca**	**condujera** *or* **condujese**
(tú)	**conduzcas**	**condujeras** *or* **condujeses**
(él/ella/usted)	**conduzca**	**condujera** *or* **condujese**
(nosotros/as)	**conduzcamos**	**condujéramos** *or* **condujésemos**
(vosotros/as)	**conduzcáis**	**condujerais** *or* **condujeseis**
(ellos/ellas/ ustedes)	**conduzcan**	**condujeran** *or* **condujesen**

IMPERATIVE

conduce / conducid

Use the present subjunctive in all cases other than these tú and vosotros affirmative forms.

EXAMPLE PHRASES

Roberto los **conducirá** a su mesa. Roberto will show you to your table.

Remember that subject pronouns are not used very often in Spanish.

conocer (to know; to meet; to recognize)

	PRESENT	PRESENT PERFECT
(yo)	conozco	he conocido
(tú)	conoces	has conocido
(él/ella/usted)	conoce	ha conocido
(nosotros/as)	conocemos	hemos conocido
(vosotros/as)	conocéis	habéis conocido
(ellos/ellas/ ustedes)	conocen	han conocido

	PRETERITE	IMPERFECT
(yo)	conocí	conocía
(tú)	conociste	conocías
(él/ella/usted)	conoció	conocía
(nosotros/as)	conocimos	conocíamos
(vosotros/as)	conocisteis	conocíais
(ellos/ellas/ ustedes)	conocieron	conocían

GERUND	PAST PARTICIPLE
conociendo	conocido

EXAMPLE PHRASES

Conozco un restaurante donde se come bien. I know a restaurant where the food is very good.

La **conocí** en una fiesta. I met her at a party.

Nos conocíamos desde hacía años. We'd known each other for years.

Remember that subject pronouns are not used very often in Spanish.

conocer

	FUTURE	CONDITIONAL
(yo)	conoceré	conocería
(tú)	conocerás	conocerías
(él/ella/usted)	conocerá	conocería
(nosotros/as)	conoceremos	conoceríamos
(vosotros/as)	conoceréis	conoceríais
(ellos/ellas/ ustedes)	conocerán	conocerían

	PRESENT SUBJUNCTIVE	IMPERFECT SUBJUNCTIVE
(yo)	conozca	conociera *or* conociese
(tú)	conozcas	conocieras *or* conocieses
(él/ella/usted)	conozca	conociera *or* conociese
(nosotros/as)	conozcamos	conociéramos *or* conociésemos
(vosotros/as)	conozcáis	conocierais *or* conocieseis
(ellos/ellas/ ustedes)	conozcan	conocieran *or* conociesen

IMPERATIVE

conoce / conoced

Use the present subjunctive in all cases other than these tú and vosotros affirmative forms.

EXAMPLE PHRASES

No sé si la **conocerás** cuando la veas. I don't know if you'll recognize her when you see her.

No quiero que mis padres lo **conozcan**. I don't want my parents to meet him.

Si no la **conociera**, pensaría que lo hizo a propósito. If I didn't know her better, I'd think she had done it on purpose.

Remember that subject pronouns are not used very often in Spanish.

construir (to build)

	PRESENT	PRESENT PERFECT
(yo)	construyo	he construido
(tú)	construyes	has construido
(él/ella/usted)	construye	ha construido
(nosotros/as)	construimos	hemos construido
(vosotros/as)	construís	habéis construido
(ellos/ellas/ ustedes)	construyen	han construido

	PRETERITE	IMPERFECT
(yo)	construí	construía
(tú)	construiste	construías
(él/ella/usted)	construyó	construía
(nosotros/as)	construimos	construíamos
(vosotros/as)	construisteis	construíais
(ellos/ellas/ ustedes)	construyeron	construían

GERUND	PAST PARTICIPLE
construyendo	construido

EXAMPLE PHRASES

Construyen casas de madera. They build wooden houses.

Están construyendo una escuela. They're building a new school.

Construyó la casa él solo. He built the house on his own.

Su empresa **construía** puentes. His company built bridges.

Remember that subject pronouns are not used very often in Spanish.

construir

	FUTURE	CONDITIONAL
(yo)	construiré	construiría
(tú)	construirás	construirías
(él/ella/usted)	construirá	construiría
(nosotros/as)	construiremos	construiríamos
(vosotros/as)	construiréis	construiríais
(ellos/ellas/ ustedes)	construirán	construirían

	PRESENT SUBJUNCTIVE	IMPERFECT SUBJUNCTIVE
(yo)	construya	construyera *or* construyese
(tú)	construyas	construyeras *or* construyeses
(él/ella/usted)	construya	construyera *or* construyese
(nosotros/as)	construyamos	construyéramos *or* construyésemos
(vosotros/as)	construyáis	construyerais *or* construyeseis
(ellos/ellas/ ustedes)	construyan	construyeran *or* construyesen

IMPERATIVE

construye / construid

Use the present subjunctive in all cases other than these tú *and* vosotros *affirmative forms.*

EXAMPLE PHRASES

Construirán una nueva autopista. They're going to build a new highway.

Yo **construiría** la oración de otra forma. I'd construct the sentence differently.

Le pedí que lo **construyera** así. I asked him to build it like this.

Remember that subject pronouns are not used very often in Spanish.

contar (to tell; to count)

	PRESENT	PRESENT PERFECT
(yo)	cuento	he contado
(tú)	cuentas	has contado
(él/ella/usted)	cuenta	ha contado
(nosotros/as)	contamos	hemos contado
(vosotros/as)	contáis	habéis contado
(ellos/ellas/ustedes)	cuentan	han contado

	PRETERITE	IMPERFECT
(yo)	conté	contaba
(tú)	contaste	contabas
(él/ella/usted)	contó	contaba
(nosotros/as)	contamos	contábamos
(vosotros/as)	contasteis	contabais
(ellos/ellas/ustedes)	contaron	contaban

GERUND	PAST PARTICIPLE
contando	contado

EXAMPLE PHRASES

Sabe **contar** hasta diez. She can count up to ten.

Estoy contando los días. I'm counting the days.

Nos **contó** un secreto. He told us a secret.

Para él sólo **contaba** su carrera. The only thing that mattered to him was his career.

Remember that subject pronouns are not used very often in Spanish.

contar

	FUTURE	CONDITIONAL
(yo)	contaré	contaría
(tú)	contarás	contarías
(él/ella/usted)	contará	contaría
(nosotros/as)	contaremos	contaríamos
(vosotros/as)	contaréis	contaríais
(ellos/ellas/ ustedes)	contarán	contarían

	PRESENT SUBJUNCTIVE	IMPERFECT SUBJUNCTIVE
(yo)	cuente	contara *or* contase
(tú)	cuentes	contaras *or* contases
(él/ella/usted)	cuente	contara *or* contase
(nosotros/as)	contemos	contáramos *or* contásemos
(vosotros/as)	contéis	contarais *or* contaseis
(ellos/ellas/ ustedes)	cuenten	contaran *or* contasen

IMPERATIVE

cuenta / contad

Use the present subjunctive in all cases other than these tú and vosotros affirmative forms.

EXAMPLE PHRASES

Prométeme que no se lo **contarás** a nadie. Promise me you won't tell anyone.

Quiero que me **cuente** exactamente qué pasó. I want you to tell me exactly what happened.

Quería que le **contara** un cuento. She wanted me to tell her a story.

No **cuentes** conmigo. Don't count on me.

Remember that subject pronouns are not used very often in Spanish.

crecer (to grow; to rise)

	PRESENT	PRESENT PERFECT
(yo)	**crezco**	**he crecido**
(tú)	**creces**	**has crecido**
(él/ella/usted)	**crece**	**ha crecido**
(nosotros/as)	**crecemos**	**hemos crecido**
(vosotros/as)	**crecéis**	**habéis crecido**
(ellos/ellas/ ustedes)	**crecen**	**han crecido**

	PRETERITE	IMPERFECT
(yo)	**crecí**	**crecía**
(tú)	**creciste**	**crecías**
(él/ella/usted)	**creció**	**crecía**
(nosotros/as)	**crecimos**	**crecíamos**
(vosotros/as)	**crecisteis**	**crecíais**
(ellos/ellas/ ustedes)	**crecieron**	**crecían**

GERUND	PAST PARTICIPLE
creciendo	**crecido**

EXAMPLE PHRASES

Esas plantas **crecen** en Chile. Those plants grow in Chile.

¡Cómo **has crecido**! Haven't you grown!

Crecimos juntos. We grew up together.

La ciudad **crecía** a pasos agigantados. The city was growing by leaps and bounds.

Sigue **creciendo** la inflación. Inflation is still rising.

Remember that subject pronouns are not used very often in Spanish.

crecer

	FUTURE	CONDITIONAL
(yo)	**creceré**	**crecería**
(tú)	**crecerás**	**crecerías**
(él/ella/usted)	**crecerá**	**crecería**
(nosotros/as)	**creceremos**	**creceríamos**
(vosotros/as)	**creceréis**	**creceríais**
(ellos/ellas/ ustedes)	**crecerán**	**crecerían**

	PRESENT SUBJUNCTIVE	IMPERFECT SUBJUNCTIVE
(yo)	**crezca**	**creciera** *or* **creciese**
(tú)	**crezcas**	**crecieras** *or* **crecieses**
(él/ella/usted)	**crezca**	**creciera** *or* **creciese**
(nosotros/as)	**crezcamos**	**creciéramos** *or* **creciésemos**
(vosotros/as)	**crezcáis**	**crecierais** *or* **crecieseis**
(ellos/ellas/ ustedes)	**crezcan**	**crecieran** *or* **creciesen**

IMPERATIVE

crece / creced

Use the present subjunctive in all cases other than these tú and vosotros affirmative forms.

EXAMPLE PHRASES

Este año la economía **crecerá** un 2%. The economy will grow by 2% this year.

Crecería mejor en un ambiente húmedo. It would grow better in a humid environment.

Quería que sus hijos **crecieran** en otro ambiente. She wanted her children to grow up in a different environment.

Remember that subject pronouns are not used very often in Spanish.

cruzar (to cross)

	PRESENT	PRESENT PERFECT
(yo)	cruzo	he cruzado
(tú)	cruzas	has cruzado
(él/ella/usted)	cruza	ha cruzado
(nosotros/as)	cruzamos	hemos cruzado
(vosotros/as)	cruzáis	habéis cruzado
(ellos/ellas/ ustedes)	cruzan	han cruzado

	PRETERITE	IMPERFECT
(yo)	crucé	cruzaba
(tú)	cruzaste	cruzabas
(él/ella/usted)	cruzó	cruzaba
(nosotros/as)	cruzamos	cruzábamos
(vosotros/as)	cruzasteis	cruzabais
(ellos/ellas/ ustedes)	cruzaron	cruzaban

GERUND	PAST PARTICIPLE
cruzando	cruzado

EXAMPLE PHRASES

Hace tiempo que no **me cruzo** con él. I haven't seen him for a long time.

La caravana **está cruzando** el desierto. The caravan is crossing the desert.

Cruzaron el puente. They crossed the bridge.

La carretera **cruzaba** el pueblo. The road went through the village.

Remember that subject pronouns are not used very often in Spanish.

cruzar

	FUTURE	CONDITIONAL
(yo)	**cruzaré**	**cruzaría**
(tú)	**cruzarás**	**cruzarías**
(él/ella/usted)	**cruzará**	**cruzaría**
(nosotros/as)	**cruzaremos**	**cruzaríamos**
(vosotros/as)	**cruzaréis**	**cruzaríais**
(ellos/ellas/ ustedes)	**cruzarán**	**cruzarían**

	PRESENT SUBJUNCTIVE	IMPERFECT SUBJUNCTIVE
(yo)	**cruce**	**cruzara** *or* **cruzase**
(tú)	**cruces**	**cruzaras** *or* **cruzases**
(él/ella/usted)	**cruce**	**cruzara** *or* **cruzase**
(nosotros/as)	**crucemos**	**cruzáramos** *or* **cruzásemos**
(vosotros/as)	**crucéis**	**cruzarais** *or* **cruzaseis**
(ellos/ellas/ ustedes)	**crucen**	**cruzaran** *or* **cruzasen**

IMPERATIVE

cruza / cruzad

Use the present subjunctive in all cases other than these tú and vosotros affirmative forms.

EXAMPLE PHRASES

Cruzarán varias especies distintas. They'll cross several different species.

Crucemos los dedos. Let's keep our fingers crossed.

Le dije que **cruzara** con cuidado. I told her to be careful crossing the street.

No **cruces** la calle con el semáforo en rojo. Don't cross the street when the signal's red.

Remember that subject pronouns are not used very often in Spanish.

cubrir (to cover)

	PRESENT	PRESENT PERFECT
(yo)	cubro	he cubierto
(tú)	cubres	has cubierto
(él/ella/usted)	cubre	ha cubierto
(nosotros/as)	cubrimos	hemos cubierto
(vosotros/as)	cubrís	habéis cubierto
(ellos/ellas/ ustedes)	cubren	han cubierto

	PRETERITE	IMPERFECT
(yo)	cubrí	cubría
(tú)	cubriste	cubrías
(él/ella/usted)	cubrió	cubría
(nosotros/as)	cubrimos	cubríamos
(vosotros/as)	cubristeis	cubríais
(ellos/ellas/ ustedes)	cubrieron	cubrían

GERUND	PAST PARTICIPLE
cubriendo	cubierto

EXAMPLE PHRASES

Esto no **cubre** los gastos. This isn't enough to cover expenses.

Lo **cubrieron** con una manta. They covered him with a blanket.

Se cubrió la cara con las manos. She covered her face with her hands.

La nieve **cubría** la montaña. The mountain was covered in snow.

Remember that subject pronouns are not used very often in Spanish.

cubrir

	FUTURE	CONDITIONAL
(yo)	**cubriré**	**cubriría**
(tú)	**cubrirás**	**cubrirías**
(él/ella/usted)	**cubrirá**	**cubriría**
(nosotros/as)	**cubriremos**	**cubriríamos**
(vosotros/as)	**cubriréis**	**cubriríais**
(ellos/ellas/ ustedes)	**cubrirán**	**cubrirían**

	PRESENT SUBJUNCTIVE	IMPERFECT SUBJUNCTIVE
(yo)	**cubra**	**cubriera** *or* **cubriese**
(tú)	**cubras**	**cubrieras** *or* **cubrieses**
(él/ella/usted)	**cubra**	**cubriera** *or* **cubriese**
(nosotros/as)	**cubramos**	**cubriéramos** *or* **cubriésemos**
(vosotros/as)	**cubráis**	**cubrierais** *or* **cubrieseis**
(ellos/ellas/ ustedes)	**cubran**	**cubrieran** *or* **cubriesen**

IMPERATIVE

cubre / cubrid

Use the present subjunctive in all cases other than these tú and vosotros affirmative forms.

EXAMPLE PHRASES

Los corredores **cubrirán** una distancia de 2 km. The runners will cover a distance of 2 km.

¿Quién **cubriría** la vacante? Who'd fill the vacancy?

Quiero que **cubras** la noticia. I want you to cover the story.

Remember that subject pronouns are not used very often in Spanish.

dar (to give)

	PRESENT	PRESENT PERFECT
(yo)	**doy**	**he dado**
(tú)	**das**	**has dado**
(él/ella/usted)	**da**	**ha dado**
(nosotros/as)	**damos**	**hemos dado**
(vosotros/as)	**dais**	**habéis dado**
(ellos/ellas/ ustedes)	**dan**	**han dado**

	PRETERITE	IMPERFECT
(yo)	**di**	**daba**
(tú)	**diste**	**dabas**
(él/ella/usted)	**dio**	**daba**
(nosotros/as)	**dimos**	**dábamos**
(vosotros/as)	**disteis**	**dabais**
(ellos/ellas/ ustedes)	**dieron**	**daban**

GERUND	PAST PARTICIPLE
dando	**dado**

EXAMPLE PHRASES

Me **da** miedo la oscuridad. I'm afraid of the dark.

Nos **dieron** un par de entradas gratis. They gave us a pair of free tickets.

Mi ventana **daba** al jardín. My window looked out on the garden.

Remember that subject pronouns are not used very often in Spanish.

dar

	FUTURE	CONDITIONAL
(yo)	**daré**	**daría**
(tú)	**darás**	**darías**
(él/ella/usted)	**dará**	**daría**
(nosotros/as)	**daremos**	**daríamos**
(vosotros/as)	**daréis**	**daríais**
(ellos/ellas/ ustedes)	**darán**	**darían**

	PRESENT SUBJUNCTIVE	IMPERFECT SUBJUNCTIVE
(yo)	**dé**	**diera** *or* **diese**
(tú)	**des**	**dieras** *or* **dieses**
(él/ella/usted)	**dé**	**diera** *or* **diese**
(nosotros/as)	**demos**	**diéramos** *or* **diésemos**
(vosotros/as)	**deis**	**dierais** *or* **dieseis**
(ellos/ellas/ ustedes)	**den**	**dieran** *or* **diesen**

IMPERATIVE

da / dad

Use the present subjunctive in all cases other than these tú and vosotros affirmative forms.

EXAMPLE PHRASES

Te **daré** el número de mi celular. I'll give you my cell phone number.

Me **daría** mucha alegría volver a verla. It would be really good to see her again.

Quiero que me lo **des** ahora mismo. I want you to give it to me right now.

Déme 2 kilos. 2 kilos, please.

Remember that subject pronouns are not used very often in Spanish.

decir (to say; to tell)

	PRESENT	PRESENT PERFECT
(yo)	digo	he dicho
(tú)	dices	has dicho
(él/ella/usted)	dice	ha dicho
(nosotros/as)	decimos	hemos dicho
(vosotros/as)	decís	habéis dicho
(ellos/ellas/ ustedes)	dicen	han dicho

	PRETERITE	IMPERFECT
(yo)	dije	decía
(tú)	dijiste	decías
(él/ella/usted)	dijo	decía
(nosotros/as)	dijimos	decíamos
(vosotros/as)	dijisteis	decíais
(ellos/ellas/ ustedes)	dijeron	decían

GERUND
diciendo

PAST PARTICIPLE
dicho

EXAMPLE PHRASES

Pero ¿qué **dices**? What are you saying?

¿Te **dijo** lo de la boda? Did he tell you about the wedding?

Ya me lo había **dicho**. He had already told me.

Siempre nos **decía** que tuviéramos cuidado. She always used to tell us to be careful.

Remember that subject pronouns are not used very often in Spanish.

decir

	FUTURE	CONDITIONAL
(yo)	**diré**	**diría**
(tú)	**dirás**	**dirías**
(él/ella/usted)	**dirá**	**diría**
(nosotros/as)	**diremos**	**diríamos**
(vosotros/as)	**diréis**	**diríais**
(ellos/ellas/ ustedes)	**dirán**	**dirían**

	PRESENT SUBJUNCTIVE	IMPERFECT SUBJUNCTIVE
(yo)	**diga**	**dijera** *or* **dijese**
(tú)	**digas**	**dijeras** *or* **dijeses**
(él/ella/usted)	**diga**	**dijera** *or* **dijese**
(nosotros/as)	**digamos**	**dijéramos** *or* **dijésemos**
(vosotros/as)	**digáis**	**dijerais** *or* **dijeseis**
(ellos/ellas/ ustedes)	**digan**	**dijeran** *or* **dijesen**

IMPERATIVE

di / decid

Use the present subjunctive in all cases other than these tú and vosotros affirmative forms.

EXAMPLE PHRASES

Yo **diría** que miente. I'd say he's lying.

Si me **dijeras** lo que pasa, a lo mejor podría ayudar. If you told me what was going on, maybe I could help.

No le **digas** que me viste. Don't tell him you saw me.

Remember that subject pronouns are not used very often in Spanish.

despreocuparse (to stop worrying)

	PRESENT	PRESENT PERFECT
(yo)	me despreocupo	me he despreocupado
(tú)	te despreocupas	te has despreocupado
(él/ella/usted)	se despreocupa	se ha despreocupado
(nosotros/as)	nos despreocupamos	nos hemos despreocupado
(vosotros/as)	os despreocupáis	os habéis despreocupado
(ellos/ellas/ ustedes)	se despreocupan	se han despreocupado

	PRETERITE	IMPERFECT
(yo)	me despreocupé	me despreocupaba
(tú)	te despreocupaste	te despreocupabas
(él/ella/usted)	se despreocupó	se despreocupaba
(nosotros/as)	nos despreocupamos	nos despreocupábamos
(vosotros/as)	os despreocupasteis	os despreocupabais
(ellos/ellas/ ustedes)	se despreocuparon	se despreocupaban

GERUND
despreocupándose, etc

PAST PARTICIPLE
despreocupado

EXAMPLE PHRASES

Deberías **despreocuparte** un poco más de las cosas. You shouldn't worry so much about things.

Se despreocupa de todo. He shows no concern for anything.

Se despreocupó del asunto. He forgot about the matter.

Remember that subject pronouns are not used very often in Spanish.

despreocuparse

	FUTURE	CONDITIONAL
(yo)	me despreocuparé	me despreocuparía
(tú)	te despreocuparás	te despreocuparías
(él/ella/usted)	se despreocupará	se despreocuparía
(nosotros/as)	nos despreocuparemos	nos despreocuparíamos
(vosotros/as)	os despreocuparéis	os despreocuparíais
(ellos/ellas/ ustedes)	se despreocuparán	se despreocuparían

	PRESENT SUBJUNCTIVE	IMPERFECT SUBJUNCTIVE
(yo)	me despreocupe	me despreocupara *or* despreocupase
(tú)	te despreocupes	te despreocuparas *or* despreocupases
(él/ella/usted)	se despreocupe	se despreocupara *or* despreocupase
(nosotros/as)	nos despreocupemos	nos despreocupáramos *or* despreocupásemos
(vosotros/as)	os despreocupéis	os despreocuparais *or* despreocupaseis
(ellos/ellas/ ustedes)	se despreocupen	se despreocuparan *or* despreocupasen

IMPERATIVE

despreocúpate / despreocupaos

Use the present subjunctive in all cases other than these tú and vosotros affirmative forms.

EXAMPLE PHRASES

Yo **me despreocuparía** de él. I wouldn't worry about him.

Despreocúpate de todo. Don't worry about a thing.

detener (to stop; to arrest)

	PRESENT	PRESENT PERFECT
(yo)	detengo	he detenido
(tú)	detienes	has detenido
(él/ella/usted)	detiene	ha detenido
(nosotros/as)	detenemos	hemos detenido
(vosotros/as)	detenéis	habéis detenido
(ellos/ellas/ ustedes)	detienen	han detenido

	PRETERITE	IMPERFECT
(yo)	detuve	detenía
(tú)	detuviste	detenías
(él/ella/usted)	detuvo	detenía
(nosotros/as)	detuvimos	deteníamos
(vosotros/as)	detuvisteis	deteníais
(ellos/ellas/ ustedes)	detuvieron	detenían

GERUND	PAST PARTICIPLE
deteniendo	detenido

EXAMPLE PHRASES

Detuvieron a los ladrones. They arrested the thieves.

Nos detuvimos en el semáforo. We stopped at the light.

¡Queda **detenido**! You are under arrest!

Remember that subject pronouns are not used very often in Spanish.

detener

	FUTURE	CONDITIONAL
(yo)	**detendré**	**detendría**
(tú)	**detendrás**	**detendrías**
(él/ella/usted)	**detendrá**	**detendría**
(nosotros/as)	**detendremos**	**detendríamos**
(vosotros/as)	**detendréis**	**detendríais**
(ellos/ellas/ ustedes)	**detendrán**	**detendrían**

	PRESENT SUBJUNCTIVE	IMPERFECT SUBJUNCTIVE
(yo)	**detenga**	**detuviera** *or* **detuviese**
(tú)	**detengas**	**detuvieras** *or* **detuvieses**
(él/ella/usted)	**detenga**	**detuviera** *or* **detuviese**
(nosotros/as)	**detengamos**	**detuviéramos** *or* **detuviésemos**
(vosotros/as)	**detengáis**	**detuvierais** *or* **detuvieseis**
(ellos/ellas/ ustedes)	**detengan**	**detuvieran** *or* **detuviesen**

IMPERATIVE

detén / detened

Use the present subjunctive in all cases other than these tú and vosotros affirmative forms.

EXAMPLE PHRASES

Nada la **detendrá**. Nothing will stop her.

Si **te detuvieras** a pensar, nunca harías nada. If you stopped to think, you'd never do anything.

¡**Deténgase**! Stop!

¡No **te detengas!** Don't stop!

Remember that subject pronouns are not used very often in Spanish.

dirigir (to direct; to run)

	PRESENT	PRESENT PERFECT
(yo)	**dirijo**	**he dirigido**
(tú)	**diriges**	**has dirigido**
(él/ella/usted)	**dirige**	**ha dirigido**
(nosotros/as)	**dirigimos**	**hemos dirigido**
(vosotros/as)	**dirigís**	**habéis dirigido**
(ellos/ellas/ ustedes)	**dirigen**	**han dirigido**

	PRETERITE	IMPERFECT
(yo)	**dirigí**	**dirigía**
(tú)	**dirigiste**	**dirigías**
(él/ella/usted)	**dirigió**	**dirigía**
(nosotros/as)	**dirigimos**	**dirigíamos**
(vosotros/as)	**dirigisteis**	**dirigíais**
(ellos/ellas/ ustedes)	**dirigieron**	**dirigían**

GERUND	PAST PARTICIPLE
dirigiendo	**dirigido**

EXAMPLE PHRASES

Dirijo esta empresa desde hace dos años. I've been running this company for two years.

Ha dirigido varias películas. She has directed several movies.

No le **dirigió** la palabra. She didn't say a word to him.

Se dirigía a su casa. He was making his way home.

Remember that subject pronouns are not used very often in Spanish.

dirigir

	FUTURE	CONDITIONAL
(yo)	**dirigiré**	**dirigiría**
(tú)	**dirigirás**	**dirigirías**
(él/ella/usted)	**dirigirá**	**dirigiría**
(nosotros/as)	**dirigiremos**	**dirigiríamos**
(vosotros/as)	**dirigiréis**	**dirigiríais**
(ellos/ellas/ ustedes)	**dirigirán**	**dirigirían**

	PRESENT SUBJUNCTIVE	IMPERFECT SUBJUNCTIVE
(yo)	**dirija**	**dirigiera** *or* **dirigiese**
(tú)	**dirijas**	**dirigieras** *or* **dirigieses**
(él/ella/usted)	**dirija**	**dirigiera** *or* **dirigiese**
(nosotros/as)	**dirijamos**	**dirigiéramos** *or* **dirigiésemos**
(vosotros/as)	**dirijáis**	**dirigierais** *or* **dirigieseis**
(ellos/ellas/ ustedes)	**dirijan**	**dirigieran** *or* **dirigiesen**

IMPERATIVE

dirige / dirigid

Use the present subjunctive in all cases other than these tú and vosotros affirmative forms.

EXAMPLE PHRASES

Dirigirá la expedición. He'll be leading the expedition.

Para más información **diríjase** a la página 82. For more information turn to page 82.

distinguir (to distinguish)

	PRESENT	PRESENT PERFECT
(yo)	**distingo**	**he distinguido**
(tú)	**distingues**	**has distinguido**
(él/ella/usted)	**distingue**	**ha distinguido**
(nosotros/as)	**distinguimos**	**hemos distinguido**
(vosotros/as)	**distinguís**	**habéis distinguido**
(ellos/ellas/ ustedes)	**distinguen**	**han distinguido**

	PRETERITE	IMPERFECT
(yo)	**distinguí**	**distinguía**
(tú)	**distinguiste**	**distinguías**
(él/ella/usted)	**distinguió**	**distinguía**
(nosotros/as)	**distinguimos**	**distinguíamos**
(vosotros/as)	**distinguisteis**	**distinguíais**
(ellos/ellas/ ustedes)	**distinguieron**	**distinguían**

GERUND	PAST PARTICIPLE
distinguiendo	**distinguido**

EXAMPLE PHRASES

No lo **distingo** del azul. I can't tell the difference between it and the blue one.
Se distinguió por su valentía. He distinguished himself with his bravery.
Se distinguía desde lejos. You could see it from a distance.

Remember that subject pronouns are not used very often in Spanish.

distinguir

	FUTURE	CONDITIONAL
(yo)	**distinguiré**	**distinguiría**
(tú)	**distinguirás**	**distinguirías**
(él/ella/usted)	**distinguirá**	**distinguiría**
(nosotros/as)	**distinguiremos**	**distinguiríamos**
(vosotros/as)	**distinguiréis**	**distinguiríais**
(ellos/ellas/ ustedes)	**distinguirán**	**distinguirían**

	PRESENT SUBJUNCTIVE	IMPERFECT SUBJUNCTIVE
(yo)	**distinga**	**distinguiera** *or* **distinguiese**
(tú)	**distingas**	**distinguieras** *or* **distinguieses**
(él/ella/usted)	**distinga**	**distinguiera** *or* **distinguiese**
(nosotros/as)	**distingamos**	**distinguiéramos** *or* **distinguiésemos**
(vosotros/as)	**distingáis**	**distinguierais** *or* **distinguieseis**
(ellos/ellas/ ustedes)	**distingan**	**distinguieran** *or* **distinguiesen**

IMPERATIVE

distingue / distinguid

Use the present subjunctive in all cases other than these tú and vosotros affirmative forms.

EXAMPLE PHRASES

No los **distinguiría**. I wouldn't be able to tell them apart.

Nos **distinguirá** con su presencia. She will honor us with her presence.

divertir (to entertain; to amuse)

	PRESENT	PRESENT PERFECT
(yo)	**divierto**	**he divertido**
(tú)	**diviertes**	**has divertido**
(él/ella/usted)	**divierte**	**ha divertido**
(nosotros/as)	**divertimos**	**hemos divertido**
(vosotros/as)	**divertís**	**habéis divertido**
(ellos/ellas/ ustedes)	**divierten**	**han divertido**

	PRETERITE	IMPERFECT
(yo)	**divertí**	**divertía**
(tú)	**divertiste**	**divertías**
(él/ella/usted)	**divirtió**	**divertía**
(nosotros/as)	**divertimos**	**divertíamos**
(vosotros/as)	**divertisteis**	**divertíais**
(ellos/ellas/ ustedes)	**divirtieron**	**divertían**

GERUND	PAST PARTICIPLE
divirtiendo	**divertido**

EXAMPLE PHRASES

Cantamos sólo para **divertirnos**. We sing just for fun.

Me **divierte** verlos tan serios. It's amusing to see them looking so serious.

¿**Se divirtieron** en la fiesta? Did you enjoy the party?

Nos **divirtió** con sus anécdotas. He entertained us with his stories.

Nos divertíamos mucho jugando en la playa. We were having a great time playing on the beach.

Remember that subject pronouns are not used very often in Spanish.

divertir

	FUTURE	CONDITIONAL
(yo)	**divertiré**	**divertiría**
(tú)	**divertirás**	**divertirías**
(él/ella/usted)	**divertirá**	**divertiría**
(nosotros/as)	**divertiremos**	**divertiríamos**
(vosotros/as)	**divertiréis**	**divertiríais**
(ellos/ellas/ ustedes)	**divertirán**	**divertirían**

	PRESENT SUBJUNCTIVE	IMPERFECT SUBJUNCTIVE
(yo)	**divierta**	**divirtiera** *or* **divirtiese**
(tú)	**diviertas**	**divirtieras** *or* **divirtieses**
(él/ella/usted)	**divierta**	**divirtiera** *or* **divirtiese**
(nosotros/as)	**divirtamos**	**divirtiéramos** *or* **divirtiésemos**
(vosotros/as)	**divirtáis**	**divirtierais** *or* **divirtieseis**
(ellos/ellas/ ustedes)	**diviertan**	**divirtieran** *or* **divirtiesen**

IMPERATIVE

divierte / divertid

Use the present subjunctive in all cases other than these tú and vosotros affirmative forms.

EXAMPLE PHRASES

Si fueras, **te divertirías** mucho. If you went, you'd have a great time.

Hizo lo posible por que **se divirtieran**. He did everything he could to make it fun for them.

¡Que **te diviertas**! Have a good time!

Remember that subject pronouns are not used very often in Spanish.

dormir (to sleep)

	PRESENT	PRESENT PERFECT
(yo)	duermo	he dormido
(tú)	duermes	has dormido
(él/ella/usted)	duerme	ha dormido
(nosotros/as)	dormimos	hemos dormido
(vosotros/as)	dormís	habéis dormido
(ellos/ellas/ ustedes)	duermen	han dormido

	PRETERITE	IMPERFECT
(yo)	dormí	dormía
(tú)	dormiste	dormías
(él/ella/usted)	durmió	dormía
(nosotros/as)	dormimos	dormíamos
(vosotros/as)	dormisteis	dormíais
(ellos/ellas/ ustedes)	durmieron	dormían

GERUND	PAST PARTICIPLE
durmiendo	dormido

EXAMPLE PHRASES

No **duermo** muy bien. I don't sleep very well.

Está durmiendo. She's asleep.

Dormí de un tirón. I slept like a log.

Se me **durmió** la pierna. My leg went to sleep.

Se dormía en clase. She would fall asleep in class.

Remember that subject pronouns are not used very often in Spanish.

dormir

	FUTURE	CONDITIONAL
(yo)	**dormiré**	**dormiría**
(tú)	**dormirás**	**dormirías**
(él/ella/usted)	**dormirá**	**dormiría**
(nosotros/as)	**dormiremos**	**dormiríamos**
(vosotros/as)	**dormiréis**	**dormiríais**
(ellos/ellas/ ustedes)	**dormirán**	**dormirían**

	PRESENT SUBJUNCTIVE	IMPERFECT SUBJUNCTIVE
(yo)	**duerma**	**durmiera** *or* **durmiese**
(tú)	**duermas**	**durmieras** *or* **durmieses**
(él/ella/usted)	**duerma**	**durmiera** *or* **durmiese**
(nosotros/as)	**durmamos**	**durmiéramos** *or* **durmiésemos**
(vosotros/as)	**durmáis**	**durmierais** *or* **durmieseis**
(ellos/ellas/ ustedes)	**duerman**	**durmieran** *or* **durmiesen**

IMPERATIVE

duerme / dormid

Use the present subjunctive in all cases other than these tú and vosotros affirmative forms.

EXAMPLE PHRASES

Si no tomo café, **me dormiré**. I'll fall asleep if I don't have some coffee.

Yo no **dormiría** en esa casa. I wouldn't sleep in that house.

Quiero que **duermas** la siesta. I want you to take a nap.

Si **durmieras** más horas, no estarías tan cansada. You wouldn't be so tired if you got more sleep.

Remember that subject pronouns are not used very often in Spanish.

elegir (to choose; to elect)

	PRESENT	PRESENT PERFECT
(yo)	**elijo**	**he elegido**
(tú)	**eliges**	**has elegido**
(él/ella/usted)	**elige**	**ha elegido**
(nosotros/as)	**elegimos**	**hemos elegido**
(vosotros/as)	**elegís**	**habéis elegido**
(ellos/ellas/ ustedes)	**eligen**	**han elegido**

	PRETERITE	IMPERFECT
(yo)	**elegí**	**elegía**
(tú)	**elegiste**	**elegías**
(él/ella/usted)	**eligió**	**elegía**
(nosotros/as)	**elegimos**	**elegíamos**
(vosotros/as)	**elegisteis**	**elegíais**
(ellos/ellas/ ustedes)	**eligieron**	**elegían**

GERUND	PAST PARTICIPLE
eligiendo	**elegido**

EXAMPLE PHRASES

Te dan a **elegir** entre dos modelos. You have a choice of two models.

Nosotros no **elegimos** a nuestros padres, ni ellos nos **eligen** a nosotros.
We don't choose our parents and they don't choose us either.

Creo que **eligió** bien. I think he made a good choice.

Salió **elegido** presidente. He was elected president.

Remember that subject pronouns are not used very often in Spanish.

elegir

	FUTURE	CONDITIONAL
(yo)	**elegiré**	**elegiría**
(tú)	**elegirás**	**elegirías**
(él/ella/usted)	**elegirá**	**elegiría**
(nosotros/as)	**elegiremos**	**elegiríamos**
(vosotros/as)	**elegiréis**	**elegiríais**
(ellos/ellas/ ustedes)	**elegirán**	**elegirían**

	PRESENT SUBJUNCTIVE	IMPERFECT SUBJUNCTIVE
(yo)	**elija**	**eligiera** *or* **eligiese**
(tú)	**elijas**	**eligieras** *or* **eligieses**
(él/ella/usted)	**elija**	**eligiera** *or* **eligiese**
(nosotros/as)	**elijamos**	**eligiéramos** *or* **eligiésemos**
(vosotros/as)	**elijáis**	**eligierais** *or* **eligieseis**
(ellos/ellas/ ustedes)	**elijan**	**eligieran** *or* **eligiesen**

IMPERATIVE

elige / elegid

Use the present subjunctive in all cases other than these tú and vosotros affirmative forms.

EXAMPLE PHRASES

Yo **elegiría** el más caro. I'd choose the most expensive one.

Elija una carta. Pick a card.

empezar (to begin; to start)

	PRESENT	PRESENT PERFECT
(yo)	empiezo	he empezado
(tú)	empiezas	has empezado
(él/ella/usted)	empieza	ha empezado
(nosotros/as)	empezamos	hemos empezado
(vosotros/as)	empezáis	habéis empezado
(ellos/ellas/ ustedes)	empiezan	han empezado

	PRETERITE	IMPERFECT
(yo)	empecé	empezaba
(tú)	empezaste	empezabas
(él/ella/usted)	empezó	empezaba
(nosotros/as)	empezamos	empezábamos
(vosotros/as)	empezasteis	empezabais
(ellos/ellas/ ustedes)	empezaron	empezaban

GERUND	PAST PARTICIPLE
empezando	empezado

EXAMPLE PHRASES

Está a punto de **empezar**. It's about to start.

¿Cuándo **empiezas** a trabajar en el sitio nuevo? When do you start work at the new place?

Empezó a nevar. It started snowing.

Las vacaciones **empezaron** el quince. The vacation started on the fifteenth.

Empezaba con *p*. It began with *p*.

Remember that subject pronouns are not used very often in Spanish.

empezar

	FUTURE	CONDITIONAL
(yo)	**empezaré**	**empezaría**
(tú)	**empezarás**	**empezarías**
(él/ella/usted)	**empezará**	**empezaría**
(nosotros/as)	**empezaremos**	**empezaríamos**
(vosotros/as)	**empezaréis**	**empezaríais**
(ellos/ellas/ ustedes)	**empezarán**	**empezarían**

	PRESENT SUBJUNCTIVE	IMPERFECT SUBJUNCTIVE
(yo)	**empiece**	**empezara** *or* **empezase**
(tú)	**empieces**	**empezaras** *or* **empezases**
(él/ella/usted)	**empiece**	**empezara** *or* **empezase**
(nosotros/as)	**empecemos**	**empezáramos** *or* **empezásemos**
(vosotros/as)	**empecéis**	**empezarais** *or* **empezaseis**
(ellos/ellas/ ustedes)	**empiecen**	**empezaran** *or* **empezasen**

IMPERATIVE

empieza / empezad

Use the present subjunctive in all cases other than these tú and vosotros affirmative forms.

EXAMPLE PHRASES

La semana que viene **empezaremos** un curso nuevo. We'll start a new course next week.

Yo **empezaría** desde cero. I'd start from scratch.

Quiero que **empieces** ya. I want you to start now.

Si **empezáramos** ahora, acabaríamos a las diez. If we started now, we'd be finished by ten.

Empieza por aquí. Start here.

Remember that subject pronouns are not used very often in Spanish.

enfrentarse a/con (to face)

	PRESENT	PRESENT PERFECT
(yo)	me enfrento	me he enfrentado
(tú)	te enfrentas	te has enfrentado
(él/ella/usted)	se enfrenta	se ha enfrentado
(nosotros/as)	nos enfrentamos	nos hemos enfrentado
(vosotros/as)	os enfrentáis	os habéis enfrentado
(ellos/ellas/ ustedes)	se enfrentan	se han enfrentado

	PRETERITE	IMPERFECT
(yo)	me enfrenté	me enfrentaba
(tú)	te enfrentaste	te enfrentabas
(él/ella/usted)	se enfrentó	se enfrentaba
(nosotros/as)	nos enfrentamos	nos enfrentábamos
(vosotros/as)	os enfrentasteis	os enfrentabais
(ellos/ellas/ ustedes)	se enfrentaron	se enfrentaban

GERUND
enfrentándose, etc

PAST PARTICIPLE
enfrentado

EXAMPLE PHRASES

Tienes que **enfrentarte** al problema. You have to face up to the problem.

Hoy **se enfrentan** los dos semifinalistas. The two semifinalists meet today.

Padre e hijo **se han enfrentado** varias veces. Father and son have had several confrontations.

Se enfrentaban a un futuro incierto. They faced an uncertain future.

Remember that subject pronouns are not used very often in Spanish.

enfrentarse a/con

	FUTURE	CONDITIONAL
(yo)	me enfrentaré	me enfrentaría
(tú)	te enfrentarás	te enfrentarías
(él/ella/usted)	se enfrentará	se enfrentaría
(nosotros/as)	nos enfrentaremos	nos enfrentaríamos
(vosotros/as)	os enfrentaréis	os enfrentaríais
(ellos/ellas/ ustedes)	se enfrentarán	se enfrentarían

	PRESENT SUBJUNCTIVE	IMPERFECT SUBJUNCTIVE
(yo)	me enfrente	me enfrentara *or* enfrentase
(tú)	te enfrentes	te enfrentaras *or* enfrentases
(él/ella/usted)	se enfrente	se enfrentara *or* enfrentase
(nosotros/as)	nos enfrentemos	nos enfrentáramos *or* enfrentásemos
(vosotros/as)	os enfrentéis	os enfrentarais *or* enfrentaseis
(ellos/ellas/ ustedes)	se enfrenten	se enfrentaran *or* enfrentasen

IMPERATIVE

enfréntate / enfrentaos

Use the present subjunctive in all cases other than these tú and vosotros affirmative forms.

EXAMPLE PHRASES

Los dos equipos **se enfrentarán** mañana. The two teams will play each other tomorrow.

No **te enfrentes** con él. Don't confront him.

entender (to understand)

	PRESENT	PRESENT PERFECT
(yo)	entiendo	he entendido
(tú)	entiendes	has entendido
(él/ella/usted)	entiende	ha entendido
(nosotros/as)	entendemos	hemos entendido
(vosotros/as)	entendéis	habéis entendido
(ellos/ellas/ ustedes)	entienden	han entendido

	PRETERITE	IMPERFECT
(yo)	entendí	entendía
(tú)	entendiste	entendías
(él/ella/usted)	entendió	entendía
(nosotros/as)	entendimos	entendíamos
(vosotros/as)	entendisteis	entendíais
(ellos/ellas/ ustedes)	entendieron	entendían

GERUND	PAST PARTICIPLE
entendiendo	entendido

EXAMPLE PHRASES

No lo vas a **entender**. You won't understand.

No lo **entiendo**. I don't understand.

Estás entendiéndolo todo al revés. You're getting me all wrong.

¿**Entendiste** lo que dijo? Did you understand what she said?

Mi padre **entendía** mucho de caballos. My father knew a lot about horses.

Remember that subject pronouns are not used very often in Spanish.

entender

	FUTURE	CONDITIONAL
(yo)	**entenderé**	**entendería**
(tú)	**entenderás**	**entenderías**
(él/ella/usted)	**entenderá**	**entendería**
(nosotros/as)	**entenderemos**	**entenderíamos**
(vosotros/as)	**entenderéis**	**entenderíais**
(ellos/ellas/ ustedes)	**entenderán**	**entenderían**

	PRESENT SUBJUNCTIVE	IMPERFECT SUBJUNCTIVE
(yo)	**entienda**	**entendiera** *or* **entendiese**
(tú)	**entiendas**	**entendieras** *or* **entendieses**
(él/ella/usted)	**entienda**	**entendiera** *or* **entendiese**
(nosotros/as)	**entendamos**	**entendiéramos** *or* **entendiésemos**
(vosotros/as)	**entendáis**	**entendierais** *or* **entendieseis**
(ellos/ellas/ ustedes)	**entiendan**	**entendieran** *or* **entendiesen**

IMPERATIVE

entiende / entended

Use the present subjunctive in all cases other than these tú and vosotros affirmative forms.

EXAMPLE PHRASES

Con el tiempo lo **entenderás**. You'll understand one day.

Yo no lo **entendería** así. I wouldn't interpret it like that.

Si de verdad me **entendieras**, no habrías dicho eso. If you really understood me, you wouldn't have said that.

No me **entiendas** mal. Don't misunderstand me.

Remember that subject pronouns are not used very often in Spanish.

enviar (to send)

	PRESENT	PRESENT PERFECT
(yo)	envío	he enviado
(tú)	envías	has enviado
(él/ella/usted)	envía	ha enviado
(nosotros/as)	enviamos	hemos enviado
(vosotros/as)	enviáis	habéis enviado
(ellos/ellas/ ustedes)	envían	han enviado

	PRETERITE	IMPERFECT
(yo)	envié	enviaba
(tú)	enviaste	enviabas
(él/ella/usted)	envió	enviaba
(nosotros/as)	enviamos	enviábamos
(vosotros/as)	enviasteis	enviabais
(ellos/ellas/ ustedes)	enviaron	enviaban

GERUND	PAST PARTICIPLE
enviando	enviado

EXAMPLE PHRASES

¿Cómo lo vas a **enviar**? How are you going to send it?

Les **envío** el trabajo por correo electrónico. I send them my work by email.

Ya **está enviando** las invitaciones. She has already started sending out the invitations.

La **han enviado** a Guatemala. They've sent her to Guatemala.

Le **envió** el regalo por correo. He mailed her the present.

Remember that subject pronouns are not used very often in Spanish.

enviar

	FUTURE	CONDITIONAL
(yo)	enviaré	enviaría
(tú)	enviarás	enviarías
(él/ella/usted)	enviará	enviaría
(nosotros/as)	enviaremos	enviaríamos
(vosotros/as)	enviaréis	enviaríais
(ellos/ellas/ ustedes)	enviarán	enviarían

	PRESENT SUBJUNCTIVE	IMPERFECT SUBJUNCTIVE
(yo)	envíe	enviara *or* enviase
(tú)	envíes	enviaras *or* enviases
(él/ella/usted)	envíe	enviara *or* enviase
(nosotros/as)	enviemos	enviáramos *or* enviásemos
(vosotros/as)	enviéis	enviarais *or* enviaseis
(ellos/ellas/ ustedes)	envíen	enviaran *or* enviasen

IMPERATIVE

envía / enviad

Use the present subjunctive in all cases other than these tú and vosotros affirmative forms.

EXAMPLE PHRASES

Nos **enviarán** más información. They'll send us more information.

Yo lo **enviaría** por mensajero. I'd send it by courier.

Necesitamos que lo **envíes** inmediatamente. We need you to send it immediately.

Si lo **enviaras** ahora, llegaría el lunes. If you sent it now it would get there on Monday.

No lo **envíes** sin repasarlo antes. Don't send it in without checking it first.

Envíe sus datos personales. Send in your details.

Remember that subject pronouns are not used very often in Spanish.

equivocarse (to make a mistake; to be wrong)

	PRESENT	PRESENT PERFECT
(yo)	me equivoco	me he equivocado
(tú)	te equivocas	te has equivocado
(él/ella/usted)	se equivoca	se ha equivocado
(nosotros/as)	nos equivocamos	nos hemos equivocado
(vosotros/as)	os equivocáis	os habéis equivocado
(ellos/ellas/ ustedes)	se equivocan	se han equivocado

	PRETERITE	IMPERFECT
(yo)	me equivoqué	me equivocaba
(tú)	te equivocaste	te equivocabas
(él/ella/usted)	se equivocó	se equivocaba
(nosotros/as)	nos equivocamos	nos equivocábamos
(vosotros/as)	os equivocasteis	os equivocabais
(ellos/ellas/ ustedes)	se equivocaron	se equivocaban

GERUND
equivocándose, etc

PAST PARTICIPLE
equivocado

EXAMPLE PHRASES

Si crees que voy a dejarte ir, **te equivocas**. If you think I'm going to let you go, you're mistaken.

Se equivocaron de tren. They took the wrong train.

Siempre **se equivocaba** de calle. He always took the wrong street.

Remember that subject pronouns are not used very often in Spanish.

equivocarse

	FUTURE	CONDITIONAL
(yo)	me equivocaré	me equivocaría
(tú)	te equivocarás	te equivocarías
(él/ella/usted)	se equivocará	se equivocaría
(nosotros/as)	nos equivocaremos	nos equivocaríamos
(vosotros/as)	os equivocaréis	os equivocaríais
(ellos/ellas/ ustedes)	se equivocarán	se equivocarían

	PRESENT SUBJUNCTIVE	IMPERFECT SUBJUNCTIVE
(yo)	me equivoque	me equivocara *or* equivocase
(tú)	te equivoques	te equivocaras *or* equivocases
(él/ella/usted)	se equivoque	se equivocara *or* equivocase
(nosotros/as)	nos equivoquemos	nos equivocáramos *or* equivocásemos
(vosotros/as)	os equivoquéis	os equivocarais *or* equivocaseis
(ellos/ellas/ ustedes)	se equivoquen	se equivocaran *or* equivocasen

IMPERATIVE

equivócate / equivocaos

Use the present subjunctive in all cases other than these tú and vosotros affirmative forms.

EXAMPLE PHRASES

Sobre todo, no **te equivoques** de hora. Above all, don't get the time wrong.

Si **te equivocaras**, quedarías eliminado del juego. If you made a mistake, you'd be out of the game.

erguir (to erect)

	PRESENT	PRESENT PERFECT
(yo)	yergo	he erguido
(tú)	yergues	has erguido
(él/ella/usted)	yergue	ha erguido
(nosotros/as)	erguimos	hemos erguido
(vosotros/as)	erguís	habéis erguido
(ellos/ellas/ ustedes)	yerguen	han erguido

	PRETERITE	IMPERFECT
(yo)	erguí	erguía
(tú)	erguiste	erguías
(él/ella/usted)	irguió	erguía
(nosotros/as)	erguimos	erguíamos
(vosotros/as)	erguisteis	erguías
(ellos/ellas/ ustedes)	irguieron	erguían

GERUND	PAST PARTICIPLE
irguiendo	erguido

EXAMPLE PHRASES

El perro **irguió** las orejas. The dog pricked up its ears.

La montaña **se erguía** majestuosa sobre el valle. The mountain rose majestically above the valley.

Tú mantén siempre la cabeza bien **erguida**. You must always hold your head high.

Remember that subject pronouns are not used very often in Spanish.

erguir

	FUTURE	CONDITIONAL
(yo)	erguiré	erguiría
(tú)	erguirás	erguirías
(él/ella/usted)	erguirá	erguiría
(nosotros/as)	erguiremos	erguiríamos
(vosotros/as)	erguiréis	erguiríais
(ellos/ellas/ ustedes)	erguirán	erguirían

	PRESENT SUBJUNCTIVE	IMPERFECT SUBJUNCTIVE
(yo)	yerga	irguiera *or* irguiese
(tú)	yergas	irguieras *or* irguieses
(él/ella/usted)	yerga	irguiera *or* irguiese
(nosotros/as)	irgamos	irguiéramos *or* irguiésemos
(vosotros/as)	irgáis	irguierais *or* irguieseis
(ellos/ellas/ ustedes)	yergan	irguieran *or* irguiesen

IMPERATIVE

yergue / erguid

Use the present subjunctive in all cases other than these tú and vosotros affirmative forms.

errar (to err)

	PRESENT	PRESENT PERFECT
(yo)	yerro	he errado
(tú)	yerras	has errado
(él/ella/usted)	yerra	ha errado
(nosotros/as)	erramos	hemos errado
(vosotros/as)	erráis	habéis errado
(ellos/ellas/ ustedes)	yerran	han errado

	PRETERITE	IMPERFECT
(yo)	erré	erraba
(tú)	erraste	errabas
(él/ella/usted)	erró	erraba
(nosotros/as)	erramos	errábamos
(vosotros/as)	errasteis	errabais
(ellos/ellas/ ustedes)	erraron	erraban

GERUND	PAST PARTICIPLE
errando	errado

EXAMPLE PHRASES

Errar es humano. To err is human.

Había errado en su decisión. She had made the wrong decision.

Erró el tiro. He missed.

Remember that subject pronouns are not used very often in Spanish.

errar

	FUTURE	CONDITIONAL
(yo)	erraré	erraría
(tú)	errarás	errarías
(él/ella/usted)	errará	erraría
(nosotros/as)	erraremos	erraríamos
(vosotros/as)	erraréis	erraríais
(ellos/ellas/ ustedes)	errarán	errarían

	PRESENT SUBJUNCTIVE	IMPERFECT SUBJUNCTIVE
(yo)	yerre	errara *or* errase
(tú)	yerres	erraras *or* errases
(él/ella/usted)	yerre	errara *or* errase
(nosotros/as)	erremos	erráramos *or* errásemos
(vosotros/as)	erréis	errarais *or* erraseis
(ellos/ellas/ ustedes)	yerren	erraran *or* errasen

IMPERATIVE

yerra / errad

Use the present subjunctive in all cases other than these tú and vosotros affirmative forms.

Remember that subject pronouns are not used very often in Spanish.

escoger (to choose; to pick)

	PRESENT	PRESENT PERFECT
(yo)	escojo	he escogido
(tú)	escoges	has escogido
(él/ella/usted)	escoge	ha escogido
(nosotros/as)	escogemos	hemos escogido
(vosotros/as)	escogéis	habéis escogido
(ellos/ellas/ ustedes)	escogen	han escogido

	PRETERITE	IMPERFECT
(yo)	escogí	escogía
(tú)	escogiste	escogías
(él/ella/usted)	escogió	escogía
(nosotros/as)	escogimos	escogíamos
(vosotros/as)	escogisteis	escogíais
(ellos/ellas/ ustedes)	escogieron	escogían

GERUND	PAST PARTICIPLE
escogiendo	escogido

EXAMPLE PHRASES

Escogió el más caro. He chose the most expensive one.

Escogía siempre al mismo alumno. She always picked the same student.

escoger

	FUTURE	CONDITIONAL
(yo)	escogeré	escogería
(tú)	escogerás	escogerías
(él/ella/usted)	escogerá	escogería
(nosotros/as)	escogeremos	escogeríamos
(vosotros/as)	escogeréis	escogeríais
(ellos/ellas/ ustedes)	escogerán	escogerían

	PRESENT SUBJUNCTIVE	IMPERFECT SUBJUNCTIVE
(yo)	escoja	escogiera *or* escogiese
(tú)	escojas	escogieras *or* escogieses
(él/ella/usted)	escoja	escogiera *or* escogiese
(nosotros/as)	escojamos	escogiéramos *or* escogiésemos
(vosotros/as)	escojáis	escogierais *or* escogieseis
(ellos/ellas/ ustedes)	escojan	escogieran *or* escogiesen

IMPERATIVE

escoge / escoged

Use the present subjunctive in all cases other than these tú and vosotros affirmative forms.

EXAMPLE PHRASES

Yo **escogería** el azul. I'd choose the blue one.

Escoja el que más le guste. Pick the one you like best.

Remember that subject pronouns are not used very often in Spanish.

escribir (to write)

	PRESENT	PRESENT PERFECT
(yo)	escribo	he escrito
(tú)	escribes	has escrito
(él/ella/usted)	escribe	ha escrito
(nosotros/as)	escribimos	hemos escrito
(vosotros/as)	escribís	habéis escrito
(ellos/ellas/ ustedes)	escriben	han escrito

	PRETERITE	IMPERFECT
(yo)	escribí	escribía
(tú)	escribiste	escribías
(él/ella/usted)	escribió	escribía
(nosotros/as)	escribimos	escribíamos
(vosotros/as)	escribisteis	escribíais
(ellos/ellas/ ustedes)	escribieron	escribían

GERUND	PAST PARTICIPLE
escribiendo	escrito

EXAMPLE PHRASES

¿Cómo se **escribe** su nombre? How do you spell your name?

¿**Estás escribiendo** la carta? Are you writing the letter?

Eso lo **escribí** yo. I wrote that.

Nos escribimos durante un tiempo. We wrote to each other for a while.

Escribía canciones. She wrote songs.

Remember that subject pronouns are not used very often in Spanish.

escribir

	FUTURE	CONDITIONAL
(yo)	**escribiré**	**escribiría**
(tú)	**escribirás**	**escribirías**
(él/ella/usted)	**escribirá**	**escribiría**
(nosotros/as)	**escribiremos**	**escribiríamos**
(vosotros/as)	**escribiréis**	**escribiríais**
(ellos/ellas/ ustedes)	**escribirán**	**escribirían**

	PRESENT SUBJUNCTIVE	IMPERFECT SUBJUNCTIVE
(yo)	**escriba**	**escribiera** *or* **escribiese**
(tú)	**escribas**	**escribieras** *or* **escribieses**
(él/ella/usted)	**escriba**	**escribiera** *or* **escribiese**
(nosotros/as)	**escribamos**	**escribiéramos** *or* **escribiésemos**
(vosotros/as)	**escribáis**	**escribierais** *or* **escribieseis**
(ellos/ellas/ ustedes)	**escriban**	**escribieran** *or* **escribiesen**

IMPERATIVE

escribe / escribid

Use the present subjunctive in all cases other than these **tú** *and* **vosotros** *affirmative forms.*

EXAMPLE PHRASES

¿Me **escribirás**? Will you write to me?

Yo lo **escribiría** con mayúscula. I'd write it with a capital letter.

No **escribas** en la mesa. Don't write on the table.

Si de verdad **escribiera** bien, ya le habrían publicado algún libro. If he really was a good writer, he'd have had a book published by now.

Escríbelo en el pizarrón. Write it on the blackboard.

Remember that subject pronouns are not used very often in Spanish.

esforzarse (to make an effort)

	PRESENT	PRESENT PERFECT
(yo)	me esfuerzo	me he esforzado
(tú)	te esfuerzas	te has esforzado
(él/ella/usted)	se esfuerza	se ha esforzado
(nosotros/as)	nos esforzamos	nos hemos esforzado
(vosotros/as)	os esforzáis	os habéis esforzado
(ellos/ellas/ ustedes)	se esfuerzan	se han esforzado

	PRETERITE	IMPERFECT
(yo)	me esforcé	me esforzaba
(tú)	te esforzaste	te esforzabas
(él/ella/usted)	se esforzó	se esforzaba
(nosotros/as)	nos esforzamos	nos esforzábamos
(vosotros/as)	os esforzasteis	os esforzabais
(ellos/ellas/ ustedes)	se esforzaron	se esforzaban

GERUND
esforzándose, etc

PAST PARTICIPLE
esforzado

EXAMPLE PHRASES

Tienes que **esforzarte** si quieres ganar. You have to make an effort if you want to win.

No **te esfuerzas** lo suficiente. You don't make enough effort.

Se esforzó todo lo que pudo por aprobar el examen. He did his best to pass the test.

Me esforzaba por entenderla. I tried hard to understand her.

Remember that subject pronouns are not used very often in Spanish.

esforzarse

	FUTURE	CONDITIONAL
(yo)	me esforzaré	me esforzaría
(tú)	te esforzarás	te esforzarías
(él/ella/usted)	se esforzará	se esforzaría
(nosotros/as)	nos esforzaremos	nos esforzaríamos
(vosotros/as)	os esforzaréis	os esforzaríais
(ellos/ellas/ ustedes)	se esforzarán	se esforzarían

	PRESENT SUBJUNCTIVE	IMPERFECT SUBJUNCTIVE
(yo)	me esfuerce	me esforzara *or* esforzase
(tú)	te esfuerces	te esforzaras *or* esforzases
(él/ella/usted)	se esfuerce	se esforzara *or* esforzase
(nosotros/as)	nos esforcemos	nos esforzáramos *or* esforzásemos
(vosotros/as)	os esforcéis	os esforzarais *or* esforzaseis
(ellos/ellas/ ustedes)	se esfuercen	se esforzaran *or* esforzasen

IMPERATIVE

esfuérzate / esforzaos

Use the present subjunctive in all cases other than these tú and vosotros affirmative forms.

EXAMPLE PHRASES

No **te esfuerces**, no me vas a convencer. Don't bother trying, you're not going to convince me.

Si **te esforzaras** un poco más, lo conseguirías. You'd manage it if you made a little more effort.

Remember that subject pronouns are not used very often in Spanish.

establecer (to establish)

	PRESENT	PRESENT PERFECT
(yo)	**establezco**	**he establecido**
(tú)	**estableces**	**has establecido**
(él/ella/usted)	**establece**	**ha establecido**
(nosotros/as)	**establecemos**	**hemos establecido**
(vosotros/as)	**establecéis**	**habéis establecido**
(ellos/ellas/ ustedes)	**establecen**	**han establecido**

	PRETERITE	IMPERFECT
(yo)	**establecí**	**establecía**
(tú)	**estableciste**	**establecías**
(él/ella/usted)	**estableció**	**establecía**
(nosotros/as)	**establecimos**	**establecíamos**
(vosotros/as)	**establecisteis**	**establecíais**
(ellos/ellas/ ustedes)	**establecieron**	**establecían**

GERUND	PAST PARTICIPLE
estableciendo	**establecido**

EXAMPLE PHRASES

Lograron **establecer** contacto con el barco. They managed to make contact with the boat.

La ley **establece** que... The law states that...

Se ha establecido una buena relación entre los dos países. A good relationship has been established between the two countries.

En 1945, la familia **se estableció** en Lima. In 1945, the family settled in Lima.

Remember that subject pronouns are not used very often in Spanish.

establecer

	FUTURE	CONDITIONAL
(yo)	**estableceré**	**establecería**
(tú)	**establecerás**	**establecerías**
(él/ella/usted)	**establecerá**	**establecería**
(nosotros/as)	**estableceremos**	**estableceríamos**
(vosotros/as)	**estableceréis**	**estableceríais**
(ellos/ellas/ ustedes)	**establecerán**	**establecerían**

	PRESENT SUBJUNCTIVE	IMPERFECT SUBJUNCTIVE
(yo)	**establezca**	**estableciera** *or* **estableciese**
(tú)	**establezcas**	**establecieras** *or* **establecieses**
(él/ella/usted)	**establezca**	**estableciera** *or* **estableciese**
(nosotros/as)	**establezcamos**	**estableciéramos** *or* **estableciésemos**
(vosotros/as)	**establezcáis**	**establecierais** *or* **estableciese**is
(ellos/ellas/ ustedes)	**establezcan**	**establecieran** *or* **estableciesen**

IMPERATIVE

establece / estableced

Use the present subjunctive in all cases other than these **tú** *and* **vosotros** *affirmative forms.*

EXAMPLE PHRASES

El año que viene **se establecerá** por su cuenta. Next year she'll set up on her own.

Remember that subject pronouns are not used very often in Spanish.

estar (to be)

	PRESENT	PRESENT PERFECT
(yo)	estoy	he estado
(tú)	estás	has estado
(él/ella/usted)	está	ha estado
(nosotros/as)	estamos	hemos estado
(vosotros/as)	estáis	habéis estado
(ellos/ellas/ ustedes)	están	han estado

	PRETERITE	IMPERFECT
(yo)	estuve	estaba
(tú)	estuviste	estabas
(él/ella/usted)	estuvo	estaba
(nosotros/as)	estuvimos	estábamos
(vosotros/as)	estuvisteis	estabais
(ellos/ellas/ ustedes)	estuvieron	estaban

GERUND
estando

PAST PARTICIPLE
estado

EXAMPLE PHRASES

Estoy cansado. I'm tired.
¿Cómo **estás**? How are you?
¿No **había estado** nunca en París? He'd never been to Paris?
Estuvimos en casa de mis padres. We were at my parents'.
¿Dónde **estabas**? Where were you?

Remember that subject pronouns are not used very often in Spanish.

estar

	FUTURE	CONDITIONAL
(yo)	estaré	estaría
(tú)	estarás	estarías
(él/ella/usted)	estará	estaría
(nosotros/as)	estaremos	estaríamos
(vosotros/as)	estaréis	estaríais
(ellos/ellas/ ustedes)	estarán	estarían

	PRESENT SUBJUNCTIVE	IMPERFECT SUBJUNCTIVE
(yo)	esté	estuviera *or* estuviese
(tú)	estés	estuvieras *or* estuvieses
(él/ella/usted)	esté	estuviera *or* estuviese
(nosotros/as)	estemos	estuviéramos *or* estuviésemos
(vosotros/as)	estéis	estuvierais *or* estuvieseis
(ellos/ellas/ ustedes)	estén	estuvieran *or* estuviesen

IMPERATIVE

está / estad

Use the present subjunctive in all cases other than these tú and vosotros affirmative forms.

EXAMPLE PHRASES

¿A qué hora **estarás** en casa? What time will you be home?

Dijo que **estaría** aquí a las ocho. She said she'd be here at eight o'clock.

Avísame cuando **estés** lista. Let me know when you're ready.

¡**Estáte** quieto! Keep still!

Si **estuviera** enfermo, habría llamado. If he were sick, he would have called.

Remember that subject pronouns are not used very often in Spanish.

evacuar (to evacuate)

	PRESENT	PRESENT PERFECT
(yo)	evacuo	he evacuado
(tú)	evacuas	has evacuado
(él/ella/usted)	evacua	ha evacuado
(nosotros/as)	evacuamos	hemos evacuado
(vosotros/as)	evacuáis	habéis evacuado
(ellos/ellas/ ustedes)	evacuan	han evacuado

	PRETERITE	IMPERFECT
(yo)	evacué	evacuaba
(tú)	evacuaste	evacuabas
(él/ella/usted)	evacuó	evacuaba
(nosotros/as)	evacuamos	evacuábamos
(vosotros/as)	evacuasteis	evacuabais
(ellos/ellas/ ustedes)	evacuaron	evacuaban

GERUND
evacuando

PAST PARTICIPLE
evacuado

EXAMPLE PHRASES

Van a **evacuar** a los heridos. They're going to evacuate the injured.

Han evacuado la zona. The area has been evacuated.

Remember that subject pronouns are not used very often in Spanish.

evacuar

	FUTURE	CONDITIONAL
(yo)	**evacuaré**	**evacuaría**
(tú)	**evacuarás**	**evacuarías**
(él/ella/usted)	**evacuará**	**evacuaría**
(nosotros/as)	**evacuaremos**	**evacuaríamos**
(vosotros/as)	**evacuaréis**	**evacuaríais**
(ellos/ellas/ ustedes)	**evacuarán**	**evacuarían**

	PRESENT SUBJUNCTIVE	IMPERFECT SUBJUNCTIVE
(yo)	**evacue**	**evacuara** *or* **evacuase**
(tú)	**evacues**	**evacuaras** *or* **evacuases**
(él/ella/usted)	**evacue**	**evacuara** *or* **evacuase**
(nosotros/as)	**evacuemos**	**evacuáramos** *or* **evacuásemos**
(vosotros/as)	**evacuéis**	**evacuarais** *or* **evacuaseis**
(ellos/ellas/ ustedes)	**evacuen**	**evacuaran** *or* **evacuasen**

IMPERATIVE

evacua / evacuad

Use the present subjunctive in all cases other than these **tú** *and* **vosotros** *affirmative forms.*

EXAMPLE PHRASES

Seguirá existiendo peligro mientras no **evacuen** el edificio. The danger won't be over until the building has been evacuated.

forzar (to force)

	PRESENT	PRESENT PERFECT
(yo)	fuerzo	he forzado
(tú)	fuerzas	has forzado
(él/ella/usted)	fuerza	ha forzado
(nosotros/as)	forzamos	hemos forzado
(vosotros/as)	forzáis	habéis forzado
(ellos/ellas/ ustedes)	fuerzan	han forzado

	PRETERITE	IMPERFECT
(yo)	forcé	forzaba
(tú)	forzaste	forzabas
(él/ella/usted)	forzó	forzaba
(nosotros/as)	forzamos	forzábamos
(vosotros/as)	forzasteis	forzabais
(ellos/ellas/ ustedes)	forzaron	forzaban

GERUND
forzando

PAST PARTICIPLE
forzado

EXAMPLE PHRASES

Nos **forzaron** a hacerlo. They forced us to do it.
Habían forzado la puerta de entrada. They had forced the front door.
Los **forzaban** a trabajar largas horas. They would force them to work long hours.

Remember that subject pronouns are not used very often in Spanish.

forzar

	FUTURE	CONDITIONAL
(yo)	forzaré	forzaría
(tú)	forzarás	forzarías
(él/ella/usted)	forzará	forzaría
(nosotros/as)	forzaremos	forzaríamos
(vosotros/as)	forzaréis	forzaríais
(ellos/ellas/ ustedes)	forzarán	forzarían

	PRESENT SUBJUNCTIVE	IMPERFECT SUBJUNCTIVE
(yo)	fuerce	forzara *or* forzase
(tú)	fuerces	forzaras *or* forzases
(él/ella/usted)	fuerce	forzara *or* forzase
(nosotros/as)	forcemos	forzáramos *or* forzásemos
(vosotros/as)	forcéis	forzarais *or* forzaseis
(ellos/ellas/ ustedes)	fuercen	forzaran *or* forzasen

IMPERATIVE

fuerza/forzad

Use the present subjunctive in all cases other than these tú and vosotros affirmative forms.

EXAMPLE PHRASES

No te **forzaremos** a ir. We won't force you to go.

No **fuerces** la cerradura. Don't force the lock.

Lo hizo sin que nadie lo **forzara**. He did it without anybody forcing him to.

freír (to fry)

	PRESENT	PRESENT PERFECT
(yo)	**frío**	**he frito**
(tú)	**fríes**	**has frito**
(él/ella/usted)	**fríe**	**ha frito**
(nosotros/as)	**freímos**	**hemos frito**
(vosotros/as)	**freís**	**habéis frito**
(ellos/ellas/ ustedes)	**fríen**	**han frito**

	PRETERITE	IMPERFECT
(yo)	**freí**	**freía**
(tú)	**freíste**	**freías**
(él/ella/usted)	**frio**	**freía**
(nosotros/as)	**freímos**	**freíamos**
(vosotros/as)	**freísteis**	**freíais**
(ellos/ellas/ ustedes)	**frieron**	**freían**

GERUND	PAST PARTICIPLE
friendo	**frito**

EXAMPLE PHRASES

No sabe ni **freír** un huevo. He can't even fry an egg.

Había frito el pescado. He had fried the fish.

Se está friendo demasiado por ese lado. It's getting overdone on that side.

Lo **frio** en mantequilla. She fried it in butter.

Nos **freíamos** de calor. We were roasting in the heat.

Remember that subject pronouns are not used very often in Spanish.

freír

	FUTURE	CONDITIONAL
(yo)	**freiré**	**freiría**
(tú)	**freirás**	**freirías**
(él/ella/usted)	**freirá**	**freiría**
(nosotros/as)	**freiremos**	**freiríamos**
(vosotros/as)	**freiréis**	**freiríais**
(ellos/ellas/ ustedes)	**freirán**	**freirían**

	PRESENT SUBJUNCTIVE	IMPERFECT SUBJUNCTIVE
(yo)	**fría**	**friera** *or* **friese**
(tú)	**frías**	**frieras** *or* **frieses**
(él/ella/usted)	**fría**	**friera** *or* **friese**
(nosotros/as)	**friamos**	**friéramos** *or* **friésemos**
(vosotros/as)	**friais**	**frierais** *or* **frieseis**
(ellos/ellas/ ustedes)	**frían**	**frieran** *or* **friesen**

IMPERATIVE

fríe / freíd

Use the present subjunctive in all cases other than these **tú** *and* **vosotros** *affirmative forms.*

EXAMPLE PHRASES

Fríelo en aceite de oliva. Fry it in olive oil.

Me dijo que **friera** la cebolla. She told me to fry the onion.

Remember that subject pronouns are not used very often in Spanish.

gruñir (to grumble; to growl)

	PRESENT	PRESENT PERFECT
(yo)	gruño	he gruñido
(tú)	gruñes	has gruñido
(él/ella/usted)	gruñe	ha gruñido
(nosotros/as)	gruñimos	hemos gruñido
(vosotros/as)	gruñís	habéis gruñido
(ellos/ellas/ustedes)	gruñen	han gruñido

	PRETERITE	IMPERFECT
(yo)	gruñí	gruñía
(tú)	gruñiste	gruñías
(él/ella/usted)	gruñó	gruñía
(nosotros/as)	gruñimos	gruñíamos
(vosotros/as)	gruñisteis	gruñíais
(ellos/ellas/ustedes)	gruñeron	gruñían

GERUND	PAST PARTICIPLE
gruñendo	gruñido

EXAMPLE PHRASES

¿A quién le **gruñe** el perro? Who's the dog growling at?

Siempre **está gruñendo**. He's always grumbling.

El oso nos **gruñía** sin parar. The bear kept growling at us.

Remember that subject pronouns are not used very often in Spanish.

gruñir

	FUTURE	CONDITIONAL
(yo)	gruñiré	gruñiría
(tú)	gruñirás	gruñirías
(él/ella/usted)	gruñirá	gruñiría
(nosotros/as)	gruñiremos	gruñiríamos
(vosotros/as)	gruñiréis	gruñiríais
(ellos/ellas/ ustedes)	gruñirán	gruñirían

	PRESENT SUBJUNCTIVE	IMPERFECT SUBJUNCTIVE
(yo)	gruña	gruñera *or* gruñese
(tú)	gruñas	gruñeras *or* gruñeses
(él/ella/usted)	gruña	gruñera *or* gruñese
(nosotros/as)	gruñamos	gruñéramos *or* gruñésemos
(vosotros/as)	gruñáis	gruñerais *or* gruñeseis
(ellos/ellas/ ustedes)	gruñan	gruñeran *or* gruñesen

IMPERATIVE

gruñe / gruñid

Use the present subjunctive in all cases other than these tú and vosotros affirmative forms.

EXAMPLE PHRASES

¡No **gruñas** tanto! Don't grumble so much.

guiar (to guide)

	PRESENT	PRESENT PERFECT
(yo)	**guío**	**he guiado**
(tú)	**guías**	**has guiado**
(él/ella/usted)	**guía**	**ha guiado**
(nosotros/as)	**guiamos**	**hemos guiado**
(vosotros/as)	**guiais**	**habéis guiado**
(ellos/ellas/ ustedes)	**guían**	**han guiado**

	PRETERITE	IMPERFECT
(yo)	**guie**	**guiaba**
(tú)	**guiaste**	**guiabas**
(él/ella/usted)	**guio**	**guiaba**
(nosotros/as)	**guiamos**	**guiábamos**
(vosotros/as)	**guiasteis**	**guiabais**
(ellos/ellas/ ustedes)	**guiaron**	**guiaban**

GERUND	PAST PARTICIPLE
guiando	**guiado**

EXAMPLE PHRASES

Los perros **se guían** por su olfato. Dogs follow their sense of smell.

Me guié por el instinto. I followed my instinct.

Nos guiamos por un mapa que teníamos. We found our way using a map we had.

Siempre me protegía y me **guiaba**. He always protected me and guided me.

Remember that subject pronouns are not used very often in Spanish.

guiar

	FUTURE	CONDITIONAL
(yo)	**guiaré**	**guiaría**
(tú)	**guiarás**	**guiarías**
(él/ella/usted)	**guiará**	**guiaría**
(nosotros/as)	**guiaremos**	**guiaríamos**
(vosotros/as)	**guiaréis**	**guiaríais**
(ellos/ellas/ ustedes)	**guiarán**	**guiarían**

	PRESENT SUBJUNCTIVE	IMPERFECT SUBJUNCTIVE
(yo)	**guíe**	**guiara** *or* **guiase**
(tú)	**guíes**	**guiaras** *or* **guiases**
(él/ella/usted)	**guíe**	**guiara** *or* **guiase**
(nosotros/as)	**guiemos**	**guiáramos** *or* **guiásemos**
(vosotros/as)	**guieis**	**guiarais** *or* **guiaseis**
(ellos/ellas/ ustedes)	**guíen**	**guiaran** *or* **guiasen**

IMPERATIVE

guía / guiad

Use the present subjunctive in all cases other than these tú and vosotros affirmative forms.

EXAMPLE PHRASES

Los **guiaré** hasta allí. I'll take you there.

Guíate por la razón. Use reason as your guide.

haber (to have – *auxiliary*)

	PRESENT	PRESENT PERFECT
(yo)	**he**	*not used except impersonally*
(tú)	**has**	*See* hay
(él/ella/usted)	**ha**	
(nosotros/as)	**hemos**	
(vosotros/as)	**habéis**	
(ellos/ellas/ ustedes)	**han**	

	PRETERITE	IMPERFECT
(yo)	**hube**	**había**
(tú)	**hubiste**	**habías**
(él/ella/usted)	**hubo**	**había**
(nosotros/as)	**hubimos**	**habíamos**
(vosotros/as)	**hubisteis**	**habíais**
(ellos/ellas/ ustedes)	**hubieron**	**habían**

GERUND	PAST PARTICIPLE
habiendo	**habido**

EXAMPLE PHRASES

De **haber**lo sabido, **habría** ido. If I'd known, I would have gone.

¿**Has** visto eso? Did you see that?

Eso nunca **había** pasado antes. That had never happened before.

Remember that subject pronouns are not used very often in Spanish.

haber

	FUTURE	CONDITIONAL
(yo)	**habré**	**habría**
(tú)	**habrás**	**habrías**
(él/ella/usted)	**habrá**	**habría**
(nosotros/as)	**habremos**	**habríamos**
(vosotros/as)	**habréis**	**habríais**
(ellos/ellas/ ustedes)	**habrán**	**habrían**

	PRESENT SUBJUNCTIVE	IMPERFECT SUBJUNCTIVE
(yo)	**haya**	**hubiera** *or* **hubiese**
(tú)	**hayas**	**hubieras** *or* **hubieses**
(él/ella/usted)	**haya**	**hubiera** *or* **hubiese**
(nosotros/as)	**hayamos**	**hubiéramos** *or* **hubiésemos**
(vosotros/as)	**hayáis**	**hubierais** *or* **hubieseis**
(ellos/ellas/ ustedes)	**hayan**	**hubieran** *or* **hubiesen**

IMPERATIVE

not used

EXAMPLE PHRASES

Como se **hayan** olvidado, los mato. I'll kill them if they've forgotten.

Si me lo **hubieras** dicho, te lo **habría** traído. I'd have brought it, if you'd told me.

Para esa hora ya **habremos** terminado. We'll have finished by that time.

Lo **habrías** logrado si **hubieras** intentado. You'd have succeeded if you'd tried.

Remember that subject pronouns are not used very often in Spanish.

hablar (to speak; to talk)

	PRESENT	PRESENT PERFECT
(yo)	**hablo**	**he hablado**
(tú)	**hablas**	**has hablado**
(él/ella/usted)	**habla**	**ha hablado**
(nosotros/as)	**hablamos**	**hemos hablado**
(vosotros/as)	**habláis**	**habéis hablado**
(ellos/ellas/ ustedes)	**hablan**	**han hablado**

	PRETERITE	IMPERFECT
(yo)	**hablé**	**hablaba**
(tú)	**hablaste**	**hablabas**
(él/ella/usted)	**habló**	**hablaba**
(nosotros/as)	**hablamos**	**hablábamos**
(vosotros/as)	**hablasteis**	**hablabais**
(ellos/ellas/ ustedes)	**hablaron**	**hablaban**

GERUND	PAST PARTICIPLE
hablando	**hablado**

EXAMPLE PHRASES

María no **habla** inglés. María doesn't speak English.

No **nos hablamos** desde hace tiempo. We haven't spoken to each other for a long time.

Está hablando por teléfono. He's on the phone.

Hoy **hablé** con mi hermana. I spoke to my sister today.

Hablaba rapidísimo. He spoke really fast.

Remember that subject pronouns are not used very often in Spanish.

hablar

	FUTURE	CONDITIONAL
(yo)	**hablaré**	**hablaría**
(tú)	**hablarás**	**hablarías**
(él/ella/usted)	**hablará**	**hablaría**
(nosotros/as)	**hablaremos**	**hablaríamos**
(vosotros/as)	**hablaréis**	**hablaríais**
(ellos/ellas/ ustedes)	**hablarán**	**hablarían**

	PRESENT SUBJUNCTIVE	IMPERFECT SUBJUNCTIVE
(yo)	**hable**	**hablara** *or* **hablase**
(tú)	**hables**	**hablaras** *or* **hablases**
(él/ella/usted)	**hable**	**hablara** *or* **hablase**
(nosotros/as)	**hablemos**	**habláramos** *or* **hablásemos**
(vosotros/as)	**habléis**	**hablarais** *or* **hablaseis**
(ellos/ellas/ ustedes)	**hablen**	**hablaran** *or* **hablasen**

IMPERATIVE

habla / hablad

Use the present subjunctive in all cases other than these tú and vosotros affirmative forms.

EXAMPLE PHRASES

Luego **hablaremos** de ese tema. We'll talk about that later.

Recuérdame que **hable** con Daniel. Remind me to speak to Daniel.

¿Quieres que **hablemos**? Shall we talk?

Hay que darles una oportunidad para que **hablen**. We need to give them an opportunity to speak.

Remember that subject pronouns are not used very often in Spanish.

hacer (to do; to make)

	PRESENT	PRESENT PERFECT
(yo)	**hago**	**he hecho**
(tú)	**haces**	**has hecho**
(él/ella/usted)	**hace**	**ha hecho**
(nosotros/as)	**hacemos**	**hemos hecho**
(vosotros/as)	**hacéis**	**habéis hecho**
(ellos/ellas/ ustedes)	**hacen**	**han hecho**

	PRETERITE	IMPERFECT
(yo)	**hice**	**hacía**
(tú)	**hiciste**	**hacías**
(él/ella/usted)	**hizo**	**hacía**
(nosotros/as)	**hicimos**	**hacíamos**
(vosotros/as)	**hicisteis**	**hacíais**
(ellos/ellas/ ustedes)	**hicieron**	**hacían**

GERUND	PAST PARTICIPLE
haciendo	**hecho**

EXAMPLE PHRASES

¿Qué **hace** tu padre? What does your father do?

Están haciendo mucho ruido. They're making a lot of noise.

¿Quién **hizo** eso? Who did that?

Hicieron pintar la fachada del colegio. They had the front of the school painted.

Lo **hacía** para molestarme. He was doing it to annoy me.

Remember that subject pronouns are not used very often in Spanish.

hacer

	FUTURE	CONDITIONAL
(yo)	**haré**	**haría**
(tú)	**harás**	**harías**
(él/ella/usted)	**hará**	**haría**
(nosotros/as)	**haremos**	**haríamos**
(vosotros/as)	**haréis**	**haríais**
(ellos/ellas/ ustedes)	**harán**	**harían**

	PRESENT SUBJUNCTIVE	IMPERFECT SUBJUNCTIVE
(yo)	**haga**	**hiciera** *or* **hiciese**
(tú)	**hagas**	**hicieras** *or* **hicieses**
(él/ella/usted)	**haga**	**hiciera** *or* **hiciese**
(nosotros/as)	**hagamos**	**hiciéramos** *or* **hiciésemos**
(vosotros/as)	**hagáis**	**hicierais** *or* **hicieseis**
(ellos/ellas/ ustedes)	**hagan**	**hicieran** *or* **hiciesen**

IMPERATIVE

haz / haced

Use the present subjunctive in all cases other than these tú and vosotros affirmative forms.

EXAMPLE PHRASES

Lo **haré** yo mismo. I'll do it myself.

Dijiste que lo **harías.** You said you'd do it.

¿Quieres que **haga** las camas? Do you want me to make the beds?

Preferiría que **hiciera** menos calor. I wish it wasn't so hot.

Hazlo como te dije. Do it the way I told you.

Remember that subject pronouns are not used very often in Spanish.

hay (there is; there are)

PRESENT
hay

PRESENT PERFECT
ha habido

PRETERITE
hubo

IMPERFECT
había

GERUND
habiendo

PAST PARTICIPLE
habido

EXAMPLE PHRASES

Esta tarde va a **haber** una manifestación. There's going to be a demonstration this evening.

Hay una iglesia en la esquina. There's a church on the corner.

Ha habido muchos problemas. There have been a lot of problems.

Hubo una guerra. There was a war.

Había mucha gente. There were a lot of people.

Remember that subject pronouns are not used very often in Spanish.

hay

FUTURE
habrá

CONDITIONAL
habría

PRESENT SUBJUNCTIVE
haya

IMPERFECT SUBJUNCTIVE
hubiera *or* **hubiese**

IMPERATIVE
not used

EXAMPLE PHRASES

Habrá que repasarlo. We'll have to check it.

Habría que limpiarlo. We should clean it.

No creo que **haya** mucha gente en el recital. I don't think there'll be many people at the concert.

Si **hubiera** más espacio, pondría un sofá. I'd have a sofa if there was more room.

Remember that subject pronouns are not used very often in Spanish.

herir (to injure)

	PRESENT	PRESENT PERFECT
(yo)	**hiero**	**he herido**
(tú)	**hieres**	**has herido**
(él/ella/usted)	**hiere**	**ha herido**
(nosotros/as)	**herimos**	**hemos herido**
(vosotros/as)	**herís**	**habéis herido**
(ellos/ellas/ustedes)	**hieren**	**han herido**

	PRETERITE	IMPERFECT
(yo)	**herí**	**hería**
(tú)	**heriste**	**herías**
(él/ella/usted)	**hirió**	**hería**
(nosotros/as)	**herimos**	**heríamos**
(vosotros/as)	**heristeis**	**heríais**
(ellos/ellas/ustedes)	**hirieron**	**herían**

GERUND	PAST PARTICIPLE
hiriendo	**herido**

EXAMPLE PHRASES

Vas a **herir** sus sentimientos. You're going to hurt her feelings.

Me **hiere** que me digas eso. I'm hurt that you should say such a thing.

Lo **hirieron** en el pecho. He was wounded in the chest.

Su actitud la **hería** en lo más hondo. She was deeply hurt by his attitude.

Remember that subject pronouns are not used very often in Spanish.

herir

	FUTURE	CONDITIONAL
(yo)	**heriré**	**heriría**
(tú)	**herirás**	**heririas**
(él/ella/usted)	**herirá**	**heriría**
(nosotros/as)	**heriremos**	**heririamos**
(vosotros/as)	**heriréis**	**heririais**
(ellos/ellas/ ustedes)	**herirán**	**heririan**

	PRESENT SUBJUNCTIVE	IMPERFECT SUBJUNCTIVE
(yo)	**hiera**	**hiriera** *or* **hiriese**
(tú)	**hieras**	**hirieras** *or* **hirieses**
(él/ella/usted)	**hiera**	**hiriera** *or* **hiriese**
(nosotros/as)	**hiramos**	**hiriéramos** *or* **hiriésemos**
(vosotros/as)	**hiráis**	**hirierais** *or* **hirieseis**
(ellos/ellas/ ustedes)	**hieran**	**hirieran** *or* **hiriesen**

IMPERATIVE

hiere / herid

Use the present subjunctive in all cases other than these tú and vosotros affirmative forms.

EXAMPLE PHRASES

Mi madre siempre tenía miedo que nos **hiriéramos**. My mom was always scared we'd hurt ourselves.

Remember that subject pronouns are not used very often in Spanish.

huir (to escape; to run away; to flee)

	PRESENT	PRESENT PERFECT
(yo)	**huyo**	**he huido**
(tú)	**huyes**	**has huido**
(él/ella/usted)	**huye**	**ha huido**
(nosotros/as)	**huimos**	**hemos huido**
(vosotros/as)	**huis**	**habéis huido**
(ellos/ellas/ ustedes)	**huyen**	**han huido**

	PRETERITE	IMPERFECT
(yo)	**hui**	**huía**
(tú)	**huiste**	**huías**
(él/ella/usted)	**huyó**	**huía**
(nosotros/as)	**huimos**	**huíamos**
(vosotros/as)	**huisteis**	**huíais**
(ellos/ellas/ ustedes)	**huyeron**	**huían**

GERUND	PAST PARTICIPLE
huyendo	**huido**

EXAMPLE PHRASES

Salió **huyendo.** He ran away.

Huyeron del país. They fled the country.

huir

	FUTURE	CONDITIONAL
(yo)	**huiré**	**huiría**
(tú)	**huirás**	**huirías**
(él/ella/usted)	**huirá**	**huiría**
(nosotros/as)	**huiremos**	**huiríamos**
(vosotros/as)	**huiréis**	**huiríais**
(ellos/ellas/ ustedes)	**huirán**	**huirían**

	PRESENT SUBJUNCTIVE	IMPERFECT SUBJUNCTIVE
(yo)	**huya**	**huyera** *or* **huyese**
(tú)	**huyas**	**huyeras** *or* **huyeses**
(él/ella/usted)	**huya**	**huyera** *or* **huyese**
(nosotros/as)	**huyamos**	**huyéramos** *or* **huyésemos**
(vosotros/as)	**huyáis**	**huyerais** *or* **huyeseis**
(ellos/ellas/ ustedes)	**huyan**	**huyeran** *or* **huyesen**

IMPERATIVE

huye / huid

Use the present subjunctive in all cases other than these **tú** *and* **vosotros** *affirmative forms.*

EXAMPLE PHRASES

No quiero que **huyas** como un cobarde. I don't want you to run away like a coward.

¡**Huye**! Si te atrapan, te matarán. Run! If they catch you, they'll kill you.

imponer (to impose)

	PRESENT	PRESENT PERFECT
(yo)	impongo	he impuesto
(tú)	impones	has impuesto
(él/ella/usted)	impone	ha impuesto
(nosotros/as)	imponemos	hemos impuesto
(vosotros/as)	imponéis	habéis impuesto
(ellos/ellas/ ustedes)	imponen	han impuesto

	PRETERITE	IMPERFECT
(yo)	impuse	imponía
(tú)	impusiste	imponías
(él/ella/usted)	impuso	imponía
(nosotros/as)	impusimos	imponíamos
(vosotros/as)	impusisteis	imponíais
(ellos/ellas/ ustedes)	impusieron	imponían

GERUND	PAST PARTICIPLE
imponiendo	impuesto

EXAMPLE PHRASES

La minifalda **se está imponiendo** de nuevo. The miniskirt is coming back into fashion.

Habían impuesto la enseñanza religiosa. They had made religious education compulsory.

El corredor nigeriano **se impuso** en la segunda carrera. The Nigerian runner triumphed in the second race.

Mi abuelo **imponía** mucho respeto. My grandfather commanded a lot of respect.

Remember that subject pronouns are not used very often in Spanish.

imponer

	FUTURE	CONDITIONAL
(yo)	impondré	impondría
(tú)	impondrás	impondrías
(él/ella/usted)	impondrá	impondría
(nosotros/as)	impondremos	impondríamos
(vosotros/as)	impondréis	impondríais
(ellos/ellas/ ustedes)	impondrán	impondrían

	PRESENT SUBJUNCTIVE	IMPERFECT SUBJUNCTIVE
(yo)	imponga	impusiera *or* impusiese
(tú)	impongas	impusieras *or* impusieses
(él/ella/usted)	imponga	impusiera *or* impusiese
(nosotros/as)	impongamos	impusiéramos *or* impusiésemos
(vosotros/as)	impongáis	impusierais *or* impusieseis
(ellos/ellas/ ustedes)	impongan	impusieran *or* impusiesen

IMPERATIVE

impón / imponed

Use the present subjunctive in all cases other than these tú and vosotros affirmative forms.

EXAMPLE PHRASES

Impondrán cuantiosas multas. They'll impose heavy fines.

imprimir (to print)

	PRESENT	PRESENT PERFECT
(yo)	imprimo	he imprimido
(tú)	imprimes	has imprimido
(él/ella/usted)	imprime	ha imprimido
(nosotros/as)	imprimimos	hemos imprimido
(vosotros/as)	imprimís	habéis imprimido
(ellos/ellas/ ustedes)	imprimen	han imprimido

	PRETERITE	IMPERFECT
(yo)	imprimí	imprimía
(tú)	imprimiste	imprimías
(él/ella/usted)	imprimió	imprimía
(nosotros/as)	imprimimos	imprimíamos
(vosotros/as)	imprimisteis	imprimíais
(ellos/ellas/ ustedes)	imprimieron	imprimían

GERUND	PAST PARTICIPLE
imprimiendo	imprimido, impreso

EXAMPLE PHRASES

¿Puedes **imprimir** el documento? Can you print the document?

Se imprimieron sólo doce copias del libro. Only twelve copies of the book were printed.

Una experiencia así **imprime** carácter. An experience like that is character-building.

Remember that subject pronouns are not used very often in Spanish.

imprimir

	FUTURE	CONDITIONAL
(yo)	imprimiré	imprimiría
(tú)	imprimirás	imprimirías
(él/ella/usted)	imprimirá	imprimiría
(nosotros/as)	imprimiremos	imprimiríamos
(vosotros/as)	imprimiréis	imprimiríais
(ellos/ellas/ ustedes)	imprimirán	imprimirían

	PRESENT SUBJUNCTIVE	IMPERFECT SUBJUNCTIVE
(yo)	imprima	imprimiera *or* imprimiese
(tú)	imprimas	imprimieras *or* imprimieses
(él/ella/usted)	imprima	imprimiera *or* imprimiese
(nosotros/as)	imprimamos	imprimiéramos *or* imprimiésemos
(vosotros/as)	imprimáis	imprimierais *or* imprimieseis
(ellos/ellas/ ustedes)	impriman	imprimieran *or* imprimiesen

IMPERATIVE

imprime / imprimid

Use the present subjunctive in all cases other than these **tú** *and* **vosotros** *affirmative forms.*

EXAMPLE PHRASE

Imprímelo en blanco y negro. Print it in black and white.

Remember that subject pronouns are not used very often in Spanish.

ir (to go)

	PRESENT	PRESENT PERFECT
(yo)	**voy**	**he ido**
(tú)	**vas**	**has ido**
(él/ella/usted)	**va**	**ha ido**
(nosotros/as)	**vamos**	**hemos ido**
(vosotros/as)	**vais**	**habéis ido**
(ellos/ellas/ ustedes)	**van**	**han ido**

	PRETERITE	IMPERFECT
(yo)	**fui**	**iba**
(tú)	**fuiste**	**ibas**
(él/ella/usted)	**fue**	**iba**
(nosotros/as)	**fuimos**	**íbamos**
(vosotros/as)	**fuisteis**	**ibais**
(ellos/ellas/ ustedes)	**fueron**	**iban**

GERUND	PAST PARTICIPLE
yendo	**ido**

EXAMPLE PHRASES

¿Puedo **ir** contigo? Can I come with you?

Estoy yendo a clases de natación. I'm taking swimming classes.

Había ido a comprar el pan. She'd gone to buy the bread.

Anoche **fuimos** al cine. We went to the movies last night.

Remember that subject pronouns are not used very often in Spanish.

ir

	FUTURE	CONDITIONAL
(yo)	**iré**	**iría**
(tú)	**irás**	**irías**
(él/ella/usted)	**irá**	**iría**
(nosotros/as)	**iremos**	**iríamos**
(vosotros/as)	**iréis**	**iríais**
(ellos/ellas/ ustedes)	**irán**	**irían**

	PRESENT SUBJUNCTIVE	IMPERFECT SUBJUNCTIVE
(yo)	**vaya**	**fuera** *or* **fuese**
(tú)	**vayas**	**fueras** *or* **fueses**
(él/ella/usted)	**vaya**	**fuera** *or* **fuese**
(nosotros/as)	**vayamos**	**fuéramos** *or* **fuésemos**
(vosotros/as)	**vayáis**	**fuerais** *or* **fueseis**
(ellos/ellas/ ustedes)	**vayan**	**fueran** *or* **fuesen**

IMPERATIVE

ve / id

Use the present subjunctive in most cases other than these tú and vosotros affirmative forms. However, in the 'let's' affirmative form, vamos is more common than vayamos.

EXAMPLE PHRASES

El domingo **iré** a verla. I'll go to see her on Sunday.

Dijeron que **irían** en tren. They said they'd go by train.

¡Que te **vaya** bien! Take care of yourself!

Quería pedirte que **fueras** en mi lugar. I wanted to ask you if you'd go instead of me.

No **te vayas** sin despedirte. Don't go without saying goodbye.

Remember that subject pronouns are not used very often in Spanish.

jugar (to play)

	PRESENT	PRESENT PERFECT
(yo)	juego	he jugado
(tú)	juegas	has jugado
(él/ella/usted)	juega	ha jugado
(nosotros/as)	jugamos	hemos jugado
(vosotros/as)	jugáis	habéis jugado
(ellos/ellas/ ustedes)	juegan	han jugado

	PRETERITE	IMPERFECT
(yo)	jugué	jugaba
(tú)	jugaste	jugabas
(él/ella/usted)	jugó	jugaba
(nosotros/as)	jugamos	jugábamos
(vosotros/as)	jugasteis	jugabais
(ellos/ellas/ ustedes)	jugaron	jugaban

GERUND	PAST PARTICIPLE
jugando	jugado

EXAMPLE PHRASES

Juego futbol todos los domingos. I play soccer every Sunday.

Están jugando en el jardín. They're playing in the yard.

Le **jugaron** una mala pasada. They played a dirty trick on him.

Se jugaba la vida continuamente. She was constantly risking her life.

Remember that subject pronouns are not used very often in Spanish.

jugar

	FUTURE	CONDITIONAL
(yo)	**jugaré**	**jugaría**
(tú)	**jugarás**	**jugarías**
(él/ella/usted)	**jugará**	**jugaría**
(nosotros/as)	**jugaremos**	**jugaríamos**
(vosotros/as)	**jugaréis**	**jugaríais**
(ellos/ellas/ ustedes)	**jugarán**	**jugarían**

	PRESENT SUBJUNCTIVE	IMPERFECT SUBJUNCTIVE
(yo)	**juegue**	**jugara** *or* **jugase**
(tú)	**juegues**	**jugaras** *or* **jugases**
(él/ella/usted)	**juegue**	**jugara** *or* **jugase**
(nosotros/as)	**juguemos**	**jugáramos** *or* **jugásemos**
(vosotros/as)	**juguéis**	**jugarais** *or* **jugaseis**
(ellos/ellas/ ustedes)	**jueguen**	**jugaran** *or* **jugasen**

IMPERATIVE

juega / jugad

Use the present subjunctive in all cases other than these **tú** *and* **vosotros** *affirmative forms.*

EXAMPLE PHRASES

Ambos partidos se **jugarán** el domingo. Both games will be played on Sunday.

Jugarías mejor si estuvieras más relajado. You'd play better if you were more relaxed.

No **juegues** con tu salud. Don't take risks with your health.

El médico le aconsejó que **jugara** más y leyera menos. The doctor advised him to play more and read less.

Remember that subject pronouns are not used very often in Spanish.

leer (to read)

	PRESENT	PRESENT PERFECT
(yo)	**leo**	**he leído**
(tú)	**lees**	**has leído**
(él/ella/usted)	**lee**	**ha leído**
(nosotros/as)	**leemos**	**hemos leído**
(vosotros/as)	**leéis**	**habéis leído**
(ellos/ellas/ ustedes)	**leen**	**han leído**

	PRETERITE	IMPERFECT
(yo)	**leí**	**leía**
(tú)	**leíste**	**leías**
(él/ella/usted)	**leyó**	**leía**
(nosotros/as)	**leímos**	**leíamos**
(vosotros/as)	**leísteis**	**leíais**
(ellos/ellas/ ustedes)	**leyeron**	**leían**

GERUND
leyendo

PAST PARTICIPLE
leído

EXAMPLE PHRASES

Hace mucho tiempo que no **leo** nada. I haven't read anything for ages.
Estoy leyendo un libro muy interesante. I'm reading a very interesting book.
No **había leído** nada suyo. I hadn't read anything by her.
Lo **leí** hace tiempo. I read it a while ago.
Antes **leía** mucho más. I used to read a lot more before.

Remember that subject pronouns are not used very often in Spanish.

leer

	FUTURE	CONDITIONAL
(yo)	**leeré**	**leería**
(tú)	**leerás**	**leerías**
(él/ella/usted)	**leerá**	**leería**
(nosotros/as)	**leeremos**	**leeríamos**
(vosotros/as)	**leeréis**	**leeríais**
(ellos/ellas/ ustedes)	**leerán**	**leerían**

	PRESENT SUBJUNCTIVE	IMPERFECT SUBJUNCTIVE
(yo)	**lea**	**leyera** *or* **leyese**
(tú)	**leas**	**leyeras** *or* **leyeses**
(él/ella/usted)	**lea**	**leyera** *or* **leyese**
(nosotros/as)	**leamos**	**leyéramos** *or* **leyésemos**
(vosotros/as)	**leáis**	**leyerais** *or* **leyeseis**
(ellos/ellas/ ustedes)	**lean**	**leyeran** *or* **leyesen**

IMPERATIVE

lee / leed

Use the present subjunctive in all cases other than these tú and vosotros affirmative forms.

EXAMPLE PHRASES

Si se portan bien, les **leeré** un cuento. If you behave yourselves, I'll read you a story.

Yo **leería** también la letra pequeña. I'd read the fine print as well.

Quiero que lo **leas** y me digas qué piensas. I want you to read it and tell me what you think.

No **leas** tan rápido. Don't read so fast.

Remember that subject pronouns are not used very often in Spanish.

levantar (to lift; to raise; to pick up)

	PRESENT	PRESENT PERFECT
(yo)	**levanto**	**he levantado**
(tú)	**levantas**	**has levantado**
(él/ella/usted)	**levanta**	**ha levantado**
(nosotros/as)	**levantamos**	**hemos levantado**
(vosotros/as)	**levantáis**	**habéis levantado**
(ellos/ellas/ ustedes)	**levantan**	**han levantado**

	PRETERITE	IMPERFECT
(yo)	**levanté**	**levantaba**
(tú)	**levantaste**	**levantabas**
(él/ella/usted)	**levantó**	**levantaba**
(nosotros/as)	**levantamos**	**levantábamos**
(vosotros/as)	**levantasteis**	**levantabais**
(ellos/ellas/ ustedes)	**levantaron**	**levantaban**

GERUND	PAST PARTICIPLE
levantando	**levantado**

EXAMPLE PHRASES

Fue la primera en **levantar** la mano. She was the first to raise her hand.

Siempre **se levanta** de mal humor. He's always in a bad mood when he gets up.

Hoy **me levanté** temprano. I got up early this morning.

Levantó la maleta como si no pesara nada. He lifted up the suitcase as if it weighed nothing.

Me levanté y seguí caminando. I got up and continued walking.

Remember that subject pronouns are not used very often in Spanish.

levantar

	FUTURE	CONDITIONAL
(yo)	**levantaré**	**levantaría**
(tú)	**levantarás**	**levantarías**
(él/ella/usted)	**levantará**	**levantaría**
(nosotros/as)	**levantaremos**	**levantaríamos**
(vosotros/as)	**levantaréis**	**levantaríais**
(ellos/ellas/ ustedes)	**levantarán**	**levantarían**

	PRESENT SUBJUNCTIVE	IMPERFECT SUBJUNCTIVE
(yo)	**levante**	**levantara** *or* **levantase**
(tú)	**levantes**	**levantaras** *or* **levantases**
(él/ella/usted)	**levante**	**levantara** *or* **levantase**
(nosotros/as)	**levantemos**	**levantáramos** *or* **levantásemos**
(vosotros/as)	**levantéis**	**levantarais** *or* **levantaseis**
(ellos/ellas/ ustedes)	**levanten**	**levantaran** *or* **levantasen**

IMPERATIVE

levanta / levantad

Use the present subjunctive in all cases other than these tú and vosotros affirmative forms.

EXAMPLE PHRASES

La noticia le **levantará** el ánimo. This news will raise her spirits.

Si pudiera **me levantaría** siempre tarde. I'd sleep in every day, if I could.

No me **levantes** la voz. Don't raise your voice to me.

Levanta la tapa. Lift the lid.

Levanten la mano si tienen alguna duda. Raise your hands if you are unclear about anything.

Remember that subject pronouns are not used very often in Spanish.

llover (to rain)

PRESENT
llueve

PRESENT PERFECT
ha llovido

PRETERITE
llovió

IMPERFECT
llovía

GERUND
lloviendo

PAST PARTICIPLE
llovido

EXAMPLE PHRASES

Hace semanas que no **llueve**. It hasn't rained in weeks.
Está lloviendo. It's raining.
Le **llovieron** las ofertas. He received a lot of offers.
Llovió sin parar. It rained nonstop.
Llovía a cántaros. It was pouring rain.

Remember that subject pronouns are not used very often in Spanish.

llover

FUTURE
lloverá

CONDITIONAL
llovería

PRESENT SUBJUNCTIVE
llueva

IMPERFECT SUBJUNCTIVE
lloviera *or* lloviese

IMPERATIVE
not used

EXAMPLE PHRASES

Sabía que le **lloverían** las críticas. She knew she would come in for a lot of criticism.

Espero que no **llueva** este fin de semana. I hope it won't rain this weekend.

Si no **lloviera**, podríamos salir a dar una vuelta. We could go for a walk if it didn't rain.

Remember that subject pronouns are not used very often in Spanish.

lucir (to look; to shine; to show off)

	PRESENT	PRESENT PERFECT
(yo)	**luzco**	**he lucido**
(tú)	**luces**	**has lucido**
(él/ella/usted)	**luce**	**ha lucido**
(nosotros/as)	**lucimos**	**hemos lucido**
(vosotros/as)	**lucís**	**habéis lucido**
(ellos/ellas/ ustedes)	**lucen**	**han lucido**

	PRETERITE	IMPERFECT
(yo)	**lucí**	**lucía**
(tú)	**luciste**	**lucías**
(él/ella/usted)	**lució**	**lucía**
(nosotros/as)	**lucimos**	**lucíamos**
(vosotros/as)	**lucisteis**	**lucíais**
(ellos/ellas/ ustedes)	**lucieron**	**lucían**

GERUND	PAST PARTICIPLE
luciendo	**lucido**

EXAMPLE PHRASES

Luces muy bien. You look very well.

Quería **lucir** sus conocimientos. He wanted to show off his knowledge.

Te luciste con la comida. You've outdone yourself with the meal.

Remember that subject pronouns are not used very often in Spanish.

lucir

	FUTURE	CONDITIONAL
(yo)	**luciré**	**luciría**
(tú)	**lucirás**	**lucirías**
(él/ella/usted)	**lucirá**	**luciría**
(nosotros/as)	**luciremos**	**luciríamos**
(vosotros/as)	**luciréis**	**luciríais**
(ellos/ellas/ ustedes)	**lucirán**	**lucirían**

	PRESENT SUBJUNCTIVE	IMPERFECT SUBJUNCTIVE
(yo)	**luzca**	**luciera** *or* **luciese**
(tú)	**luzcas**	**lucieras** *or* **lucieses**
(él/ella/usted)	**luzca**	**luciera** *or* **luciese**
(nosotros/as)	**luzcamos**	**luciéramos** *or* **luciésemos**
(vosotros/as)	**luzcáis**	**lucierais** *or* **lucieseis**
(ellos/ellas/ ustedes)	**luzcan**	**lucieran** *or* **luciesen**

IMPERATIVE

luce / lucid

Use the present subjunctive in all cases other than these **tú** *and* **vosotros** *affirmative forms.*

EXAMPLE PHRASES

Lucirá un traje muy elegante. She will be wearing a very elegant outfit.

Luciría más con otros zapatos. It would look better with a different pair of shoes.

Quiero que esta noche **luzcas** tú el collar. I want you to wear the necklace tonight.

Remember that subject pronouns are not used very often in Spanish.

morir (to die)

	PRESENT	PRESENT PERFECT
(yo)	muero	he muerto
(tú)	mueres	has muerto
(él/ella/usted)	muere	ha muerto
(nosotros/as)	morimos	hemos muerto
(vosotros/as)	morís	habéis muerto
(ellos/ellas/ ustedes)	mueren	han muerto

	PRETERITE	IMPERFECT
(yo)	morí	moría
(tú)	moriste	morías
(él/ella/usted)	murió	moría
(nosotros/as)	morimos	moríamos
(vosotros/as)	moristeis	moríais
(ellos/ellas/ ustedes)	murieron	morían

GERUND
muriendo

PAST PARTICIPLE
muerto

EXAMPLE PHRASES

¡**Me muero** de hambre! I'm starving!
Se está muriendo. She's dying.
Se le **había muerto** el gato. His cat had died.
Se murió el mes pasado. He died last month.
Me moría de ganas de contárselo. I was dying to tell her.

Remember that subject pronouns are not used very often in Spanish

morir

	FUTURE	CONDITIONAL
(yo)	**moriré**	**moriría**
(tú)	**morirás**	**morirías**
(él/ella/usted)	**morirá**	**moriría**
(nosotros/as)	**moriremos**	**moriríamos**
(vosotros/as)	**moriréis**	**moriríais**
(ellos/ellas/ ustedes)	**morirán**	**morirían**

	PRESENT SUBJUNCTIVE	IMPERFECT SUBJUNCTIVE
(yo)	**muera**	**muriera** *or* **muriese**
(tú)	**mueras**	**murieras** *or* **murieses**
(él/ella/usted)	**muera**	**muriera** *or* **muriese**
(nosotros/as)	**muramos**	**muriéramos** *or* **muriésemos**
(vosotros/as)	**muráis**	**murierais** *or* **murieseis**
(ellos/ellas/ ustedes)	**mueran**	**murieran** *or* **muriesen**

IMPERATIVE

muere / morid

Use the present subjunctive in all cases other than these tú and vosotros affirmative forms.

EXAMPLE PHRASES

Cuando te lo cuente **te morirás** de risa. You'll die laughing when I tell you.

Yo **me moriría** de vergüenza. I'd die of shame.

Cuando **me muera**... When I die...

¡Por favor, no **te mueras**! Please don't die!

Remember that subject pronouns are not used very often in Spanish.

mover (to move)

	PRESENT	PRESENT PERFECT
(yo)	**muevo**	**he movido**
(tú)	**mueves**	**has movido**
(él/ella/usted)	**mueve**	**ha movido**
(nosotros/as)	**movemos**	**hemos movido**
(vosotros/as)	**movéis**	**habéis movido**
(ellos/ellas/ ustedes)	**mueven**	**han movido**

	PRETERITE	IMPERFECT
(yo)	**moví**	**movía**
(tú)	**moviste**	**movías**
(él/ella/usted)	**movió**	**movía**
(nosotros/as)	**movimos**	**movíamos**
(vosotros/as)	**movisteis**	**movíais**
(ellos/ellas/ ustedes)	**movieron**	**movían**

GERUND	PAST PARTICIPLE
moviendo	**movido**

EXAMPLE PHRASES

El perro no dejaba de **mover** la cola. The dog kept wagging its tail.

Se está moviendo. It's moving.

No **se movieron** de casa. They didn't leave the house.

Antes **se movía** en esos ambientes. He used to move in those circles.

Remember that subject pronouns are not used very often in Spanish.

mover

	FUTURE	CONDITIONAL
(yo)	**moveré**	**movería**
(tú)	**moverás**	**moverías**
(él/ella/usted)	**moverá**	**movería**
(nosotros/as)	**moveremos**	**moveríamos**
(vosotros/as)	**moveréis**	**moveríais**
(ellos/ellas/ ustedes)	**moverán**	**moverían**

	PRESENT SUBJUNCTIVE	IMPERFECT SUBJUNCTIVE
(yo)	**mueva**	**moviera** *or* **moviese**
(tú)	**muevas**	**movieras** *or* **movieses**
(él/ella/usted)	**mueva**	**moviera** *or* **moviese**
(nosotros/as)	**movamos**	**moviéramos** *or* **moviésemos**
(vosotros/as)	**mováis**	**movierais** *or* **movieseis**
(ellos/ellas/ ustedes)	**muevan**	**movieran** *or* **moviesen**

IMPERATIVE

mueve / moved

Use the present subjunctive in all cases other than these tú and vosotros affirmative forms.

EXAMPLE PHRASES

Prométeme que no **te moverás** de aquí. Promise me you won't move from here.

No **te muevas**. Don't move.

Mueve un poco las cajas para que podamos pasar. Move the boxes a bit so that we can get past.

Remember that subject pronouns are not used very often in Spanish.

nacer (to be born)

	PRESENT	PRESENT PERFECT
(yo)	**nazco**	**he nacido**
(tú)	**naces**	**has nacido**
(él/ella/usted)	**nace**	**ha nacido**
(nosotros/as)	**nacemos**	**hemos nacido**
(vosotros/as)	**nacéis**	**habéis nacido**
(ellos/ellas/ ustedes)	**nacen**	**han nacido**

	PRETERITE	IMPERFECT
(yo)	**nací**	**nacía**
(tú)	**naciste**	**nacías**
(él/ella/usted)	**nació**	**nacía**
(nosotros/as)	**nacimos**	**nacíamos**
(vosotros/as)	**nacisteis**	**nacíais**
(ellos/ellas/ ustedes)	**nacieron**	**nacían**

GERUND	PAST PARTICIPLE
naciendo	**nacido**

EXAMPLE PHRASES

Nacen cuatro niños por minuto. Four children are born every minute.

Nació en 1980. He was born in 1980.

¿Cuándo **naciste**? When were you born?

Tu todavía no **habías nacido**. You hadn't been born yet.

nacer

	FUTURE	CONDITIONAL
(yo)	**naceré**	**nacería**
(tú)	**nacerás**	**nacerías**
(él/ella/usted)	**nacerá**	**nacería**
(nosotros/as)	**naceremos**	**naceríamos**
(vosotros/as)	**naceréis**	**naceríais**
(ellos/ellas/ ustedes)	**nacerán**	**nacerían**

	PRESENT SUBJUNCTIVE	IMPERFECT SUBJUNCTIVE
(yo)	**nazca**	**naciera** *or* **naciese**
(tú)	**nazcas**	**nacieras** *or* **nacieses**
(él/ella/usted)	**nazca**	**naciera** *or* **naciese**
(nosotros/as)	**nazcamos**	**naciéramos** *or* **naciésemos**
(vosotros/as)	**nazcáis**	**nacierais** *or* **nacieseis**
(ellos/ellas/ ustedes)	**nazcan**	**nacieran** *or* **naciesen**

IMPERATIVE

nace / naced

Use the present subjunctive in all cases other than these tú and vosotros affirmative forms.

EXAMPLE PHRASES

Nacerá el año que viene. It will be born next year.

Queremos que **nazca** en México. We want it to be born in Mexico.

Si **naciera** hoy, sería tauro. He'd be a Taurus if he were born today.

negar (to deny; to refuse)

	PRESENT	PRESENT PERFECT
(yo)	**niego**	**he negado**
(tú)	**niegas**	**has negado**
(él/ella/usted)	**niega**	**ha negado**
(nosotros/as)	**negamos**	**hemos negado**
(vosotros/as)	**negáis**	**habéis negado**
(ellos/ellas/ ustedes)	**niegan**	**han negado**

	PRETERITE	IMPERFECT
(yo)	**negué**	**negaba**
(tú)	**negaste**	**negabas**
(él/ella/usted)	**negó**	**negaba**
(nosotros/as)	**negamos**	**negábamos**
(vosotros/as)	**negasteis**	**negabais**
(ellos/ellas/ ustedes)	**negaron**	**negaban**

GERUND	PAST PARTICIPLE
negando	**negado**

EXAMPLE PHRASES

No lo puedes **negar**. You can't deny it.

Me niego a creerlo. I refuse to believe it.

Se negó a venir con nosotros. She refused to come with us.

Decían que era el ladrón, pero él lo **negaba**. They said that he was the thief, but he denied it.

negar

	FUTURE	CONDITIONAL
(yo)	**negaré**	**negaría**
(tú)	**negarás**	**negarías**
(él/ella/usted)	**negará**	**negaría**
(nosotros/as)	**negaremos**	**negaríamos**
(vosotros/as)	**negaréis**	**negaríais**
(ellos/ellas/ ustedes)	**negarán**	**negarían**

	PRESENT SUBJUNCTIVE	IMPERFECT SUBJUNCTIVE
(yo)	**niegue**	**negara** *or* **negase**
(tú)	**niegues**	**negaras** *or* **negases**
(él/ella/usted)	**niegue**	**negara** *or* **negase**
(nosotros/as)	**neguemos**	**negáramos** *or* **negásemos**
(vosotros/as)	**neguéis**	**negarais** *or* **negaseis**
(ellos/ellas/ ustedes)	**nieguen**	**negaran** *or* **negasen**

IMPERATIVE

niega / negad

Use the present subjunctive in all cases other than these tú and vosotros affirmative forms.

EXAMPLE PHRASES

No me **negarás** que es barato. You can't say it's not cheap.

Si lo **negaras**, nadie te creería. If you denied it, nobody would believe you.

No lo **niegues**. Don't deny it.

oír (to hear; to listen)

	PRESENT	PRESENT PERFECT
(yo)	**oigo**	**he oído**
(tú)	**oyes**	**has oído**
(él/ella/usted)	**oye**	**ha oído**
(nosotros/as)	**oímos**	**hemos oído**
(vosotros/as)	**oís**	**habéis oído**
(ellos/ellas/ ustedes)	**oyen**	**han oído**

	PRETERITE	IMPERFECT
(yo)	**oí**	**oía**
(tú)	**oíste**	**oías**
(él/ella/usted)	**oyó**	**oía**
(nosotros/as)	**oímos**	**oíamos**
(vosotros/as)	**oísteis**	**oíais**
(ellos/ellas/ ustedes)	**oyeron**	**oían**

GERUND	PAST PARTICIPLE
oyendo	**oído**

EXAMPLE PHRASES

No **oigo** nada. I can't hear anything.

Estábamos oyendo las noticias. We were listening to the news.

¿**Oíste** eso? Did you hear that?

Lo **oí** por casualidad. I heard it by chance.

No **oía** muy bien. He couldn't hear very well.

Remember that subject pronouns are not used very often in Spanish.

oír

	FUTURE	CONDITIONAL
(yo)	oiré	oiría
(tú)	oirás	oirías
(él/ella/usted)	oirá	oiría
(nosotros/as)	oiremos	oiríamos
(vosotros/as)	oiréis	oiríais
(ellos/ellas/ ustedes)	oirán	oirían

	PRESENT SUBJUNCTIVE	IMPERFECT SUBJUNCTIVE
(yo)	oiga	oyera *or* oyese
(tú)	oigas	oyeras *or* oyeses
(él/ella/usted)	oiga	oyera *or* oyese
(nosotros/as)	oigamos	oyéramos *or* oyésemos
(vosotros/as)	oigáis	oyerais *or* oyeseis
(ellos/ellas/ ustedes)	oigan	oyeran *or* oyesen

IMPERATIVE

oye / oíd

Use the present subjunctive in all cases other than these tú and vosotros affirmative forms.

EXAMPLE PHRASES

Oye, ¿tú qué te crees? Listen, who do you think you are?

Oigan bien. Listen carefully.

oler (to smell)

	PRESENT	PRESENT PERFECT
(yo)	**huelo**	**he olido**
(tú)	**hueles**	**has olido**
(él/ella/usted)	**huele**	**ha olido**
(nosotros/as)	**olemos**	**hemos olido**
(vosotros/as)	**oléis**	**habéis olido**
(ellos/ellas/ ustedes)	**huelen**	**han olido**

	PRETERITE	IMPERFECT
(yo)	**olí**	**olía**
(tú)	**oliste**	**olías**
(él/ella/usted)	**olió**	**olía**
(nosotros/as)	**olimos**	**olíamos**
(vosotros/as)	**olisteis**	**olíais**
(ellos/ellas/ ustedes)	**olieron**	**olían**

GERUND	PAST PARTICIPLE
oliendo	**olido**

EXAMPLE PHRASES

Huele a pescado. It smells of fish.

El perro **estaba oliendo** la basura. The dog was sniffing the trash.

A mí el asunto me **olió** mal. I thought there was something fishy about it.

Olía muy bien. It smelled really nice.

Remember that subject pronouns are not used very often in Spanish.

oler

	FUTURE	CONDITIONAL
(yo)	**oleré**	**olería**
(tú)	**olerás**	**olerías**
(él/ella/usted)	**olerá**	**olería**
(nosotros/as)	**oleremos**	**oleríamos**
(vosotros/as)	**oleréis**	**oleríais**
(ellos/ellas/ ustedes)	**olerán**	**olerían**

	PRESENT SUBJUNCTIVE	IMPERFECT SUBJUNCTIVE
(yo)	**huela**	**oliera** *or* **oliese**
(tú)	**huelas**	**olieras** *or* **olieses**
(él/ella/usted)	**huela**	**oliera** *or* **oliese**
(nosotros/as)	**olamos**	**oliéramos** *or* **oliésemos**
(vosotros/as)	**oláis**	**olierais** *or* **olieseis**
(ellos/ellas/ ustedes)	**huelan**	**olieran** *or* **oliesen**

IMPERATIVE

huele / oled

Use the present subjunctive in all cases other than these **tú** *and* **vosotros** *affirmative forms.*

EXAMPLE PHRASES

Con esto ya no **olerá**. This will take the smell away.

Si estuviera fresco, no **olería** así. If it were fresh, it wouldn't smell like that.

pagar (to pay; to pay for)

	PRESENT	PRESENT PERFECT
(yo)	pago	he pagado
(tú)	pagas	has pagado
(él/ella/usted)	paga	ha pagado
(nosotros/as)	pagamos	hemos pagado
(vosotros/as)	pagáis	habéis pagado
(ellos/ellas/ ustedes)	pagan	han pagado

	PRETERITE	IMPERFECT
(yo)	pagué	pagaba
(tú)	pagaste	pagabas
(él/ella/usted)	pagó	pagaba
(nosotros/as)	pagamos	pagábamos
(vosotros/as)	pagasteis	pagabais
(ellos/ellas/ ustedes)	pagaron	pagaban

GERUND	PAST PARTICIPLE
pagando	pagado

EXAMPLE PHRASES

Se puede **pagar** con tarjeta de crédito. You can pay by credit card.

¿Cuánto te **pagan** al mes? How much do they pay you a month?

Lo **pagué** en efectivo. I paid for it in cash.

Me **pagaban** muy poco. I got paid very little.

Remember that subject pronouns are not used very often in Spanish.

pagar

	FUTURE	CONDITIONAL
(yo)	**pagaré**	**pagaría**
(tú)	**pagarás**	**pagarías**
(él/ella/usted)	**pagará**	**pagaría**
(nosotros/as)	**pagaremos**	**pagaríamos**
(vosotros/as)	**pagaréis**	**pagaríais**
(ellos/ellas/ ustedes)	**pagarán**	**pagarían**

	PRESENT SUBJUNCTIVE	IMPERFECT SUBJUNCTIVE
(yo)	**pague**	**pagara** *or* **pagase**
(tú)	**pagues**	**pagaras** *or* **pagases**
(él/ella/usted)	**pague**	**pagara** *or* **pagase**
(nosotros/as)	**paguemos**	**pagáramos** *or* **pagásemos**
(vosotros/as)	**paguéis**	**pagarais** *or* **pagaseis**
(ellos/ellas/ ustedes)	**paguen**	**pagaran** *or* **pagasen**

IMPERATIVE

paga / pagad

Use the present subjunctive in all cases other than these tú and vosotros affirmative forms.

EXAMPLE PHRASES

Yo te **pagaré** la entrada. I'll pay for your ticket.

¡Quiero que **pague** por lo que me ha hecho! I want him to pay for what he's done to me!

Si **pagara** sus deudas, se quedaría sin nada. He'd be left with nothing if he paid his debts.

No les **pagues** hasta que lo hayan hecho. Don't pay them until they've done it.

Págame lo que me debes. Pay me what you owe me.

Remember that subject pronouns are not used very often in Spanish.

partir (to cut; to leave)

	PRESENT	PRESENT PERFECT
(yo)	parto	he partido
(tú)	partes	has partido
(él/ella/usted)	parte	ha partido
(nosotros/as)	partimos	hemos partido
(vosotros/as)	partís	habéis partido
(ellos/ellas/ ustedes)	parten	han partido

	PRETERITE	IMPERFECT
(yo)	partí	partía
(tú)	partiste	partías
(él/ella/usted)	partió	partía
(nosotros/as)	partimos	partíamos
(vosotros/as)	partisteis	partíais
(ellos/ellas/ ustedes)	partieron	partían

GERUND	PAST PARTICIPLE
partiendo	partido

EXAMPLE PHRASES

¿Te **parto** un trozo de queso? Shall I cut you a piece of cheese?

Partiendo de la base de que... Assuming that...

El remo **se partió** en dos. The oar broke in two.

Remember that subject pronouns are not used very often in Spanish.

partir

	FUTURE	CONDITIONAL
(yo)	**partiré**	**partiría**
(tú)	**partirás**	**partirías**
(él/ella/usted)	**partirá**	**partiría**
(nosotros/as)	**partiremos**	**partiríamos**
(vosotros/as)	**partiréis**	**partiríais**
(ellos/ellas/ ustedes)	**partirán**	**partirían**

	PRESENT SUBJUNCTIVE	IMPERFECT SUBJUNCTIVE
(yo)	**parta**	**partiera** *or* **partiese**
(tú)	**partas**	**partieras** *or* **partieses**
(él/ella/usted)	**parta**	**partiera** *or* **partiese**
(nosotros/as)	**partamos**	**partiéramos** *or* **partiésemos**
(vosotros/as)	**partáis**	**partierais** *or* **partieseis**
(ellos/ellas/ ustedes)	**partan**	**partieran** *or* **partiesen**

IMPERATIVE

parte / partid

Use the present subjunctive in all cases other than these tú and vosotros affirmative forms.

EXAMPLE PHRASES

La expedición **partirá** mañana de París. The expedition will leave from Paris tomorrow.

Eso le **partiría** el corazón. That would break his heart.

Pártelo por la mitad. Cut it in half.

Remember that subject pronouns are not used very often in Spanish.

pedir (to ask for; to ask)

	PRESENT	PRESENT PERFECT
(yo)	**pido**	**he pedido**
(tú)	**pides**	**has pedido**
(él/ella/usted)	**pide**	**ha pedido**
(nosotros/as)	**pedimos**	**hemos pedido**
(vosotros/as)	**pedís**	**habéis pedido**
(ellos/ellas/ ustedes)	**piden**	**han pedido**

	PRETERITE	IMPERFECT
(yo)	**pedí**	**pedía**
(tú)	**pediste**	**pedías**
(él/ella/usted)	**pidió**	**pedía**
(nosotros/as)	**pedimos**	**pedíamos**
(vosotros/as)	**pedisteis**	**pedíais**
(ellos/ellas/ ustedes)	**pidieron**	**pedían**

GERUND	PAST PARTICIPLE
pidiendo	**pedido**

EXAMPLE PHRASES

¿Cuánto **pide** por el carro? How much is he asking for the car?

La casa **está pidiendo** a gritos una mano de pintura. The house is crying out to be painted.

Pedimos dos cervezas. We ordered two beers.

No nos **pidieron** el pasaporte. They didn't ask us for our passports.

Pedían dos millones de rescate. They were demanding two million in ransom.

Remember that subject pronouns are not used very often in Spanish.

pedir

	FUTURE	CONDITIONAL
(yo)	**pediré**	**pediría**
(tú)	**pedirás**	**pedirías**
(él/ella/usted)	**pedirá**	**pediría**
(nosotros/as)	**pediremos**	**pediríamos**
(vosotros/as)	**pediréis**	**pediríais**
(ellos/ellas/ ustedes)	**pedirán**	**pedirían**

	PRESENT SUBJUNCTIVE	IMPERFECT SUBJUNCTIVE
(yo)	**pida**	**pidiera** *or* **pidiese**
(tú)	**pidas**	**pidieras** *or* **pidieses**
(él/ella/usted)	**pida**	**pidiera** *or* **pidiese**
(nosotros/as)	**pidamos**	**pidiéramos** *or* **pidiésemos**
(vosotros/as)	**pidáis**	**pidierais** *or* **pidieseis**
(ellos/ellas/ ustedes)	**pidan**	**pidieran** *or* **pidiesen**

IMPERATIVE

pide / pedid

Use the present subjunctive in all cases other than these tú and vosotros affirmative forms.

EXAMPLE PHRASES

Si se entera, te **pedirá** explicaciones. If he finds out, he'll ask you for an explanation.

Nunca te **pediría** que hicieras una cosa así. I'd never ask you to do anything like that.

Y que sea lo último que me **pidas**. And don't ask me for anything else.

Pídele el teléfono. Ask her for her phone number.

Remember that subject pronouns are not used very often in Spanish.

pensar (to think)

	PRESENT	PRESENT PERFECT
(yo)	pienso	he pensado
(tú)	piensas	has pensado
(él/ella/usted)	piensa	ha pensado
(nosotros/as)	pensamos	hemos pensado
(vosotros/as)	pensáis	habéis pensado
(ellos/ellas/ ustedes)	piensan	han pensado

	PRETERITE	IMPERFECT
(yo)	pensé	pensaba
(tú)	pensaste	pensabas
(él/ella/usted)	pensó	pensaba
(nosotros/as)	pensamos	pensábamos
(vosotros/as)	pensasteis	pensabais
(ellos/ellas/ ustedes)	pensaron	pensaban

GERUND	PAST PARTICIPLE
pensando	pensado

EXAMPLE PHRASES

¿**Piensas** que vale la pena? Do you think it's worth it?

¿Qué **piensas** del aborto? What do you think about abortion?

Está pensando en comprarse una casa. He's thinking about buying a house.

¿Lo **pensaste** bien? Have you thought about it carefully?

Pensaba que vendrías. I thought you'd come.

Remember that subject pronouns are not used very often in Spanish.

pensar

	FUTURE	CONDITIONAL
(yo)	**pensaré**	**pensaría**
(tú)	**pensarás**	**pensarías**
(él/ella/usted)	**pensará**	**pensaría**
(nosotros/as)	**pensaremos**	**pensaríamos**
(vosotros/as)	**pensaréis**	**pensaríais**
(ellos/ellas/ ustedes)	**pensarán**	**pensarían**

	PRESENT SUBJUNCTIVE	IMPERFECT SUBJUNCTIVE
(yo)	**piense**	**pensara** *or* **pensase**
(tú)	**pienses**	**pensaras** *or* **pensases**
(él/ella/usted)	**piense**	**pensara** *or* **pensase**
(nosotros/as)	**pensemos**	**pensáramos** *or* **pensásemos**
(vosotros/as)	**penséis**	**pensarais** *or* **pensaseis**
(ellos/ellas/ ustedes)	**piensen**	**pensaran** *or* **pensasen**

IMPERATIVE

piensa / pensad

Use the present subjunctive in all cases other than these tú and vosotros affirmative forms.

EXAMPLE PHRASES

Yo no me lo **pensaría** dos veces. I wouldn't think twice.

Me da igual lo que **piensen**. I don't care what they think.

Si **pensara** eso, te lo diría. If I thought that, I'd tell you.

No **pienses** que no quiero ir. Don't think that I don't want to go.

No lo **pienses** más. Don't give it another thought.

Remember that subject pronouns are not used very often in Spanish.

perder (to lose)

	PRESENT	PRESENT PERFECT
(yo)	pierdo	he perdido
(tú)	pierdes	has perdido
(él/ella/usted)	pierde	ha perdido
(nosotros/as)	perdemos	hemos perdido
(vosotros/as)	perdéis	habéis perdido
(ellos/ellas/ ustedes)	pierden	han perdido

	PRETERITE	IMPERFECT
(yo)	perdí	perdía
(tú)	perdiste	perdías
(él/ella/usted)	perdió	perdía
(nosotros/as)	perdimos	perdíamos
(vosotros/as)	perdisteis	perdíais
(ellos/ellas/ ustedes)	perdieron	perdían

GERUND	PAST PARTICIPLE
perdiendo	perdido

EXAMPLE PHRASES

Siempre **pierde** las llaves. He's always losing his keys.

Ana es la que saldrá **perdiendo**. Ana is the one who will lose out.

Había perdido dos kilos. He'd lost two kilos.

Perdimos dos a cero. We lost two-nothing.

Perdían siempre. They always used to lose.

Remember that subject pronouns are not used very often in Spanish.

perder

	FUTURE	CONDITIONAL
(yo)	**perderé**	**perdería**
(tú)	**perderás**	**perderías**
(él/ella/usted)	**perderá**	**perdería**
(nosotros/as)	**perderemos**	**perderíamos**
(vosotros/as)	**perderéis**	**perderíais**
(ellos/ellas/ ustedes)	**perderán**	**perderían**

	PRESENT SUBJUNCTIVE	IMPERFECT SUBJUNCTIVE
(yo)	**pierda**	**perdiera** *or* **perdiese**
(tú)	**pierdas**	**perdieras** *or* **perdieses**
(él/ella/usted)	**pierda**	**perdiera** *or* **perdiese**
(nosotros/as)	**perdamos**	**perdiéramos** *or* **perdiésemos**
(vosotros/as)	**perdáis**	**perdierais** *or* **perdieseis**
(ellos/ellas/ ustedes)	**pierdan**	**perdieran** *or* **perdiesen**

IMPERATIVE

pierde / perded

Use the present subjunctive in all cases other than these tú and vosotros affirmative forms.

EXAMPLE PHRASES

Apúrate o **perderás** el tren. Hurry up or you'll miss the train.

¡No **te** lo **pierdas**! Don't miss it!

No **pierdas** esta oportunidad. Don't miss this opportunity.

poder (to be able to)

	PRESENT	PRESENT PERFECT
(yo)	puedo	he podido
(tú)	puedes	has podido
(él/ella/usted)	puede	ha podido
(nosotros/as)	podemos	hemos podido
(vosotros/as)	podéis	habéis podido
(ellos/ellas/ ustedes)	pueden	han podido

	PRETERITE	IMPERFECT
(yo)	pude	podía
(tú)	pudiste	podías
(él/ella/usted)	pudo	podía
(nosotros/as)	pudimos	podíamos
(vosotros/as)	pudisteis	podíais
(ellos/ellas/ ustedes)	pudieron	podían

GERUND	PAST PARTICIPLE
pudiendo	podido

EXAMPLE PHRASES

¿**Puedo** entrar? Can I come in?

Puede que llegue mañana. He may arrive tomorrow.

No **pude** venir antes. I couldn't come before.

Pudiste haberte lastimado. You could have hurt yourself.

¡Me lo **podías** haber dicho! You could have told me!

Remember that subject pronouns are not used very often in Spanish.

poder

	FUTURE	CONDITIONAL
(yo)	**podré**	**podría**
(tú)	**podrás**	**podrías**
(él/ella/usted)	**podrá**	**podría**
(nosotros/as)	**podremos**	**podríamos**
(vosotros/as)	**podréis**	**podríais**
(ellos/ellas/ ustedes)	**podrán**	**podrían**

	PRESENT SUBJUNCTIVE	IMPERFECT SUBJUNCTIVE
(yo)	**pueda**	**pudiera** *or* **pudiese**
(tú)	**puedas**	**pudieras** *or* **pudieses**
(él/ella/usted)	**pueda**	**pudiera** *or* **pudiese**
(nosotros/as)	**podamos**	**pudiéramos** *or* **pudiésemos**
(vosotros/as)	**podáis**	**pudierais** *or* **pudieseis**
(ellos/ellas/ ustedes)	**puedan**	**pudieran** *or* **pudiesen**

IMPERATIVE

puede / poded

Use the present subjunctive in all cases other than these tú and vosotros affirmative forms.

EXAMPLE PHRASES

Estoy segura de que **podrá** conseguirlo. I'm sure he'll succeed.

¿**Podrías** ayudarme? Could you help me?

Ven en cuanto **puedas**. Come as soon as you can.

Me fui para que **pudieran** hablar. I left so they could talk.

Remember that subject pronouns are not used very often in Spanish.

poner (to put)

	PRESENT	PRESENT PERFECT
(yo)	pongo	he puesto
(tú)	pones	has puesto
(él/ella/usted)	pone	ha puesto
(nosotros/as)	ponemos	hemos puesto
(vosotros/as)	ponéis	habéis puesto
(ellos/ellas/ ustedes)	ponen	han puesto

	PRETERITE	IMPERFECT
(yo)	puse	ponía
(tú)	pusiste	ponías
(él/ella/usted)	puso	ponía
(nosotros/as)	pusimos	poníamos
(vosotros/as)	pusisteis	poníais
(ellos/ellas/ ustedes)	pusieron	ponían

GERUND
poniendo

PAST PARTICIPLE
puesto

EXAMPLE PHRASES

¿Dónde **pongo** mis cosas? Where shall I put my things?
¿Le **pusiste** azúcar a mi café? Did you put sugar in my coffee?
Todos **nos pusimos** de acuerdo. We all agreed.

Remember that subject pronouns are not used very often in Spanish.

poner

	FUTURE	CONDITIONAL
(yo)	**pondré**	**pondría**
(tú)	**pondrás**	**pondrías**
(él/ella/usted)	**pondrá**	**pondría**
(nosotros/as)	**pondremos**	**pondríamos**
(vosotros/as)	**pondréis**	**pondríais**
(ellos/ellas/ ustedes)	**pondrán**	**pondrían**

	PRESENT SUBJUNCTIVE	IMPERFECT SUBJUNCTIVE
(yo)	**ponga**	**pusiera** *or* **pusiese**
(tú)	**pongas**	**pusieras** *or* **pusieses**
(él/ella/usted)	**ponga**	**pusiera** *or* **pusiese**
(nosotros/as)	**pongamos**	**pusiéramos** *or* **pusiésemos**
(vosotros/as)	**pongáis**	**pusierais** *or* **pusieseis**
(ellos/ellas/ ustedes)	**pongan**	**pusieran** *or* **pusiesen**

IMPERATIVE

pon / poned

Use the present subjunctive in all cases other than these tú and vosotros affirmative forms.

EXAMPLE PHRASES

Lo **pondré** aquí. I'll put it here.

¿Le **pondrías** más sal? Would you add more salt?

Ponlo ahí. Put it over there.

Remember that subject pronouns are not used very often in Spanish.

prohibir (to ban; to prohibit)

	PRESENT	PRESENT PERFECT
(yo)	prohíbo	he prohibido
(tú)	prohíbes	has prohibido
(él/ella/usted)	prohíbe	ha prohibido
(nosotros/as)	prohibimos	hemos prohibido
(vosotros/as)	prohibís	habéis prohibido
(ellos/ellas/ ustedes)	prohíben	han prohibido

	PRETERITE	IMPERFECT
(yo)	prohibí	prohibía
(tú)	prohibiste	prohibías
(él/ella/usted)	prohibió	prohibía
(nosotros/as)	prohibimos	prohibíamos
(vosotros/as)	prohibisteis	prohibíais
(ellos/ellas/ ustedes)	prohibieron	prohibían

GERUND
prohibiendo

PAST PARTICIPLE
prohibido

EXAMPLE PHRASES

Deberían **prohibirlo**. It should be banned.

Te **prohíbo** que me hables así. I won't have you talking to me like that!

Le **prohibieron** la entrada. She was not allowed in.

El tratado **prohibía** el uso de armas químicas. The treaty prohibited the use of chemical weapons.

Remember that subject pronouns are not used very often in Spanish.

prohibir

	FUTURE	CONDITIONAL
(yo)	**prohibiré**	**prohibiría**
(tú)	**prohibirás**	**prohibirías**
(él/ella/usted)	**prohibirá**	**prohibiría**
(nosotros/as)	**prohibiremos**	**prohibiríamos**
(vosotros/as)	**prohibiréis**	**prohibiríais**
(ellos/ellas/ ustedes)	**prohibirán**	**prohibirían**

	PRESENT SUBJUNCTIVE	IMPERFECT SUBJUNCTIVE
(yo)	**prohíba**	**prohibiera** *or* **prohibiese**
(tú)	**prohíbas**	**prohibieras** *or* **prohibieses**
(él/ella/usted)	**prohíba**	**prohibiera** *or* **prohibiese**
(nosotros/as)	**prohibamos**	**prohibiéramos** *or* **prohibiésemos**
(vosotros/as)	**prohibáis**	**prohibierais** *or* **prohibieseis**
(ellos/ellas/ ustedes)	**prohíban**	**prohibieran** *or* **prohibiesen**

IMPERATIVE

prohíbe / prohibid

Use the present subjunctive in all cases other than these tú and vosotros affirmative forms.

EXAMPLE PHRASES

Tarde o temprano lo **prohibirán**. Sooner or later they'll ban it.

Yo esa música la **prohibiría**. If it were up to me, that music would be banned.

"**prohibido** fumar" "no smoking"

querer (to want; to love)

	PRESENT	PRESENT PERFECT
(yo)	quiero	he querido
(tú)	quieres	has querido
(él/ella/usted)	quiere	ha querido
(nosotros/as)	queremos	hemos querido
(vosotros/as)	queréis	habéis querido
(ellos/ellas/ ustedes)	quieren	han querido

	PRETERITE	IMPERFECT
(yo)	quise	quería
(tú)	quisiste	querías
(él/ella/usted)	quiso	quería
(nosotros/as)	quisimos	queríamos
(vosotros/as)	quisisteis	queríais
(ellos/ellas/ ustedes)	quisieron	querían

GERUND
queriendo

PAST PARTICIPLE
querido

EXAMPLE PHRASES

Lo hice sin **querer.** I didn't mean to do it.
Te **quiero**. I love you.
Quiero que vayas. I want you to go.
No **quería** decírmelo. She didn't want to tell me.

Remember that subject pronouns are not used very often in Spanish.

querer

	FUTURE	CONDITIONAL
(yo)	**querré**	**querría**
(tú)	**querrás**	**querrías**
(él/ella/usted)	**querrá**	**querría**
(nosotros/as)	**querremos**	**querríamos**
(vosotros/as)	**querréis**	**querríais**
(ellos/ellas/ ustedes)	**querrán**	**querrían**

	PRESENT SUBJUNCTIVE	IMPERFECT SUBJUNCTIVE
(yo)	**quiera**	**quisiera** *or* **quisiese**
(tú)	**quieras**	**quisieras** *or* **quisieses**
(él/ella/usted)	**quiera**	**quisiera** *or* **quisiese**
(nosotros/as)	**queramos**	**quisiéramos** *or* **quisiésemos**
(vosotros/as)	**queráis**	**quisierais** *or* **quisieseis**
(ellos/ellas/ ustedes)	**quieran**	**quisieran** *or* **quisiesen**

IMPERATIVE

quiere / quered

Use the present subjunctive in all cases other than these tú and vosotros affirmative forms.

EXAMPLE PHRASES

Siempre la **querré**. I will always love her.

Querría que no hubiera pasado nunca. I wish it had never happened.

¡Por lo que más **quieras**, cállate! For goodness sake, shut up!

Quisiera preguntar una cosa. I'd like to ask something.

Remember that subject pronouns are not used very often in Spanish.

reducir (to reduce)

	PRESENT	PRESENT PERFECT
(yo)	reduzco	he reducido
(tú)	reduces	has reducido
(él/ella/usted)	reduce	ha reducido
(nosotros/as)	reducimos	hemos reducido
(vosotros/as)	reducís	habéis reducido
(ellos/ellas/ ustedes)	reducen	han reducido

	PRETERITE	IMPERFECT
(yo)	reduje	reducía
(tú)	redujiste	reducías
(él/ella/usted)	redujo	reducía
(nosotros/as)	redujimos	reducíamos
(vosotros/as)	redujisteis	reducíais
(ellos/ellas/ ustedes)	redujeron	reducían

GERUND	PAST PARTICIPLE
reduciendo	reducido

EXAMPLE PHRASES

Al final todo **se reduce** a eso. In the end it all comes down to that.

Se había reducido la tasa de natalidad. The birth rate had fallen.

Sus gastos **se redujeron** a la mitad. Their expenses were cut by half.

Remember that subject pronouns are not used very often in Spanish.

reducir

	FUTURE	CONDITIONAL
(yo)	**reduciré**	**reduciría**
(tú)	**reducirás**	**reducirías**
(él/ella/usted)	**reducirá**	**reduciría**
(nosotros/as)	**reduciremos**	**reduciríamos**
(vosotros/as)	**reduciréis**	**reduciríais**
(ellos/ellas/ ustedes)	**reducirán**	**reducirían**

	PRESENT SUBJUNCTIVE	IMPERFECT SUBJUNCTIVE
(yo)	**reduzca**	**redujera** *or* **redujese**
(tú)	**reduzcas**	**redujeras** *or* **redujeses**
(él/ella/usted)	**reduzca**	**redujera** *or* **redujese**
(nosotros/as)	**reduzcamos**	**redujéramos** *or* **redujésemos**
(vosotros/as)	**reduzcáis**	**redujerais** *or* **redujeseis**
(ellos/ellas/ ustedes)	**reduzcan**	**redujeran** *or* **redujesen**

IMPERATIVE

reduce / reducid

Use the present subjunctive in all cases other than these tú and vosotros affirmative forms.

EXAMPLE PHRASES

Reducirán la producción en un 20%. They'll cut production by 20%.

Reduzca la velocidad. Reduce speed.

rehusar (to refuse)

	PRESENT	PRESENT PERFECT
(yo)	rehúso	he rehusado
(tú)	rehúsas	has rehusado
(él/ella/usted)	rehúsa	ha rehusado
(nosotros/as)	rehusamos	hemos rehusado
(vosotros/as)	rehusáis	habéis rehusado
(ellos/ellas/ustedes)	rehúsan	han rehusado

	PRETERITE	IMPERFECT
(yo)	rehusé	rehusaba
(tú)	rehusaste	rehusabas
(él/ella/usted)	rehusó	rehusaba
(nosotros/as)	rehusamos	rehusábamos
(vosotros/as)	rehusasteis	rehusabais
(ellos/ellas/ustedes)	rehusaron	rehusaban

GERUND
rehusando

PAST PARTICIPLE
rehusado

EXAMPLE PHRASES

Rehúso tomar parte en esto. I refuse to take part in this.
Había rehusado varias ofertas de trabajo. He had declined several job offers.
Su familia **rehusó** hacer declaraciones. His family refused to comment.

Remember that subject pronouns are not used very often in Spanish.

rehusar

	FUTURE	CONDITIONAL
(yo)	rehusaré	rehusaría
(tú)	rehusarás	rehusarías
(él/ella/usted)	rehusará	rehusaría
(nosotros/as)	rehusaremos	rehusaríamos
(vosotros/as)	rehusaréis	rehusaríais
(ellos/ellas/ ustedes)	rehusarán	rehusarían

	PRESENT SUBJUNCTIVE	IMPERFECT SUBJUNCTIVE
(yo)	rehúse	rehusara *or* rehusase
(tú)	rehúses	rehusaras *or* rehusases
(él/ella/usted)	rehúse	rehusara *or* rehusase
(nosotros/as)	rehusemos	rehusáramos *or* rehusásemos
(vosotros/as)	rehuséis	rehusarais *or* rehusaseis
(ellos/ellas/ ustedes)	rehúsen	rehusaran *or* rehusasen

IMPERATIVE

rehúsa / rehusad

Use the present subjunctive in all cases other than these tú and vosotros affirmative forms.

reír (to laugh)

	PRESENT	PRESENT PERFECT
(yo)	**río**	**he reído**
(tú)	**ríes**	**has reído**
(él/ella/usted)	**ríe**	**ha reído**
(nosotros/as)	**reímos**	**hemos reído**
(vosotros/as)	**reís**	**habéis reído**
(ellos/ellas/ ustedes)	**ríen**	**han reído**

	PRETERITE	IMPERFECT
(yo)	**reí**	**reía**
(tú)	**reíste**	**reías**
(él/ella/usted)	**rio**	**reía**
(nosotros/as)	**reímos**	**reíamos**
(vosotros/as)	**reísteis**	**reíais**
(ellos/ellas/ ustedes)	**rieron**	**reían**

GERUND	PAST PARTICIPLE
riendo	**reído**

EXAMPLE PHRASES

Se echó a **reír**. She burst out laughing.

Se ríe de todo. She doesn't take anything seriously.

¿De qué **te ríes**? What are you laughing at?

Siempre **están riéndose** en clase. They're always laughing in class.

Me reía mucho con él. I always had a good laugh with him.

Remember that subject pronouns are not used very often in Spanish.

reír

	FUTURE	CONDITIONAL
(yo)	**reiré**	**reiría**
(tú)	**reirás**	**reirías**
(él/ella/usted)	**reirá**	**reiría**
(nosotros/as)	**reiremos**	**reiríamos**
(vosotros/as)	**reiréis**	**reiríais**
(ellos/ellas/ ustedes)	**reirán**	**reirían**

	PRESENT SUBJUNCTIVE	IMPERFECT SUBJUNCTIVE
(yo)	**ría**	**riera** *or* **riese**
(tú)	**rías**	**rieras** *or* **rieses**
(él/ella/usted)	**ría**	**riera** *or* **riese**
(nosotros/as)	**riamos**	**riéramos** *or* **riésemos**
(vosotros/as)	**riais**	**rierais** *or* **rieseis**
(ellos/ellas/ ustedes)	**rían**	**rieran** *or* **riesen**

IMPERATIVE

ríe / reíd

Use the present subjunctive in all cases other than these tú and vosotros affirmative forms.

EXAMPLE PHRASES

Te reirás cuando te lo cuente. You'll laugh when I tell you about it.

Que **se rían** lo que quieran. Let them laugh as much as they want.

No **te rías** de mí. Don't laugh at me.

¡Tú **ríete**, pero pasé muchísimo miedo! You may laugh, but I was really frightened.

Remember that subject pronouns are not used very often in Spanish.

reñir (to quarrel; to argue)

	PRESENT	PRESENT PERFECT
(yo)	**riño**	**he reñido**
(tú)	**riñes**	**has reñido**
(él/ella/usted)	**riñe**	**ha reñido**
(nosotros/as)	**reñimos**	**hemos reñido**
(vosotros/as)	**reñís**	**habéis reñido**
(ellos/ellas/ ustedes)	**riñen**	**han reñido**

	PRETERITE	IMPERFECT
(yo)	**reñí**	**reñía**
(tú)	**reñiste**	**reñías**
(él/ella/usted)	**riñó**	**reñía**
(nosotros/as)	**reñimos**	**reñíamos**
(vosotros/as)	**reñisteis**	**reñíais**
(ellos/ellas/ ustedes)	**riñeron**	**reñían**

GERUND	PAST PARTICIPLE
riñendo	**reñido**

EXAMPLE PHRASES

Se pasan el día entero **riñendo**. They spend the whole day quarreling.

Reñimos por una tontería. We argued over something stupid.

Remember that subject pronouns are not used very often in Spanish.

reñir

	FUTURE	CONDITIONAL
(yo)	**reñiré**	**reñiría**
(tú)	**reñirás**	**reñirías**
(él/ella/usted)	**reñirá**	**reñiría**
(nosotros/as)	**reñiremos**	**reñiríamos**
(vosotros/as)	**reñiréis**	**reñiríais**
(ellos/ellas/ ustedes)	**reñirán**	**reñirían**

	PRESENT SUBJUNCTIVE	IMPERFECT SUBJUNCTIVE
(yo)	**riña**	**riñera** *or* **riñese**
(tú)	**riñas**	**riñeras** *or* **riñeses**
(él/ella/usted)	**riña**	**riñera** *or* **riñese**
(nosotros/as)	**riñamos**	**riñéramos** *or* **riñésemos**
(vosotros/as)	**riñáis**	**riñerais** *or* **riñeseis**
(ellos/ellas/ ustedes)	**riñan**	**riñeran** *or* **riñesen**

IMPERATIVE

riñe / reñid

Use the present subjunctive in all cases other than these tú and vosotros affirmative forms.

EXAMPLE PHRASES

¡No **riñán** más! Stop fighting!

Remember that subject pronouns are not used very often in Spanish.

repetir (to repeat)

	PRESENT	PRESENT PERFECT
(yo)	**repito**	**he repetido**
(tú)	**repites**	**has repetido**
(él/ella/usted)	**repite**	**ha repetido**
(nosotros/as)	**repetimos**	**hemos repetido**
(vosotros/as)	**repetís**	**habéis repetido**
(ellos/ellas/ ustedes)	**repiten**	**han repetido**

	PRETERITE	IMPERFECT
(yo)	**repetí**	**repetía**
(tú)	**repetiste**	**repetías**
(él/ella/usted)	**repitió**	**repetía**
(nosotros/as)	**repetimos**	**repetíamos**
(vosotros/as)	**repetisteis**	**repetíais**
(ellos/ellas/ ustedes)	**repitieron**	**repetían**

GERUND	PAST PARTICIPLE
repitiendo	**repetido**

EXAMPLE PHRASES

¿Podría **repetir**lo, por favor? Could you repeat that, please?

Le **repito** que es imposible. I'm telling you again that it is impossible.

Se lo **he repetido** mil veces, pero no escucha. I've told him hundreds of times but he won't listen.

Repetía una y otra vez que era inocente. He kept repeating that he was innocent.

Remember that subject pronouns are not used very often in Spanish.

repetir

	FUTURE	CONDITIONAL
(yo)	**repetiré**	repetiría
(tú)	**repetirás**	repetirías
(él/ella/usted)	**repetirá**	repetiría
(nosotros/as)	**repetiremos**	repetiríamos
(vosotros/as)	**repetiréis**	repetiríais
(ellos/ellas/ ustedes)	**repetirán**	repetirían

	PRESENT SUBJUNCTIVE	IMPERFECT SUBJUNCTIVE
(yo)	**repita**	repitiera *or* repitiese
(tú)	**repitas**	repitieras *or* repitieses
(él/ella/usted)	**repita**	repitiera *or* repitiese
(nosotros/as)	**repitamos**	repitiéramos *or* repitiésemos
(vosotros/as)	**repitáis**	repitierais *or* repitieseis
(ellos/ellas/ ustedes)	**repitan**	repitieran *or* repitiesen

IMPERATIVE

repite / repetid

Use the present subjunctive in all cases other than these tú and vosotros affirmative forms.

EXAMPLE PHRASES

Espero que no se **repita**. I hope this won't happen again.

Repitan el ejercicio. Repeat the exercise.

resolver (to solve)

	PRESENT	PRESENT PERFECT
(yo)	resuelvo	he resuelto
(tú)	resuelves	has resuelto
(él/ella/usted)	resuelve	ha resuelto
(nosotros/as)	resolvemos	hemos resuelto
(vosotros/as)	resolvéis	habéis resuelto
(ellos/ellas/ ustedes)	resuelven	han resuelto

	PRETERITE	IMPERFECT
(yo)	resolví	resolvía
(tú)	resolviste	resolvías
(él/ella/usted)	resolvió	resolvía
(nosotros/as)	resolvimos	resolvíamos
(vosotros/as)	resolvisteis	resolvíais
(ellos/ellas/ ustedes)	resolvieron	resolvían

GERUND	PAST PARTICIPLE
resolviendo	resuelto

EXAMPLE PHRASES

Trataré de **resolver** tus dudas. I'll try to answer your questions.

Enojarse no **resuelve** nada. Getting angry doesn't help at all.

Resolvimos el problema entre todos. We solved the problem together.

Remember that subject pronouns are not used very often in Spanish.

resolver

	FUTURE	CONDITIONAL
(yo)	resolveré	resolvería
(tú)	resolverás	resolverías
(él/ella/usted)	resolverá	resolvería
(nosotros/as)	resolveremos	resolveríamos
(vosotros/as)	resolveréis	resolveríais
(ellos/ellas/ ustedes)	resolverán	resolverían

	PRESENT SUBJUNCTIVE	IMPERFECT SUBJUNCTIVE
(yo)	resuelva	resolviera *or* resolviese
(tú)	resuelvas	resolvieras *or* resolvieses
(él/ella/usted)	resuelva	resolviera *or* resolviese
(nosotros/as)	resolvamos	resolviéramos *or* resolviésemos
(vosotros/as)	resolváis	resolvierais *or* resolvieseis
(ellos/ellas/ ustedes)	resuelvan	resolvieran *or* resolviesen

IMPERATIVE

resuelve / resolved

Use the present subjunctive in all cases other than these tú and vosotros affirmative forms.

EXAMPLE PHRASES

No te preocupes, ya lo **resolveremos**. Don't worry, we'll sort it out.

Yo lo **resolvería** de otra forma. I'd sort it out another way.

Hasta que no lo **resuelva** no descansaré. I won't rest until I've sorted it out.

Remember that subject pronouns are not used very often in Spanish.

reunir (to put together; to gather)

	PRESENT	PRESENT PERFECT
(yo)	reúno	he reunido
(tú)	reúnes	has reunido
(él/ella/usted)	reúne	ha reunido
(nosotros/as)	reunimos	hemos reunido
(vosotros/as)	reunís	habéis reunido
(ellos/ellas/ ustedes)	reúnen	han reunido

	PRETERITE	IMPERFECT
(yo)	reuní	reunía
(tú)	reuniste	reunías
(él/ella/usted)	reunió	reunía
(nosotros/as)	reunimos	reuníamos
(vosotros/as)	reunisteis	reuníais
(ellos/ellas/ ustedes)	reunieron	reunían

GERUND	PAST PARTICIPLE
reuniendo	reunido

EXAMPLE PHRASES

Hemos conseguido **reunir** suficiente dinero. We've managed to raise enough money.

Hace tiempo que no **me reúno** con ellos. I haven't seen them in ages.

Reunió a todos para comunicarles la noticia. He called them all together to tell them the news.

No **reunía** los requisitos. She didn't satisfy the requirements.

Remember that subject pronouns are not used very often in Spanish.

reunir

	FUTURE	CONDITIONAL
(yo)	reuniré	reuniría
(tú)	reunirás	reunirías
(él/ella/usted)	reunirá	reuniría
(nosotros/as)	reuniremos	reuniríamos
(vosotros/as)	reuniréis	reuniríais
(ellos/ellas/ ustedes)	reunirán	reunirían

	PRESENT SUBJUNCTIVE	IMPERFECT SUBJUNCTIVE
(yo)	reúna	reuniera *or* reuniese
(tú)	reúnas	reunieras *or* reunieses
(él/ella/usted)	reúna	reuniera *or* reuniese
(nosotros/as)	reunamos	reuniéramos *or* reuniésemos
(vosotros/as)	reunáis	reunierais *or* reunieseis
(ellos/ellas/ ustedes)	reúnan	reunieran *or* reuniesen

IMPERATIVE

reúne / reunid

Use the present subjunctive in all cases other than these tú and vosotros affirmative forms.

EXAMPLE PHRASES

Se reunirán el viernes. They'll meet on Friday.

Necesito encontrar un local que **reúna** las condiciones. I need to find premises that will meet the requirements.

Consiguió que su familia **se reuniera** tras una larga separación. She managed to get her family back together again after a long separation.

Remember that subject pronouns are not used very often in Spanish.

rogar (to beg; to pray)

	PRESENT	PRESENT PERFECT
(yo)	**ruego**	**he rogado**
(tú)	**ruegas**	**has rogado**
(él/ella/usted)	**ruega**	**ha rogado**
(nosotros/as)	**rogamos**	**hemos rogado**
(vosotros/as)	**rogáis**	**habéis rogado**
(ellos/ellas/ ustedes)	**ruegan**	**han rogado**

	PRETERITE	IMPERFECT
(yo)	**rogué**	**rogaba**
(tú)	**rogaste**	**rogabas**
(él/ella/usted)	**rogó**	**rogaba**
(nosotros/as)	**rogamos**	**rogábamos**
(vosotros/as)	**rogasteis**	**rogabais**
(ellos/ellas/ ustedes)	**rogaron**	**rogaban**

GERUND	PAST PARTICIPLE
rogando	**rogado**

EXAMPLE PHRASES

Les **rogamos** acepten nuestras disculpas. Please accept our apologies.

Te **ruego** que me lo devuelvas. Please give it back to me.

"Se **ruega** no fumar" "Please do not smoke"

Me **rogó** que lo perdonara. He begged me to forgive him.

Le **rogaba** a Dios que se curara. I prayed to God to make him better.

Remember that subject pronouns are not used very often in Spanish.

rogar

	FUTURE	CONDITIONAL
(yo)	rogaré	rogaría
(tú)	rogarás	rogarías
(él/ella/usted)	rogará	rogaría
(nosotros/as)	rogaremos	rogaríamos
(vosotros/as)	rogaréis	rogaríais
(ellos/ellas/ ustedes)	rogarán	rogarían

	PRESENT SUBJUNCTIVE	IMPERFECT SUBJUNCTIVE
(yo)	ruegue	rogara *or* rogase
(tú)	ruegues	rogaras *or* rogases
(él/ella/usted)	ruegue	rogara *or* rogase
(nosotros/as)	roguemos	rogáramos *or* rogásemos
(vosotros/as)	roguéis	rogarais *or* rogaseis
(ellos/ellas/ ustedes)	rueguen	rogaran *or* rogasen

IMPERATIVE

ruega / rogad

Use the present subjunctive in all cases other than these tú and vosotros affirmative forms.

EXAMPLE PHRASES

Ruega por mí. Pray for me.

Remember that subject pronouns are not used very often in Spanish.

romper (to break)

	PRESENT	PRESENT PERFECT
(yo)	rompo	he roto
(tú)	rompes	has roto
(él/ella/usted)	rompe	ha roto
(nosotros/as)	rompemos	hemos roto
(vosotros/as)	rompéis	habéis roto
(ellos/ellas/ ustedes)	rompen	han roto

	PRETERITE	IMPERFECT
(yo)	rompí	rompía
(tú)	rompiste	rompías
(él/ella/usted)	rompió	rompía
(nosotros/as)	rompimos	rompíamos
(vosotros/as)	rompisteis	rompíais
(ellos/ellas/ ustedes)	rompieron	rompían

GERUND	PAST PARTICIPLE
rompiendo	roto

EXAMPLE PHRASES

La cuerda **se** va a **romper**. The rope is going to snap.

Siempre **están rompiendo** cosas. They're always breaking things.

Se había roto una taza. A cup had gotten broken.

Se rompió el jarrón. The vase broke.

Remember that subject pronouns are not used very often in Spanish.

romper

	FUTURE	CONDITIONAL
(yo)	**romperé**	**rompería**
(tú)	**romperás**	**romperías**
(él/ella/usted)	**romperá**	**rompería**
(nosotros/as)	**romperemos**	**romperíamos**
(vosotros/as)	**romperéis**	**romperíais**
(ellos/ellas/ ustedes)	**romperán**	**romperían**

	PRESENT SUBJUNCTIVE	IMPERFECT SUBJUNCTIVE
(yo)	**rompa**	**rompiera** *or* **rompiese**
(tú)	**rompas**	**rompieras** *or* **rompieses**
(él/ella/usted)	**rompa**	**rompiera** *or* **rompiese**
(nosotros/as)	**rompamos**	**rompiéramos** *or* **rompiésemos**
(vosotros/as)	**rompáis**	**rompierais** *or* **rompieseis**
(ellos/ellas/ ustedes)	**rompan**	**rompieran** *or* **rompiesen**

IMPERATIVE

rompe / romped

Use the present subjunctive in all cases other than these tú and vosotros affirmative forms.

EXAMPLE PHRASES

Yo nunca **rompería** una promesa. I'd never break a promise.

Si lo **rompiera**, tendría que pagarlo. If you broke it, you'd have to pay for it.

Cuidado, no lo **rompas**. Careful you don't break it.

saber (to know)

	PRESENT	PRESENT PERFECT
(yo)	sé	he sabido
(tú)	sabes	has sabido
(él/ella/usted)	sabe	ha sabido
(nosotros/as)	sabemos	hemos sabido
(vosotros/as)	sabéis	habéis sabido
(ellos/ellas/ ustedes)	saben	han sabido

	PRETERITE	IMPERFECT
(yo)	supe	sabía
(tú)	supiste	sabías
(él/ella/usted)	supo	sabía
(nosotros/as)	supimos	sabíamos
(vosotros/as)	supisteis	sabíais
(ellos/ellas/ ustedes)	supieron	sabían

GERUND	PAST PARTICIPLE
sabiendo	sabido

EXAMPLE PHRASES

No lo **sé**. I don't know.

¿**Sabes** una cosa? Do you know what?

¿Cuándo lo **supiste**? When did you find out?

No **supe** qué responder. I didn't know how to answer.

Pensaba que lo **sabías**. I thought you knew.

Remember that subject pronouns are not used very often in Spanish.

saber

	FUTURE	CONDITIONAL
(yo)	**sabré**	**sabría**
(tú)	**sabrás**	**sabrías**
(él/ella/usted)	**sabrá**	**sabría**
(nosotros/as)	**sabremos**	**sabríamos**
(vosotros/as)	**sabréis**	**sabríais**
(ellos/ellas/ ustedes)	**sabrán**	**sabrían**

	PRESENT SUBJUNCTIVE	IMPERFECT SUBJUNCTIVE
(yo)	**sepa**	**supiera** *or* **supiese**
(tú)	**sepas**	**supieras** *or* **supieses**
(él/ella/usted)	**sepa**	**supiera** *or* **supiese**
(nosotros/as)	**sepamos**	**supiéramos** *or* **supiésemos**
(vosotros/as)	**sepáis**	**supierais** *or* **supieseis**
(ellos/ellas/ ustedes)	**sepan**	**supieran** *or* **supiesen**

IMPERATIVE

sabe / sabed

Use the present subjunctive in all cases other than these tú and vosotros affirmative forms.

EXAMPLE PHRASES

Nunca se **sabrá** quién la mató. We'll never know who killed her.

Si no le tuvieras tanto miedo al agua, ya **sabrías** nadar. If you weren't so afraid of water, you'd already be able to swim.

Que yo **sepa**, vive en París. As far as I know, she lives in Paris.

¡Si **supiéramos** al menos dónde está! If only we knew where he was!

Remember that subject pronouns are not used very often in Spanish.

sacar (to take out; to get)

	PRESENT	PRESENT PERFECT
(yo)	saco	he sacado
(tú)	sacas	has sacado
(él/ella/usted)	saca	ha sacado
(nosotros/as)	sacamos	hemos sacado
(vosotros/as)	sacáis	habéis sacado
(ellos/ellas/ ustedes)	sacan	han sacado

	PRETERITE	IMPERFECT
(yo)	saqué	sacaba
(tú)	sacaste	sacabas
(él/ella/usted)	sacó	sacaba
(nosotros/as)	sacamos	sacábamos
(vosotros/as)	sacasteis	sacabais
(ellos/ellas/ ustedes)	sacaron	sacaban

GERUND	PAST PARTICIPLE
sacando	sacado

EXAMPLE PHRASES

Voy a **sacar** la basura. I'm going to take out the trash.

¿Me **sacas** una foto? Will you take a photo of me?

Estás sacando las cosas de quicio. You're blowing things out of all proportion.

Ya **saqué** los boletos. I already bought the tickets.

¿De dónde **sacaba** tanto dinero? Where did he get so much money from?

Remember that subject pronouns are not used very often in Spanish.

sacar

	FUTURE	CONDITIONAL
(yo)	sacaré	sacaría
(tú)	sacarás	sacarías
(él/ella/usted)	sacará	sacaría
(nosotros/as)	sacaremos	sacaríamos
(vosotros/as)	sacaréis	sacaríais
(ellos/ellas/ ustedes)	sacarán	sacarían

	PRESENT SUBJUNCTIVE	IMPERFECT SUBJUNCTIVE
(yo)	saque	sacara *or* sacase
(tú)	saques	sacaras *or* sacases
(él/ella/usted)	saque	sacara *or* sacase
(nosotros/as)	saquemos	sacáramos *or* sacásemos
(vosotros/as)	saquéis	sacarais *or* sacaseis
(ellos/ellas/ ustedes)	saquen	sacaran *or* sacasen

IMPERATIVE

saca / sacad

Use the present subjunctive in all cases other than these tú and vosotros affirmative forms.

EXAMPLE PHRASES

Quiero que **saques** esa bicicleta de casa inmediatamente. I want you to get that bike out of the house immediately.

No **saques** la cabeza por la ventanilla. Don't lean out of the window.

Remember that subject pronouns are not used very often in Spanish.

salir (to go out; to work out)

	PRESENT	PRESENT PERFECT
(yo)	salgo	he salido
(tú)	sales	has salido
(él/ella/usted)	sale	ha salido
(nosotros/as)	salimos	hemos salido
(vosotros/as)	salís	habéis salido
(ellos/ellas/ ustedes)	salen	han salido

	PRETERITE	IMPERFECT
(yo)	salí	salía
(tú)	saliste	salías
(él/ella/usted)	salió	salía
(nosotros/as)	salimos	salíamos
(vosotros/as)	salisteis	salíais
(ellos/ellas/ ustedes)	salieron	salían

GERUND
saliendo

PAST PARTICIPLE
salido

EXAMPLE PHRASES

Hace tiempo que no **salimos**. We haven't been out for a while.

Está saliendo con un compañero de trabajo. She's dating a work colleague.

Su foto **salió** en todos los periódicos. Her picture appeared in all the newspapers.

Salía muy tarde de trabajar. He used to finish work very late.

Remember that subject pronouns are not used very often in Spanish.

salir

	FUTURE	CONDITIONAL
(yo)	**saldré**	**saldría**
(tú)	**saldrás**	**saldrías**
(él/ella/usted)	**saldrá**	**saldría**
(nosotros/as)	**saldremos**	**saldríamos**
(vosotros/as)	**saldréis**	**saldríais**
(ellos/ellas/ ustedes)	**saldrán**	**saldrían**

	PRESENT SUBJUNCTIVE	IMPERFECT SUBJUNCTIVE
(yo)	**salga**	**saliera** *or* **saliese**
(tú)	**salgas**	**salieras** *or* **salieses**
(él/ella/usted)	**salga**	**saliera** *or* **saliese**
(nosotros/as)	**salgamos**	**saliéramos** *or* **saliésemos**
(vosotros/as)	**salgáis**	**salierais** *or* **salieseis**
(ellos/ellas/ ustedes)	**salgan**	**salieran** *or* **saliesen**

IMPERATIVE

sal / salid

Use the present subjunctive in all cases other than these tú and vosotros affirmative forms.

EXAMPLE PHRASES

Te dije que **saldría** muy caro. I told you it would wind up being very expensive.

Espero que todo **salga** bien. I hope everything works out all right.

Si **saliera** elegido... If I were elected...

Por favor, **salgan** por la puerta de atrás. Please leave through the back door.

Remember that subject pronouns are not used very often in Spanish.

satisfacer (to satisfy)

	PRESENT	PRESENT PERFECT
(yo)	satisfago	he satisfecho
(tú)	satisfaces	has satisfecho
(él/ella/usted)	satisface	ha satisfecho
(nosotros/as)	satisfacemos	hemos satisfecho
(vosotros/as)	satisfacéis	habéis satisfecho
(ellos/ellas/ ustedes)	satisfacen	han satisfecho

	PRETERITE	IMPERFECT
(yo)	satisfice	satisfacía
(tú)	satisficiste	satisfacías
(él/ella/usted)	satisfizo	satisfacía
(nosotros/as)	satisficimos	satisfacíamos
(vosotros/as)	satisficisteis	satisfacíais
(ellos/ellas/ ustedes)	satisficieron	satisfacían

GERUND
satisfaciendo

PAST PARTICIPLE
satisfecho

EXAMPLE PHRASES

No me **satisface** nada el resultado. I'm not at all satisfied with the result.

Eso **satisfizo** mi curiosidad. That satisfied my curiosity.

Aquella vida **satisfacía** todas mis necesidades. That lifestyle satisfied all my needs.

Remember that subject pronouns are not used very often in Spanish.

satisfacer

	FUTURE	CONDITIONAL
(yo)	satisfaré	satisfaría
(tú)	satisfarás	satisfarías
(él/ella/usted)	satisfará	satisfaría
(nosotros/as)	satisfaremos	satisfaríamos
(vosotros/as)	satisfaréis	satisfaríais
(ellos/ellas/ ustedes)	satisfarán	satisfarían

	PRESENT SUBJUNCTIVE	IMPERFECT SUBJUNCTIVE
(yo)	satisfaga	satisficiera *or* satisficiese
(tú)	satisfagas	satisficieras *or* satisficieses
(él/ella/usted)	satisfaga	satisficiera *or* satisficiese
(nosotros/as)	satisfagamos	satisficiéramos *or* satisficiésemos
(vosotros/as)	satisfagáis	satisficierais *or* satisficieseis
(ellos/ellas/ ustedes)	satisfagan	satisficieran *or* satisficiesen

IMPERATIVE

satisfaz *or* satisface / satisfaced

Use the present subjunctive in all cases other than these tú and vosotros affirmative forms.

EXAMPLE PHRASES

Le **satisfará** saber que hemos cumplido nuestros objetivos. You'll be happy to know that we have achieved our objectives.

Tengo que aceptarlo aunque no me **satisfaga**. I have to accept it even though I'm not happy about it.

Remember that subject pronouns are not used very often in Spanish.

seguir (to follow; to go on)

	PRESENT	PRESENT PERFECT
(yo)	sigo	he seguido
(tú)	sigues	has seguido
(él/ella/usted)	sigue	ha seguido
(nosotros/as)	seguimos	hemos seguido
(vosotros/as)	seguís	habéis seguido
(ellos/ellas/ ustedes)	siguen	han seguido

	PRETERITE	IMPERFECT
(yo)	seguí	seguía
(tú)	seguiste	seguías
(él/ella/usted)	siguió	seguía
(nosotros/as)	seguimos	seguíamos
(vosotros/as)	seguisteis	seguíais
(ellos/ellas/ ustedes)	siguieron	seguían

GERUND	PAST PARTICIPLE
siguiendo	seguido

EXAMPLE PHRASES

Si **sigues** así, acabarás mal. If you go on like this you'll come to a bad end.

Siguió cantando como si nada. He went on singing as if there was nothing wrong.

Los **seguimos** mucho rato. We followed them for a long time.

Nos **habían seguido**. They had followed us.

Remember that subject pronouns are not used very often in Spanish.

seguir

	FUTURE	CONDITIONAL
(yo)	**seguiré**	**seguiría**
(tú)	**seguirás**	**seguirías**
(él/ella/usted)	**seguirá**	**seguiría**
(nosotros/as)	**seguiremos**	**seguiríamos**
(vosotros/as)	**seguiréis**	**seguiríais**
(ellos/ellas/ ustedes)	**seguirán**	**seguirían**

	PRESENT SUBJUNCTIVE	IMPERFECT SUBJUNCTIVE
(yo)	**siga**	**siguiera** *or* **siguiese**
(tú)	**sigas**	**siguieras** *or* **siguieses**
(él/ella/usted)	**siga**	**siguiera** *or* **siguiese**
(nosotros/as)	**sigamos**	**siguiéramos** *or* **siguiésemos**
(vosotros/as)	**sigáis**	**siguierais** *or* **siguieseis**
(ellos/ellas/ ustedes)	**sigan**	**siguieran** *or* **siguiesen**

IMPERATIVE

sigue / seguid

Use the present subjunctive in all cases other than these tú and vosotros affirmative forms.

EXAMPLE PHRASES

Nos seguiremos viendo. We will go on seeing each other.

Quiero que **sigas** estudiando. I want you to go on with your studies.

Si **siguieras** mis consejos, te iría muchísimo mejor. You'd be much better off if you followed my advice.

Siga por esta calle hasta el final. Go straight till you get to the end of the street.

Remember that subject pronouns are not used very often in Spanish.

sentir (to feel; to be sorry)

	PRESENT	PRESENT PERFECT
(yo)	siento	he sentido
(tú)	sientes	has sentido
(él/ella/usted)	siente	ha sentido
(nosotros/as)	sentimos	hemos sentido
(vosotros/as)	sentís	habéis sentido
(ellos/ellas/ ustedes)	sienten	han sentido

	PRETERITE	IMPERFECT
(yo)	sentí	sentía
(tú)	sentiste	sentías
(él/ella/usted)	sintió	sentía
(nosotros/as)	sentimos	sentíamos
(vosotros/as)	sentisteis	sentíais
(ellos/ellas/ ustedes)	sintieron	sentían

GERUND
sintiendo

PAST PARTICIPLE
sentido

EXAMPLE PHRASES

Te vas a **sentir** sola. You'll feel lonely.

Siento mucho lo que pasó. I'm really sorry about what happened.

Sintió mucho la muerte de su padre. He was greatly affected by his father's death.

No **sentí** nada. I didn't feel a thing.

Me sentía muy mal. I didn't feel well at all.

Remember that subject pronouns are not used very often in Spanish.

sentir

	FUTURE	CONDITIONAL
(yo)	**sentiré**	**sentiría**
(tú)	**sentirás**	**sentirías**
(él/ella/usted)	**sentirá**	**sentiría**
(nosotros/as)	**sentiremos**	**sentiríamos**
(vosotros/as)	**sentiréis**	**sentiríais**
(ellos/ellas/ ustedes)	**sentirán**	**sentirían**

	PRESENT SUBJUNCTIVE	IMPERFECT SUBJUNCTIVE
(yo)	**sienta**	**sintiera** *or* **sintiese**
(tú)	**sientas**	**sintieras** *or* **sintieses**
(él/ella/usted)	**sienta**	**sintiera** *or* **sintiese**
(nosotros/as)	**sintamos**	**sintiéramos** *or* **sintiésemos**
(vosotros/as)	**sintáis**	**sintierais** *or* **sintieseis**
(ellos/ellas/ ustedes)	**sientan**	**sintieran** *or* **sintiesen**

IMPERATIVE

siente / sentid

Use the present subjunctive in all cases other than these tú and vosotros affirmative forms.

EXAMPLE PHRASES

Al principio **te sentirás** un poco raro. You'll feel a bit strange at first.

Yo **sentiría** mucho que se fuera de la empresa. I'd be really sorry if you left the firm.

No creo que lo **sienta**. I don't think she's sorry.

Sería mucho más preocupante si no **sintiera** la pierna. It would be much more worrying if he couldn't feel his leg.

Remember that subject pronouns are not used very often in Spanish.

ser (to be)

	PRESENT	PRESENT PERFECT
(yo)	**soy**	**he sido**
(tú)	**eres**	**has sido**
(él/ella/usted)	**es**	**ha sido**
(nosotros/as)	**somos**	**hemos sido**
(vosotros/as)	**sois**	**habéis sido**
(ellos/ellas/ ustedes)	**son**	**han sido**

	PRETERITE	IMPERFECT
(yo)	**fui**	**era**
(tú)	**fuiste**	**eras**
(él/ella/usted)	**fue**	**era**
(nosotros/as)	**fuimos**	**éramos**
(vosotros/as)	**fuisteis**	**erais**
(ellos/ellas/ ustedes)	**fueron**	**eran**

GERUND	PAST PARTICIPLE
siendo	**sido**

EXAMPLE PHRASES

Soy colombiano. I'm Colombian.

Fue un duro golpe. It was a major blow.

¿**Fuiste** tú el que llamó? Was it you who called?

Era de noche. It was dark.

Había sido sacerdote. He had been a priest.

Remember that subject pronouns are not used very often in Spanish.

ser

	FUTURE	CONDITIONAL
(yo)	**seré**	**sería**
(tú)	**serás**	**serías**
(él/ella/usted)	**será**	**sería**
(nosotros/as)	**seremos**	**seríamos**
(vosotros/as)	**seréis**	**seríais**
(ellos/ellas/ ustedes)	**serán**	**serían**

	PRESENT SUBJUNCTIVE	IMPERFECT SUBJUNCTIVE
(yo)	**sea**	**fuera** *or* **fuese**
(tú)	**seas**	**fueras** *or* **fueses**
(él/ella/usted)	**sea**	**fuera** *or* **fuese**
(nosotros/as)	**seamos**	**fuéramos** *or* **fuésemos**
(vosotros/as)	**seáis**	**fuerais** *or* **fueseis**
(ellos/ellas/ ustedes)	**sean**	**fueran** *or* **fuesen**

IMPERATIVE

sé / sed

Use the present subjunctive in all cases other than these tú and vosotros affirmative forms.

EXAMPLE PHRASES

Será de Joaquín. Maybe it's Joaquín's.

Eso **sería** maravilloso. That would be wonderful.

O **sea**, que no vienes. So you're not coming.

No **seas** tan perfeccionista. Don't be such a perfectionist.

¡**Sean** buenos! Behave yourselves!

Remember that subject pronouns are not used very often in Spanish.

soler (to be in the habit of; to be accustomed to)

	PRESENT	PRESENT PERFECT
(yo)	**suelo**	*not used*
(tú)	**sueles**	
(él/ella/usted)	**suele**	
(nosotros/as)	**solemos**	
(vosotros/as)	**soléis**	
(ellos/ellas/ ustedes)	**suelen**	

	PRETERITE	IMPERFECT
(yo)	*not used*	**solía**
(tú)		**solías**
(él/ella/usted)		**solía**
(nosotros/as)		**solíamos**
(vosotros/as)		**solíais**
(ellos/ellas/ ustedes)		**solían**

GERUND	PAST PARTICIPLE
soliendo	*not used*

EXAMPLE PHRASES

Suele salir a las ocho. He usually goes out at eight.

Solíamos ir todos los años a la playa. We used to go to the beach every year.

Remember that subject pronouns are not used very often in Spanish.

soler

	FUTURE	CONDITIONAL
(yo)	*not used*	*not used*
(tú)		
(él/ella/usted)		
(nosotros/as)		
(vosotros/as)		
(ellos/ellas/ ustedes)		

	PRESENT SUBJUNCTIVE	IMPERFECT SUBJUNCTIVE
(yo)	**suela**	**soliera** *or* **soliese**
(tú)	**suelas**	**solieras** *or* **solieses**
(él/ella/usted)	**suela**	**soliera** *or* **soliese**
(nosotros/as)	**solamos**	**soliéramos** *or* **soliésemos**
(vosotros/as)	**soláis**	**solierais** *or* **solieseis**
(ellos/ellas/ ustedes)	**suelan**	**solieran** *or* **soliesen**

IMPERATIVE

not used

Remember that subject pronouns are not used very often in Spanish.

soltar (to let go of; to release)

	PRESENT	PRESENT PERFECT
(yo)	suelto	he soltado
(tú)	sueltas	has soltado
(él/ella/usted)	suelta	ha soltado
(nosotros/as)	soltamos	hemos soltado
(vosotros/as)	soltáis	habéis soltado
(ellos/ellas/ustedes)	sueltan	han soltado

	PRETERITE	IMPERFECT
(yo)	solté	soltaba
(tú)	soltaste	soltabas
(él/ella/usted)	soltó	soltaba
(nosotros/as)	soltamos	soltábamos
(vosotros/as)	soltasteis	soltabais
(ellos/ellas/ustedes)	soltaron	soltaban

GERUND	PAST PARTICIPLE
soltando	soltado

EXAMPLE PHRASES

Al final logró **soltarse**. Eventually she managed to break free.

¿Por qué no **te sueltas** el pelo? Why don't you wear your hair down?

Habían soltado a los rehenes. They had released the hostages.

Soltó una carcajada. He burst out laughing.

soltar

	FUTURE	CONDITIONAL
(yo)	**soltaré**	**soltaría**
(tú)	**soltarás**	**soltarías**
(él/ella/usted)	**soltará**	**soltaría**
(nosotros/as)	**soltaremos**	**soltaríamos**
(vosotros/as)	**soltaréis**	**soltaríais**
(ellos/ellas/ ustedes)	**soltarán**	**soltarían**

	PRESENT SUBJUNCTIVE	IMPERFECT SUBJUNCTIVE
(yo)	**suelte**	**soltara** *or* **soltase**
(tú)	**sueltes**	**soltaras** *or* **soltases**
(él/ella/usted)	**suelte**	**soltara** *or* **soltase**
(nosotros/as)	**soltemos**	**soltáramos** *or* **soltásemos**
(vosotros/as)	**soltéis**	**soltarais** *or* **soltaseis**
(ellos/ellas/ ustedes)	**suelten**	**soltaran** *or* **soltasen**

IMPERATIVE

suelta / soltad

Use the present subjunctive in all cases other than these tú and vosotros affirmative forms.

EXAMPLE PHRASES

Te **soltaré** el brazo si me dices dónde está. I'll let go of your arm if you tell me where he is.

Te dije que lo **soltaras**. I told you to let it go.

No **sueltes** la cuerda. Don't let go of the rope.

¡**Suéltame**! Let me go!

Remember that subject pronouns are not used very often in Spanish.

sonar (to sound; to ring)

	PRESENT	PRESENT PERFECT
(yo)	sueno	he sonado
(tú)	suenas	has sonado
(él/ella/usted)	suena	ha sonado
(nosotros/as)	sonamos	hemos sonado
(vosotros/as)	sonáis	habéis sonado
(ellos/ellas/ustedes)	suenan	han sonado

	PRETERITE	IMPERFECT
(yo)	soné	sonaba
(tú)	sonaste	sonabas
(él/ella/usted)	sonó	sonaba
(nosotros/as)	sonamos	sonábamos
(vosotros/as)	sonasteis	sonabais
(ellos/ellas/ustedes)	sonaron	sonaban

GERUND	PAST PARTICIPLE
sonando	sonado

EXAMPLE PHRASES

¿Te **suena** su nombre? Does her name sound familiar?

Justo en ese momento **sonó** el timbre. Just then the bell rang.

Sonabas un poco triste por teléfono. You sounded a bit sad on the phone.

Estaba sonando el teléfono. The phone was ringing.

Remember that subject pronouns are not used very often in Spanish.

sonar

	FUTURE	CONDITIONAL
(yo)	sonaré	sonaría
(tú)	sonarás	sonarías
(él/ella/usted)	sonará	sonaría
(nosotros/as)	sonaremos	sonaríamos
(vosotros/as)	sonaréis	sonaríais
(ellos/ellas/ ustedes)	sonarán	sonarían

	PRESENT SUBJUNCTIVE	IMPERFECT SUBJUNCTIVE
(yo)	suene	sonara *or* sonase
(tú)	suenes	sonaras *or* sonases
(él/ella/usted)	suene	sonara *or* sonase
(nosotros/as)	sonemos	sonáramos *or* sonásemos
(vosotros/as)	sonéis	sonarais *or* sonaseis
(ellos/ellas/ ustedes)	suenen	sonaran *or* sonasen

IMPERATIVE

suena / sonad

Use the present subjunctive in all cases other than these tú and vosotros affirmative forms.

EXAMPLE PHRASES

Hay que esperar a que **suene** un pitido. We have to wait until we hear a beep.

¡**Suénate** la nariz! Blow your nose!

Remember that subject pronouns are not used very often in Spanish.

temer (to be afraid)

	PRESENT	PRESENT PERFECT
(yo)	temo	he temido
(tú)	temes	has temido
(él/ella/usted)	teme	ha temido
(nosotros/as)	tememos	hemos temido
(vosotros/as)	teméis	habéis temido
(ellos/ellas/ ustedes)	temen	han temido

	PRETERITE	IMPERFECT
(yo)	temí	temía
(tú)	temiste	temías
(él/ella/usted)	temío	temía
(nosotros/as)	temimos	temíamos
(vosotros/as)	temisteis	temíais
(ellos/ellas/ ustedes)	temieron	temían

GERUND	PAST PARTICIPLE
temiendo	temido

EXAMPLE PHRASES

No le **teme** a nadie. He's not afraid of anyone.

Me temo que no. I'm afraid not.

Se temen lo peor. They fear the worst.

Empezó a llover. –**Me** lo **temía**. "It's started raining." – "I was afraid it would."

Temían por su seguridad. They feared for their safety.

Remember that subject pronouns are not used very often in Spanish.

temer

	FUTURE	CONDITIONAL
(yo)	**temeré**	**temería**
(tú)	**temerás**	**temerías**
(él/ella/usted)	**temerá**	**temería**
(nosotros/as)	**temeremos**	**temeríamos**
(vosotros/as)	**temeréis**	**temeríais**
(ellos/ellas/ ustedes)	**temerán**	**temerían**

	PRESENT SUBJUNCTIVE	IMPERFECT SUBJUNCTIVE
(yo)	**tema**	**temiera** *or* **temiese**
(tú)	**temas**	**temieras** *or* **temieses**
(él/ella/usted)	**tema**	**temiera** *or* **temiese**
(nosotros/as)	**temamos**	**temiéramos** *or* **temiésemos**
(vosotros/as)	**temáis**	**temierais** *or* **temieseis**
(ellos/ellas/ ustedes)	**teman**	**temieran** *or* **temiesen**

IMPERATIVE

teme / temed

Use the present subjunctive in all cases other than these tú and vosotros affirmative forms.

EXAMPLE PHRASES

No **temas.** Don't be afraid.

Remember that subject pronouns are not used very often in Spanish.

tener (to have)

	PRESENT	PRESENT PERFECT
(yo)	**tengo**	**he tenido**
(tú)	**tienes**	**has tenido**
(él/ella/usted)	**tiene**	**ha tenido**
(nosotros/as)	**tenemos**	**hemos tenido**
(vosotros/as)	**tenéis**	**habéis tenido**
(ellos/ellas/ ustedes)	**tienen**	**ha tenido**

	PRETERITE	IMPERFECT
(yo)	**tuve**	**tenía**
(tú)	**tuviste**	**tenías**
(él/ella/usted)	**tuvo**	**tenía**
(nosotros/as)	**tuvimos**	**teníamos**
(vosotros/as)	**tuvisteis**	**teníais**
(ellos/ellas/ ustedes)	**tuvieron**	**tenían**

GERUND	PAST PARTICIPLE
teniendo	**tenido**

EXAMPLE PHRASES

Tengo dos hermanos. I have two brothers.

Había tenido una gripa muy fuerte. She'd had a very bad flu.

Tuvimos que irnos. We had to leave.

No **tenía** suficiente dinero. She didn't have enough money.

Estamos teniendo muchos problemas. We're having a lot of problems.

Remember that subject pronouns are not used very often in Spanish.

tener

	FUTURE	CONDITIONAL
(yo)	tendré	tendría
(tú)	tendrás	tendrías
(él/ella/usted)	tendrá	tendría
(nosotros/as)	tendremos	tendríamos
(vosotros/as)	tendréis	tendríais
(ellos/ellas/ ustedes)	tendrán	tendrían

	PRESENT SUBJUNCTIVE	IMPERFECT SUBJUNCTIVE
(yo)	tenga	tuviera *or* tuviese
(tú)	tengas	tuvieras *or* tuvieses
(él/ella/usted)	tenga	tuviera *or* tuviese
(nosotros/as)	tengamos	tuviéramos *or* tuviésemos
(vosotros/as)	tengáis	tuvierais *or* tuvieseis
(ellos/ellas/ ustedes)	tengan	tuvieran *or* tuviesen

IMPERATIVE

ten / tened

Use the present subjunctive in all cases other than these tú and vosotros affirmative forms.

EXAMPLE PHRASES

Tendrás que pagarlo tú. You'll have to pay for it yourself.

Tendrías que comer más. You should eat more.

No creo que **tenga** suficiente dinero. I don't think he has enough money.

Si **tuviera** tiempo, haría un curso de francés. If I had time, I'd take a French course.

Ten cuidado. Be careful.

No **tengas** miedo. Don't be afraid.

Remember that subject pronouns are not used very often in Spanish.

tocar (to touch; to play)

	PRESENT	PRESENT PERFECT
(yo)	**toco**	**he tocado**
(tú)	**tocas**	**has tocado**
(él/ella/usted)	**toca**	**ha tocado**
(nosotros/as)	**tocamos**	**hemos tocado**
(vosotros/as)	**tocáis**	**habéis tocado**
(ellos/ellas/ ustedes)	**tocan**	**han tocado**

	PRETERITE	IMPERFECT
(yo)	**toqué**	**tocaba**
(tú)	**tocaste**	**tocabas**
(él/ella/usted)	**tocó**	**tocaba**
(nosotros/as)	**tocamos**	**tocábamos**
(vosotros/as)	**tocasteis**	**tocabais**
(ellos/ellas/ ustedes)	**tocaron**	**tocaban**

GERUND	PAST PARTICIPLE
tocando	**tocado**

EXAMPLE PHRASES

Toca el violín. He plays the violin.

Te **toca** manejar. It's your turn to drive.

Me **tocó** el peor asiento. I ended up with the worst seat.

Me **tocaba** tirar a mí. It was my turn.

Tocaban muy bien. They played very well.

Remember that subject pronouns are not used very often in Spanish.

tocar

	FUTURE	CONDITIONAL
(yo)	**tocaré**	**tocaría**
(tú)	**tocarás**	**tocarías**
(él/ella/usted)	**tocará**	**tocaría**
(nosotros/as)	**tocaremos**	**tocaríamos**
(vosotros/as)	**tocaréis**	**tocaríais**
(ellos/ellas/ ustedes)	**tocarán**	**tocarían**

	PRESENT SUBJUNCTIVE	IMPERFECT SUBJUNCTIVE
(yo)	**toque**	**tocara** *or* **tocase**
(tú)	**toques**	**tocaras** *or* **tocases**
(él/ella/usted)	**toque**	**tocara** *or* **tocase**
(nosotros/as)	**toquemos**	**tocáramos** *or* **tocásemos**
(vosotros/as)	**toquéis**	**tocarais** *or* **tocaseis**
(ellos/ellas/ ustedes)	**toquen**	**tocaran** *or* **tocasen**

IMPERATIVE

toca / tocad

Use the present subjunctive in all cases other than these tú and vosotros affirmative forms.

EXAMPLE PHRASES

Sabía que me **tocaría** ir a mí. I knew I'd be the one to have to go.

No lo **toques**. Don't touch it.

Tócalo, otra vez. Play it again.

torcer (to twist)

	PRESENT	PRESENT PERFECT
(yo)	tuerzo	he torcido
(tú)	tuerces	has torcido
(él/ella/usted)	tuerce	ha torcido
(nosotros/as)	torcemos	hemos torcido
(vosotros/as)	torcéis	habéis torcido
(ellos/ellas/ ustedes)	tuercen	han torcido

	PRETERITE	IMPERFECT
(yo)	torcí	torcía
(tú)	torciste	torcías
(él/ella/usted)	torció	torcía
(nosotros/as)	torcimos	torcíamos
(vosotros/as)	torcisteis	torcíais
(ellos/ellas/ ustedes)	torcieron	torcían

GERUND	PAST PARTICIPLE
torciendo	torcido

EXAMPLE PHRASES

El sendero **tuerce** luego a la derecha. Later on the path curves around to the right.

Me **torció** la muñeca. He twisted my wrist.

Las cosas se empezaron a **torcer**. Things started to go wrong.

Remember that subject pronouns are not used very often in Spanish.

torcer

	FUTURE	CONDITIONAL
(yo)	torceré	torcería
(tú)	torcerás	torcerías
(él/ella/usted)	torcerá	torcería
(nosotros/as)	torceremos	torceríamos
(vosotros/as)	torceréis	torceríais
(ellos/ellas/ ustedes)	torcerán	torcerían

	PRESENT SUBJUNCTIVE	IMPERFECT SUBJUNCTIVE
(yo)	tuerza	torciera *or* torciese
(tú)	tuerzas	torcieras *or* torcieses
(él/ella/usted)	tuerza	torciera *or* torciese
(nosotros/as)	torzamos	torciéramos *or* torciésemos
(vosotros/as)	torzáis	torcierais *or* torcieseis
(ellos/ellas/ ustedes)	tuerzan	torcieran *or* torciesen

IMPERATIVE

tuerce / torced

Use the present subjunctive in all cases other than these tú and vosotros affirmative forms.

EXAMPLE PHRASES

Tuerza a la izquierda. Turn left.

Tuércelo un poco más. Twist it a little more.

traer (to bring)

	PRESENT	PRESENT PERFECT
(yo)	traigo	he traído
(tú)	traes	has traído
(él/ella/usted)	trae	ha traído
(nosotros/as)	traemos	hemos traído
(vosotros/as)	traéis	habéis traído
(ellos/ellas/ ustedes)	traen	han traído

	PRETERITE	IMPERFECT
(yo)	traje	traía
(tú)	trajiste	traías
(él/ella/usted)	trajo	traía
(nosotros/as)	trajimos	traíamos
(vosotros/as)	trajisteis	traíais
(ellos/ellas/ ustedes)	trajeron	traían

GERUND	PAST PARTICIPLE
trayendo	traído

EXAMPLE PHRASES

¿Me puedes **traer** una toalla? Can you bring me a towel?

Nos **está trayendo** muchos problemas. It's causing us a lot of trouble.

¿**Trajiste** lo que te pedí? Did you bring what I asked for?

Traía un vestido nuevo. She was wearing a new dress.

No **trajo** el dinero. He didn't bring the money.

Remember that subject pronouns are not used very often in Spanish.

traer

	FUTURE	CONDITIONAL
(yo)	**traeré**	**traería**
(tú)	**traerás**	**traerías**
(él/ella/usted)	**traerá**	**traería**
(nosotros/as)	**traeremos**	**traeríamos**
(vosotros/as)	**traeréis**	**traeríais**
(ellos/ellas/ ustedes)	**traerán**	**traerían**

	PRESENT SUBJUNCTIVE	IMPERFECT SUBJUNCTIVE
(yo)	**traiga**	**trajera** *or* **trajese**
(tú)	**traigas**	**trajeras** *or* **trajeses**
(él/ella/usted)	**traiga**	**trajera** *or* **trajese**
(nosotros/as)	**traigamos**	**trajéramos** *or* **trajésemos**
(vosotros/as)	**traigáis**	**trajerais** *or* **trajeseis**
(ellos/ellas/ ustedes)	**traigan**	**trajeran** *or* **trajesen**

IMPERATIVE

trae / traed

Use the present subjunctive in all cases other than these tú and vosotros affirmative forms.

EXAMPLE PHRASES

Me pregunto qué **se traerán** entre manos. I wonder what they're up to.

Dile que **traiga** a algún amigo. Tell him to bring a friend with him.

Le pedí que **trajera** las fotos. I asked her to bring the photos.

Remember that subject pronouns are not used very often in Spanish.

valer (to be worth)

	PRESENT	PRESENT PERFECT
(yo)	valgo	he valido
(tú)	vales	has valido
(él/ella/usted)	vale	ha valido
(nosotros/as)	valemos	hemos valido
(vosotros/as)	valéis	habéis valido
(ellos/ellas/ ustedes)	valen	han valido

	PRETERITE	IMPERFECT
(yo)	valí	valía
(tú)	valiste	valías
(él/ella/usted)	valió	valía
(nosotros/as)	valimos	valíamos
(vosotros/as)	valisteis	valíais
(ellos/ellas/ ustedes)	valieron	valían

GERUND	PAST PARTICIPLE
valiendo	valido

EXAMPLE PHRASES

¿Cuánto **vale** eso? How much is that?

No puede **valerse** por sí mismo. He can't look after himself.

No le **valió** de nada suplicar. Begging got her nowhere.

No **valía** la pena. It wasn't worth it.

Remember that subject pronouns are not used very often in Spanish.

valer

	FUTURE	CONDITIONAL
(yo)	**valdré**	**valdría**
(tú)	**valdrás**	**valdrías**
(él/ella/usted)	**valdrá**	**valdría**
(nosotros/as)	**valdremos**	**valdríamos**
(vosotros/as)	**valdréis**	**valdríais**
(ellos/ellas/ ustedes)	**valdrán**	**valdrían**

	PRESENT SUBJUNCTIVE	IMPERFECT SUBJUNCTIVE
(yo)	**valga**	**valiera** *or* **valiese**
(tú)	**valgas**	**valieras** *or* **valieses**
(él/ella/usted)	**valga**	**valiera** *or* **valiese**
(nosotros/as)	**valgamos**	**valiéramos** *or* **valiésemos**
(vosotros/as)	**valgáis**	**valierais** *or* **valieseis**
(ellos/ellas/ ustedes)	**valgan**	**valieran** *or* **valiesen**

IMPERATIVE

vale / valed

Use the present subjunctive in all cases other than these tú and vosotros affirmative forms.

EXAMPLE PHRASES

Valdrá unos 500 dólares. It must be worth around 500 dollars.

Valdría más si fuera antiguo. It would be worth more if it were an antique.

Remember that subject pronouns are not used very often in Spanish.

vencer (to win; to beat)

	PRESENT	PRESENT PERFECT
(yo)	venzo	he vencido
(tú)	vences	has vencido
(él/ella/usted)	vence	ha vencido
(nosotros/as)	vencemos	hemos vencido
(vosotros/as)	vencéis	habéis vencido
(ellos/ellas/ ustedes)	vencen	han vencido

	PRETERITE	IMPERFECT
(yo)	vencí	vencía
(tú)	venciste	vencías
(él/ella/usted)	venció	vencía
(nosotros/as)	vencimos	vencíamos
(vosotros/as)	vencisteis	vencíais
(ellos/ellas/ ustedes)	vencieron	vencían

GERUND	PAST PARTICIPLE
venciendo	vencido

EXAMPLE PHRASES

Tienes que **vencer** el miedo. You must overcome your fear.
Finalmente lo **venció** el sueño. He was finally overcome by sleep.
Lo **vencía** la curiosidad. His curiosity got the better of him.

vencer

	FUTURE	CONDITIONAL
(yo)	**venceré**	**vencería**
(tú)	**vencerás**	**vencerías**
(él/ella/usted)	**vencerá**	**vencería**
(nosotros/as)	**venceremos**	**venceríamos**
(vosotros/as)	**venceréis**	**venceríais**
(ellos/ellas/ ustedes)	**vencerán**	**vencerían**

	PRESENT SUBJUNCTIVE	IMPERFECT SUBJUNCTIVE
(yo)	**venza**	**venciera** *or* **venciese**
(tú)	**venzas**	**vencieras** *or* **vencieses**
(él/ella/usted)	**venza**	**venciera** *or* **venciese**
(nosotros/as)	**venzamos**	**venciéramos** *or* **venciésemos**
(vosotros/as)	**venzáis**	**vencierais** *or* **vencieseis**
(ellos/ellas/ ustedes)	**venzan**	**vencieran** *or* **venciesen**

IMPERATIVE

vence / venced

Use the present subjunctive in all cases other than these tú and vosotros affirmative forms.

EXAMPLE PHRASES

Nuestro ejército **vencerá**. Our army will be victorious.

No dejes que te **venza** la impaciencia. Don't let your impatience get the better of you.

Remember that subject pronouns are not used very often in Spanish.

venir (to come)

	PRESENT	PRESENT PERFECT
(yo)	**vengo**	**he venido**
(tú)	**vienes**	**has venido**
(él/ella/usted)	**viene**	**ha venido**
(nosotros/as)	**venimos**	**hemos venido**
(vosotros/as)	**venís**	**habéis venido**
(ellos/ellas/ ustedes)	**vienen**	**han venido**

	PRETERITE	IMPERFECT
(yo)	**vine**	**venía**
(tú)	**viniste**	**venías**
(él/ella/usted)	**vino**	**venía**
(nosotros/as)	**vinimos**	**veníamos**
(vosotros/as)	**vinisteis**	**veníais**
(ellos/ellas/ ustedes)	**vinieron**	**venían**

GERUND	PAST PARTICIPLE
viniendo	**venido**

EXAMPLE PHRASES

Vengo a menudo. I come here often.

La casa **se está viniendo** abajo. The house is falling apart.

Vino en taxi. He came by taxi.

Vinieron a verme al hospital. They came to see me in the hospital.

La noticia **venía** en el periódico. The news was in the paper.

Remember that subject pronouns are not used very often in Spanish.

venir

	FUTURE	CONDITIONAL
(yo)	**vendré**	**vendría**
(tú)	**vendrás**	**vendrías**
(él/ella/usted)	**vendrá**	**vendría**
(nosotros/as)	**vendremos**	**vendríamos**
(vosotros/as)	**vendréis**	**vendríais**
(ellos/ellas/ ustedes)	**vendrán**	**vendrían**

	PRESENT SUBJUNCTIVE	IMPERFECT SUBJUNCTIVE
(yo)	**venga**	**viniera** *or* **viniese**
(tú)	**vengas**	**vinieras** *or* **vinieses**
(él/ella/usted)	**venga**	**viniera** *or* **viniese**
(nosotros/as)	**vengamos**	**viniéramos** *or* **viniésemos**
(vosotros/as)	**vengáis**	**vinierais** *or* **vinieseis**
(ellos/ellas/ ustedes)	**vengan**	**vinieran** *or* **viniesen**

IMPERATIVE

ven / venid

Use the present subjunctive in all cases other than these tú and vosotros affirmative forms.

EXAMPLE PHRASES

¿Crees que **vendrá**? Do you think he'll come?

A mí me **vendría** mejor el sábado. Saturday would be better for me.

No **vengas** si no quieres. Don't come if you don't want to.

¡**Ven** aquí! Come here!

Remember that subject pronouns are not used very often in Spanish.

ver (to see)

	PRESENT	PRESENT PERFECT
(yo)	**veo**	**he visto**
(tú)	**ves**	**has visto**
(él/ella/usted)	**ve**	**ha visto**
(nosotros/as)	**vemos**	**hemos visto**
(vosotros/as)	**veis**	**habéis visto**
(ellos/ellas/ ustedes)	**ven**	**han visto**

	PRETERITE	IMPERFECT
(yo)	**vi**	**veía**
(tú)	**viste**	**veías**
(él/ella/usted)	**vio**	**veía**
(nosotros/as)	**vimos**	**veíamos**
(vosotros/as)	**visteis**	**veíais**
(ellos/ellas/ ustedes)	**vieron**	**veían**

GERUND	PAST PARTICIPLE
viendo	**visto**

EXAMPLE PHRASES

No **veo** muy bien. I can't see very well.

Están viendo la televisión. They're watching TV.

No la **había visto**. I hadn't seen her.

¿**Viste** lo que pasó? Did you see what happened?

Los **veía** a todos desde la ventana. I could see them all from the window.

Remember that subject pronouns are not used very often in Spanish.

ver

	FUTURE	CONDITIONAL
(yo)	**veré**	**vería**
(tú)	**verás**	**verías**
(él/ella/usted)	**verá**	**vería**
(nosotros/as)	**veremos**	**veríamos**
(vosotros/as)	**veréis**	**veríais**
(ellos/ellas/ ustedes)	**verán**	**verían**

	PRESENT SUBJUNCTIVE	IMPERFECT SUBJUNCTIVE
(yo)	**vea**	**viera** *or* **viese**
(tú)	**veas**	**vieras** *or* **vieses**
(él/ella/usted)	**vea**	**viera** *or* **viese**
(nosotros/as)	**veamos**	**viéramos** *or* **viésemos**
(vosotros/as)	**veáis**	**vierais** *or* **vieseis**
(ellos/ellas/ ustedes)	**vean**	**vieran** *or* **viesen**

IMPERATIVE

ve / ved

Use the present subjunctive in all cases other than these tú and vosotros affirmative forms.

EXAMPLE PHRASES

Eso ya se **verá**. We'll see.

¡Si **vieras** cómo ha cambiado todo aquello! If you could see how all that has changed!

Veamos, ¿qué le pasa? Let's see now, what's the matter?

Remember that subject pronouns are not used very often in Spanish.

verter (to pour)

	PRESENT	PRESENT PERFECT
(yo)	vierto	he vertido
(tú)	viertes	has vertido
(él/ella/usted)	vierte	ha vertido
(nosotros/as)	vertemos	hemos vertido
(vosotros/as)	vertéis	habéis vertido
(ellos/ellas/ ustedes)	vierten	han vertido

	PRETERITE	IMPERFECT
(yo)	vertí	vertía
(tú)	vertiste	vertías
(él/ella/usted)	vertió	vertía
(nosotros/as)	vertimos	vertíamos
(vosotros/as)	vertisteis	vertíais
(ellos/ellas/ ustedes)	vertieron	vertían

GERUND
vertiendo

PAST PARTICIPLE
vertido

EXAMPLE PHRASES

Primero **viertes** el contenido del sobre en un tazón. First you empty the contents of the package into a bowl.

Vertió un poco de leche en la cacerola. He poured some milk into the saucepan.

Se vertían muchos residuos radioactivos en el mar. A lot of nuclear waste was dumped in the sea.

Remember that subject pronouns are not used very often in Spanish.

verter

	FUTURE	CONDITIONAL
(yo)	verteré	vertería
(tú)	verterás	verterías
(él/ella/usted)	verterá	vertería
(nosotros/as)	verteremos	verteríamos
(vosotros/as)	verteréis	verteríais
(ellos/ellas/ ustedes)	verterán	verterían

	PRESENT SUBJUNCTIVE	IMPERFECT SUBJUNCTIVE
(yo)	vierta	vertiera *or* vertiese
(tú)	viertas	vertieras *or* vertieses
(él/ella/usted)	vierta	vertiera *or* vertiese
(nosotros/as)	vertamos	vertiéramos *or* vertiésemos
(vosotros/as)	vertáis	vertierais *or* vertieseis
(ellos/ellas/ ustedes)	viertan	vertieran *or* vertiesen

IMPERATIVE

vierte / verted

Use the present subjunctive in all cases other than these tú and vosotros affirmative forms.

EXAMPLE PHRASES

Se verterán muchas lágrimas por esto. A lot of tears will be shed over this.

Ten cuidado no **viertas** el café. Be careful you don't knock over the coffee.

vestir (to dress)

	PRESENT	PRESENT PERFECT
(yo)	visto	he vestido
(tú)	vistes	has vestido
(él/ella/usted)	viste	ha vestido
(nosotros/as)	vestimos	hemos vestido
(vosotros/as)	vestís	habéis vestido
(ellos/ellas/ ustedes)	visten	han vestido

	PRETERITE	IMPERFECT
(yo)	vestí	vestía
(tú)	vestiste	vestías
(él/ella/usted)	vistió	vestía
(nosotros/as)	vestimos	vestíamos
(vosotros/as)	vestisteis	vestíais
(ellos/ellas/ ustedes)	vistieron	vestían

GERUND
vistiendo

PAST PARTICIPLE
vestido

EXAMPLE PHRASES

Tengo una familia que **vestir** y alimentar. I have a family to feed and clothe.
Viste bien. She's a sharp dresser.
Estaba vistiendo a los niños. I was dressing the children.
Me vestí en cinco minutos. I got dressed in five minutes.

Remember that subject pronouns are not used very often in Spanish.

vestir

	FUTURE	CONDITIONAL
(yo)	**vestiré**	**vestiría**
(tú)	**vestirás**	**vestirías**
(él/ella/usted)	**vestirá**	**vestiría**
(nosotros/as)	**vestiremos**	**vestiríamos**
(vosotros/as)	**vestiréis**	**vestiríais**
(ellos/ellas/ ustedes)	**vestirán**	**vestirían**

	PRESENT SUBJUNCTIVE	IMPERFECT SUBJUNCTIVE
(yo)	**vista**	**vistiera** *or* **vistiese**
(tú)	**vistas**	**vistieras** *or* **vistieses**
(él/ella/usted)	**vista**	**vistiera** *or* **vistiese**
(nosotros/as)	**vistamos**	**vistiéramos** *or* **vistiésemos**
(vosotros/as)	**vistáis**	**vistierais** *or* **vistieseis**
(ellos/ellas/ ustedes)	**vistan**	**vistieran** *or* **vistiesen**

IMPERATIVE

viste / vestid

Use the present subjunctive in all cases other than these **tú** *and* **vosotros** *affirmative forms.*

EXAMPLE PHRASES

Se vistió de princesa. She dressed up as a princess.

Vestía jeans y una camiseta. He was wearing jeans and a shirt.

Su padre **vestirá** de uniforme. Her father will wear a uniform.

¡**Vístete** de una vez! For the last time, go and get dressed!

Remember that subject pronouns are not used very often in Spanish.

vivir (to live)

	PRESENT	PRESENT PERFECT
(yo)	vivo	he vivido
(tú)	vives	has vivido
(él/ella/usted)	vive	ha vivido
(nosotros/as)	vivimos	hemos vivido
(vosotros/as)	vivís	habéis vivido
(ellos/ellas/ ustedes)	viven	han vivido

	PRETERITE	IMPERFECT
(yo)	viví	vivía
(tú)	viviste	vivías
(él/ella/usted)	vivió	vivía
(nosotros/as)	vivimos	vivíamos
(vosotros/as)	vivisteis	vivíais
(ellos/ellas/ ustedes)	vivieron	vivían

GERUND
viviendo

PAST PARTICIPLE
vivido

EXAMPLE PHRASES

Me gusta **vivir** sola. I like living on my own.
¿Dónde **vives**? Where do you live?
Siempre **viveron** muy bien. They always had a very comfortable life.
Vivían de su pensión. They lived on his pension.

Remember that subject pronouns are not used very often in Spanish.

vivir

	FUTURE	CONDITIONAL
(yo)	**viviré**	**viviría**
(tú)	**vivirás**	**vivirías**
(él/ella/usted)	**vivirá**	**viviría**
(nosotros/as)	**viviremos**	**viviríamos**
(vosotros/as)	**viviréis**	**viviríais**
(ellos/ellas/ ustedes)	**vivirán**	**vivirían**

	PRESENT SUBJUNCTIVE	IMPERFECT SUBJUNCTIVE
(yo)	**viva**	**viviera** *or* **viviese**
(tú)	**vivas**	**vivieras** *or* **vivieses**
(él/ella/usted)	**viva**	**viviera** *or* **viviese**
(nosotros/as)	**vivamos**	**viviéramos** *or* **viviésemos**
(vosotros/as)	**viváis**	**vivierais** *or* **vivieseis**
(ellos/ellas/ ustedes)	**vivan**	**vivieran** *or* **viviesen**

IMPERATIVE

vive / vivid

Use the present subjunctive in all cases other than these tú and vosotros affirmative forms.

EXAMPLE PHRASES

Viviremos en el centro de la ciudad. We'll live downtown.

Si pudiéramos, **viviríamos** en el campo. We'd live in the country if we could.

Si **vivieran** más cerca, nos veríamos más a menudo. We'd see each other more often if you lived nearer.

¡**Viva**! Hurray!

Remember that subject pronouns are not used very often in Spanish.

volcar (to overturn)

	PRESENT	PRESENT PERFECT
(yo)	vuelco	he volcado
(tú)	vuelcas	has volcado
(él/ella/usted)	vuelca	ha volcado
(nosotros/as)	volcamos	hemos volcado
(vosotros/as)	volcáis	habéis volcado
(ellos/ellas/ ustedes)	vuelcan	han volcado

	PRETERITE	IMPERFECT
(yo)	volqué	volcaba
(tú)	volcaste	volcabas
(él/ella/usted)	volcó	volcaba
(nosotros/as)	volcamos	volcábamos
(vosotros/as)	volcasteis	volcabais
(ellos/ellas/ ustedes)	volcaron	volcaban

GERUND
volcando

PAST PARTICIPLE
volcado

EXAMPLE PHRASES

La camioneta **volcó**. The van rolled over.

Se vuelca en su trabajo. She throws herself into her work.

volcar

	FUTURE	CONDITIONAL
(yo)	**volcaré**	**volcaría**
(tú)	**volcarás**	**volcarías**
(él/ella/usted)	**volcará**	**volcaría**
(nosotros/as)	**volcaremos**	**volcaríamos**
(vosotros/as)	**volcaréis**	**volcaríais**
(ellos/ellas/ ustedes)	**volcarán**	**volcarían**

	PRESENT SUBJUNCTIVE	IMPERFECT SUBJUNCTIVE
(yo)	**vuelque**	**volcara** *or* **volcase**
(tú)	**vuelques**	**volcaras** *or* **volcases**
(él/ella/usted)	**vuelque**	**volcara** *or* **volcase**
(nosotros/as)	**volquemos**	**volcáramos** *or* **volcásemos**
(vosotros/as)	**volquéis**	**volcarais** *or* **volcaseis**
(ellos/ellas/ ustedes)	**vuelquen**	**volcaran** *or* **volcasen**

IMPERATIVE

vuelca / volcad

Use the present subjunctive in all cases other than these **tú** *and* **vosotros** *affirmative forms.*

EXAMPLE PHRASES

Si sigues moviéndote, harás que **vuelque** el bote. If you keep on moving like that, you'll make the boat capsize.

Ten cuidado, no **vuelques** el vaso. Be careful not to knock over the glass.

Vuelca el contenido sobre la cama. Empty the contents onto the bed.

volver (to return; to go/come back)

	PRESENT	PRESENT PERFECT
(yo)	vuelvo	he vuelto
(tú)	vuelves	has vuelto
(él/ella/usted)	vuelve	ha vuelto
(nosotros/as)	volvemos	hemos vuelto
(vosotros/as)	volvéis	habéis vuelto
(ellos/ellas/ ustedes)	vuelven	han vuelto

	PRETERITE	IMPERFECT
(yo)	volví	volvía
(tú)	volviste	volvías
(él/ella/usted)	volvió	volvía
(nosotros/as)	volvimos	volvíamos
(vosotros/as)	volvisteis	volvíais
(ellos/ellas/ ustedes)	volvieron	volvían

GERUND
volviendo

PAST PARTICIPLE
vuelto

EXAMPLE PHRASES

Mi padre **vuelve** mañana. My father's coming back tomorrow.
Volvió a casa. He went back home.
Volvía agotado de trabajar. I used to come back from work exhausted.

Remember that subject pronouns are not used very often in Spanish.

volver

	FUTURE	CONDITIONAL
(yo)	**volveré**	**volvería**
(tú)	**volverás**	**volverías**
(él/ella/usted)	**volverá**	**volvería**
(nosotros/as)	**volveremos**	**volveríamos**
(vosotros/as)	**volveréis**	**volveríais**
(ellos/ellas/ ustedes)	**volverán**	**volverían**

	PRESENT SUBJUNCTIVE	IMPERFECT SUBJUNCTIVE
(yo)	**vuelva**	**volviera** *or* **volviese**
(tú)	**vuelvas**	**volvieras** *or* **volvieses**
(él/ella/usted)	**vuelva**	**volviera** *or* **volviese**
(nosotros/as)	**volvamos**	**volviéramos** *or* **volviésemos**
(vosotros/as)	**volváis**	**volvierais** *or* **volvieseis**
(ellos/ellas/ ustedes)	**vuelvan**	**volvieran** *or* **volviesen**

IMPERATIVE

vuelve / volved

Use the present subjunctive in all cases other than these tú and vosotros affirmative forms.

EXAMPLE PHRASES

Todo **volverá** a la normalidad. Everything will return to normal.

Yo **volvería** a intentarlo. I'd try again.

No quiero que **vuelvas** allí. I don't want you to go back there.

No **vuelvas** por aquí. Don't come back here.

¡**Vuelve** a la cama! Go back to bed!

Remember that subject pronouns are not used very often in Spanish.

zurcir (to darn)

	PRESENT	PRESENT PERFECT
(yo)	zurzo	he zurcido
(tú)	zurces	has zurcido
(él/ella/usted)	zurce	ha zurcido
(nosotros/as)	zurcimos	hemos zurcido
(vosotros/as)	zurcís	habéis zurcido
(ellos/ellas/ ustedes)	zurcen	han zurcido

	PRETERITE	IMPERFECT
(yo)	zurcí	zurcía
(tú)	zurciste	zurcías
(él/ella/usted)	zurció	zurcía
(nosotros/as)	zurcimos	zurcíamos
(vosotros/as)	zurcisteis	zurcíais
(ellos/ellas/ ustedes)	zurcieron	zurcían

GERUND
zurciendo

PAST PARTICIPLE
zurcido

EXAMPLE PHRASES

¿Quién le **zurce** los calcetines? Who darns his socks?

Las sábanas estaban **zurcidas**. The sheets had been mended.

Remember that subject pronouns are not used very often in Spanish.

zurcir

	FUTURE	CONDITIONAL
(yo)	zurciré	zurciría
(tú)	zurcirás	zurcirías
(él/ella/usted)	zurcirá	zurciría
(nosotros/as)	zurciremos	zurciríamos
(vosotros/as)	zurciréis	zurciríais
(ellos/ellas/ ustedes)	zurcirán	zurcirían

	PRESENT SUBJUNCTIVE	IMPERFECT SUBJUNCTIVE
(yo)	zurza	zurciera *or* zurciese
(tú)	zurzas	zurcieras *or* zurcieses
(él/ella/usted)	zurza	zurciera *or* zurciese
(nosotros/as)	zurzamos	zurciéramos *or* zurciésemos
(vosotros/as)	zurzáis	zurcierais *or* zurcieseis
(ellos/ellas/ ustedes)	zurzan	zurcieran *or* zurciesen

IMPERATIVE

zurce / zurcid

Use the present subjunctive in all cases other than these tú and vosotros affirmative forms.

Remember that subject pronouns are not used very often in Spanish.

How to use the Verb Index

The verbs in bold are the model verbs which you will find in the Verb Tables. All the other verbs follow one of these patterns, so the number next to each verb indicates which pattern fits this particular verb. For example, **acampar** (*to camp*) follows the same pattern as **hablar** (number 118 in the Verb Tables).

All the verbs are in alphabetical order. Superior numbers ([1] etc) refer you to notes on page 246. These notes explain any differences between verbs and their model.

abandonar 118
abastecer 58
abolir 2
abollar 118
abombar 118
abonar 118
abortar 118
abrasar 118
abrazar 60
abrigar 156
abrir 4
abrochar 118
absorber 48
abstenerse 214
abultar 118
aburrir 234
abusar 118
acabar 118
acampar 118
acariciar 118
acatarrarse 118
acceder 48
acelerar 118
acentuar 6
aceptar 118
acercar 194
acertar 162
aclarar 118
acobardarse 68
acoger 96
acompañar 118
aconsejar 118
acordar 56
acostar 56
acostumbrar 118
actuar 6
acudir 234
acurrucarse 68
acusar 118
adaptar 118
adecuar 118
adelantar 118
adelgazar 60
adivinar 118
admirar 118
admitir 234
adoptar 118
adorar 118
adornar 118
adquirir 8
advertir 10
afectar 118
afeitar 118
aficionar 118
afilar 118
afiliarse 68
afinar 118
afirmar 118
aflojar 118
afrontar 118
agachar 118
agarrar 118
agitar 118
aglomerarse 68
agobiar 118
agotar 118
agradar 118
agradecer 58
agrupar 118
aguantar 118
ahogar 156
ahorcar 194
ahorrar 118
ajustar 118
alabar 118
alardear 118
alargar 156
alcanzar 60
alegrar 118
alejar 118
aliarse 88
aligerar 118
alimentar 118
aliviar 118
almacenar 118
almorzar 108
alojar 118
alquilar 118
alterar 118
alternar 118
alucinar 118
aludir 234
alzar 60
amamantar 118
amanecer 12
amar 118
amargar 156
amarrar 118
amenazar 60
amontonar 118
amortiguar 30
ampliar 88
amputar 118
amueblar 118
analizar 60
andar 14
animar 118
anochecer[1] 58
anotar 118
anticipar 118
antojarse 68
anular 118
anunciar 118
añadir 234
apagar 156
apañar 118
aparcar 194
aparecer 58
aparentar 118
apartar 118
apasionarse 68
apearse 68
apellidar 118
apestar 118
apetecer 58
aplastar 118
aplaudir 234
aplazar 60
aplicar 194
apoderarse 16
aportar 118
apostar 56
apoyar 118
apreciar 118
aprender 48
apresurarse 68
apretar 162
aprobar 18
aprovechar 118
aproximar 118
apuntar 118
apuñalar 118
apurar 118
arañar 118
arar 118
archivar 118
arder 48
armar 118
arrancar 20
arrasar 118
arrastrar 118
arrebatar 118
arreglar 118
arrepentirse 22
arrestar 118
arriesgar 156
arrimar 118
arrodillarse 68
arrojar 118
arropar 118
arrugar 156
arruinar 118
asaltar 118
asar 118
ascender 86
asegurar 118
asesinar 118
asfixiar 118
asimilar 118
asistir 234
asociar 118
asolear 118
asomar 118
asombrar 118
asumir 234
asustar 118
atacar 194
atar 118
atardecer[1] 58
atender 86
aterrizar 60
atiborrar 118
atracar 194
atraer 220
atrapar 118
atravesar 24
atreverse 48
atropellar 118
aumentar 118
aunar 26
autorizar 60
avanzar 60
aventajar 118
aventar 162
avergonzar 28
averiarse 88
averiguar 30
avisar 118
ayudar 118
azotar 118
bailar 118
bajar 118
bañar 118
barnizar 60
barrer 48
basar 118
bastar 118
batir 234
beber 48
bendecir 32
beneficiar 118
besar 118

bloquear 118
bombardear 118
bordar 118
borrar 118
bostezar 60
botar 118
brillar 118
brincar 194
brindar 118
bromear 118
brotar 118
bucear 118
burlar 118
buscar 194
caber 34
caducar 194
caer 36
calar 118
calcar 194
calcular 118
calentar 162
calificar 194
callar 118
calmar 118
cambiar 38
caminar 118
cancelar 118
cansar 118
cantar 118
capacitar 118
capturar 118
cargar 156
casar 118
cascar 194
castigar 156
causar 118
cavar 118
cazar 40
ceder 48
celebrar 118
cenar 118
cepillar 118
cerrar 42
chapotear 118
charlar 118
chillar 118
chirriar 88
chocar 194
chupar 118
circular 118
citar 118
clasificar 194
clavar 118
cobrar 118
cocer 44
cocinar 118
coger 96
coincidir 234
cojear 118
colaborar 118
colar 56
coleccionar 118
colgar 46
colocar 194
colonizar 60
combinar 118
comentar 118
comenzar 82
comer 48
compadecer 58
comparar 118
compartir 234
compensar 118
competir 160
complacer 148
completar 118
complicar 194
componer 168
comportarse 68
comprar 118
comprender 48
comprobar 56
comprometer 48
comunicar 194
concebir 160
concentrar 118
concertar 162
condenar 118
conducir 50
conectar 118
confesar 162
confiar 88
confirmar 118
conformar 118
confundir 234
congelar 118
conmemorar 118
conmover 146
conocer 52
conquistar 118
conseguir 200
consentir 202
conservar 118
considerar 118
consistir 234
consolar 56
constar 118
construir 54
consultar 118
consumar 118
consumir 234
contagiar 118
contaminar 118
contar 56
contener 214
contentar 118
contestar 118
continuar 6
contradecir 66
contraer 220
contrastar 118
contratar 118
contribuir 54
controlar 118
convencer 58
convenir 226
conversar 118
convertir 202
convocar 194
cooperar 118
copiar 118
corregir 80
correr 48
corresponder 48
cortar 118
cosechar 118
coser 48
costar 56
crear 118
crecer 58
creer 136
criar 88
criticar 194
crujir 234
cruzar 60
cuadrar 118
cuajar 118
cubrir 62
cuchichear 118
cuidar 118
cultivar 118
cumplir 234
curar 118
dañar 118
dar 64
debatir 234
deber 48
debilitar 118
decepcionar 118
decidir 234
decir 66
declarar 118
decorar 118
dedicar 194
deducir 50
defender 86
definir 234
deformar 118
defraudar 118
dejar 118
delatar 118
deletrear 118
demostrar 56
denunciar 118
depender 48
deprimir 234
derramar 118
derretir 160
derribar 118
derrotar 118
derrumbar 118
desabrochar 118
desacertar 162
desafiar 88
desafinar 118
desahogar 156
desalojar 118
desanimar 118
desaparecer 58
desaprovechar 118
desarrollar 118
desatar 118
desayunar 118
decalzar 60
descansar 118
descargar 156
descender 86
descolgar 46
desconcertar 162
desconectar 118
desconfiar 88
descontar 56
descoser 48
describir 98
descubrir 62
descuidar 118
desdoblar 118
desear 118
desembarcar 194
desembocar 194
desempeñar 118
desengañar 118
desenredar 118
desenvolver 238
desesperar 118
desfilar 118
desgastar 118
deshacer 120
deshinchar 118
desilusionar 118
desinfectar 118
desinflar 118
deslizar 60
deslumbrar 118
desmayar 118
desmontar 118
desnudar 118
desobedecer 58
desorientar 118
despachar 118
despedir 160
despegar 156
despejar 118
desperezarse 60
despertar 162
despistar 118
desplegar 150
despreciar 118
desprender 48
despreocuparse 68
destacar 194
destapar 118
desteñir 180
destinar 118
destornillar 118
destrozar 60
destruir 54
desvelar 118
desviar 88
detener 70
deteriorar 118
determinar 118
detestar 118
devolver 238
devorar 118
dibujar 118
diferenciar 118
dificultar 118
digerir 202
diluir 54
dimitir 234
dirigir 72
disculpar 118
discutir 234
diseñar 118
disfrazar 60
disfrutar 118
disgustar 118
disimular 118
disminuir 54
disolver 184
disparar 118
disponer 168
disputar 118
distinguir 74
distraer 220
distribuir 54
disuadir 234
divertir 76
dividir 234
divorciarse 68
divulgar 156
doblar 118
doler 146

dominar 118
dormir 78
drogar 156
ducharse 68
durar 118
echar 118
editar 118
educar 194
efectuar 6
ejectuar 118
ejercer 224
elaborar 118
elegir 80
elevar 118
eliminar 118
elogiar 118
embalar 118
embarcar 194
emborrachar 118
embrollar 118
emigrar 118
emitir 234
emocionar 118
empalmar 118
empañar 118
empapar 118
empapelar 118
empaquetar 118
empastar 118
empatar 118
empeñar 118
empeorar 118
empezar 82
emplear 118
empujar 118
enamorar 118
encabezar 60
encajar 118
encantar 118
encarcelar 118
encargar 156
encender 86
encerrar 162
encoger 96
encontrar 56
enchufar 118
enderezar 60
endulzar 60
endurecer 58
enemistar 118
enfadar 118
enfermar 118
enfocar 194
enfrentarse 84
enfriar 88
enganchar 118
engañar 118
engordar 118
enlazar 60
enloquecer 58
enmascarar 118
enojar 118
enorgullecerse 58
enredar 118
enriquecer 58
enrollar 118
enroscar 194
ensanchar 118
ensayar 118
enseñar 118
ensuciar 118
entender 86
enterarse 68
enterrar 162
entrar 118
entregar 156
entrenarse 68
entretener 214
entrevistar 118
entrometerse 48
entusiasmar 118
enumerar 118
envejecer 58
enviar 88
envidiar 118
envolver 238
equivaler 222
equivocarse 90
erguir 92
erigir 72
errar 94
eructar 118
escabullirse 112
escalar 118
escandalizar 60
escapar 118
escarbar 118
escocer 44
escoger 96
esconder 48
escribir 98
escuchar 118
escupir 234
escurrir 234
esforzarse 100
esfumarse 68
esmerarse 68
espabilar 118
esperar 118
espiar 88
espirar 118
esquiar 88
esquivar 118
establecer 102
estacionar 118
estafar 118
estallar 118
estar 104
estimular 118
estirar 118
estorbar 118
estornudar 118
estrangular 118
estrechar 118
estrellar 118
estrenar 118
estropear 118
estrujar 118
estudiar 118
evacuar 106
evadir 234
evaluar 6
evaporar 118
evitar 118
evolucionar 118
exagerar 118
examinar 118
exceder 48
exceptuar 6
excitar 118
exclamar 118
excluir 54
exhibir 234
exigir 72
existir 234
experimentar 118
explicar 194
explorar 118
explotar 118
exponer 168
exportar 118
expresar 118
exprimir 234
expulsar 118
extender 86
extinguir 74
extraer 220
extrañar 118
extraviar 88
fabricar 194
facilitar 118
facturar 118
fallar 118
fallecer 58
falsificar 194
faltar 118
fastidiar 118
favorecer 58
felicitar 118
festejar 118
fiar 88
fichar 118
figurar 118
fijar 118
filmar 118
filtrar 118
financiar 118
fingir 72
firmar 118
fisgar 156
flotar 118
fluctuar 6
fluir 54
fomentar 118
formar 118
forrar 118
forzar 108
fotocopiar 118
fracasar 118
fregar 150
freír 110
frenar 118
frotar 118
fruncir 240
fugarse 68
fumar 118
funcionar 118
fundamentar 118
fundar 118
fundir 234
galopar 118
ganar 118
garantizar 60
gastar 118
generalizar 60
generar 118
girar 118
gobernar 162
golpear 118
gotear 118
gozar 60
grabar 118
graduar 6
granizar[1] 60
gritar 118
gruñir 112
guardar 118
guiar 114
guiñar 118
guisar 118
gustar 118
haber 116
habitar 118
habituar 6
hablar 118
hacer 120
halagar 156
hallar 118
hartar 118
hay 122
helar[1] 162
heredar 118
herir 124
hervir 202
hinchar 118
hojear 118
hospedar 118
huir 126
hundir 234
hurgar 156
idear 118
identificar 194
ignorar 118
iluminar 118
imaginar 118
imitar 118
impedir 160
imponer 128
importar 118
impresionar 118
imprimir 130
improvisar 118
impulsar 118
inaugurar 118
incendiar 118
inclinar 118
incluir 54
incorporar 118
increpar 118
indemnizar 60
indicar 194
indignar 118
inflar 118
influenciar 118
influir 54
informar 118
ingeniar 118
ingresar 118
inscribir 98
insinuar 6
insistir 234
insolarse 68
instalar 118
insultar 118
intentar 118
interesar 118
interpretar 118
interrogar 156
interrumpir 234
intervenir 226
introducir 50
inundar 118
invadir 234
inventar 118

invertir 202
invitar 118
inyectar 118
ir 132
irritar 118
izar 60
jalar 118
jubilar 118
jugar 134
juntar 118
jurar 118
justificar 194
juzgar 156
ladrar 118
lamentar 118
lamer 48
lanzar 60
latir 234
lavar 118
leer 136
levantar 138
liar 88
liberar 118
librar 118
ligar 156
limitar 118
limpiar 118
llamar 118
llegar 156
llenar 118
llevar 118
llorar 118
llover[1] 140
localizar 60
lograr 118
lucir 142
luchar 118
machacar 194
madrugar 156
malgastar 118
maltratar 118
mamar 118
manchar 118
mandar 118
manejar 118
manifestar 162
manipular 118
mantener 214
maquillar 118
marcar 194
marchar 118
marear 118
masticar 194
medir 160
mejorar 118
mencionar 118
mentir 202
merendar 162
meter 48
mirar 118
mojar 118
moler 146
montar 118
morder 146
morir 144
mover 146
mudar 118
multiplicar 194
nacer 148
nadar 118
narrar 118
naturalizarse 60
navegar 156
necesitar 118
negar 150
negociar 118
nevar[1] 162
nombrar 118
notar 118
notificar 194
nublarse[1] 68
obedecer 58
obligar 156
obrar 118
observar 118
obsesionar 118
obstinarse 68
obtener 214
ocasionar 118
ocultar 118
ocupar 118
ocurrir 234
odiar 118
ofender 48
ofrecer 58
oír 152
oler 154
olvidar 118
omitir 234
ondear 118
operar 118
opinar 118
oponer 168
optar 118
ordenar 118
ordeñar 118
organizar 60
originar 118
orinar 118
osar 118
oscilar 118
oscurecer 58
oxidar 118
padecer 58
pagar 156
palpar 118
palpitar 118
parar 118
parecer 58
parpadear 118
participar 118
partir 158
pasar 118
pasear 118
pasmar 118
pastar 118
patear 118
patinar 118
patrocinar 118
pecar 194
pedalear 118
pedir 160
pegar 156
peinar 118
pelar 118
pelear 118
pellizcar 194
pender 48
penetrar 118
pensar 162
percatarse 68
perder 164
perdonar 118
perfeccionar 118
perforar 118
perjudicar 194
perjurar 118
permanecer 58
permitir 234
perseguir 200
persuadir 234
pertenecer 58
pesar 118
pescar 194
pestañear 118
piar 88
picar 194
pillar 118
pinchar 118
pintar 118
pisar 118
pitar 118
planchar 118
planear 118
planificar 194
plantar 118
plantear 118
platicar 194
plegar 150
poder 166
podrir 234
poner 168
portarse 68
posar 118
poseer 136
posponer 168
practicar 194
precipitar 118
precisar 118
predecir 66
predicar 194
preferir 202
preguntar 118
premiar 118
prender 48
preocupar 118
preparar 118
prescindir 234
presenciar 118
presentar 118
presionar 118
prestar 118
presumir 234
pretender 48
prevenir 226
prever 228
privar 118
probar 56
proclamar 118
procurar 118
producir 50
programar 118
progresar 118
prohibir 170
prolongar 156
prometer 48
pronosticar 194
pronunciar 118
propagar 156
proponer 168
proporcionar 118
prosperar 118
proteger 96
protestar 118
provocar 194
proyectar 118
publicar 194
pudrir[2] 234
pulir 234
pulsar 118
quebrar 162
quedar 118
quejarse 68
quemar 118
querer 172
quitar 118
rajar 118
rallar 118
rapar 118
raptar 118
rascar 194
rasgar 156
rasurarse 68
rayar 118
reaccionar 118
realizar 60
rebajar 118
rebelarse 68
rebotar 118
recalcar 194
recargar 156
rechazar 60
recibir 234
reciclar 118
recitar 118
reclamar 118
recoger 96
recomendar 162
reconciliar 118
reconocer 58
reconstruir 54
recordar 56
recorrer 48
recortar 118
recostar 56
recuperar 118
recurrir 234
redactar 118
reducir 174
reembolsar 118
reemplazar 60
referir 202
reflexionar 118
reformar 118
refrescar 194
refugiarse 68
regalar 118
regañar 118
regar 150
regatear 118
registrar 118
regresar 118
regular 118
rehacer 120
rehogar 156
rehusar 176
reincorporarse 68
reír 178
relacionar 118
relajar 118
relucir 142
rellenar 118
remar 118
remedar 118

remediar 118
remitir 234
remojar 118
remover 146
rendir 160
renovar 56
rentar 118
reñir **180**
reparar 118
repartir 234
repasar 118
repetir **182**
repostar 118
reprobar 56
reprochar 118
reproducir 50
resaltar 118
resbalar 118
rescatar 118
reservar 118
resfriarse 88
resistir 234
resolver **184**
respaldar 118
respetar 118
respirar 118
responder 48
resquebrajar 118
restablecer 58
restar 118
restaurar 118
restregar 156
resultar 118
resumir 234
retar 118
retirar 118
retorcer 28
retransmitir 234
retrasar 118
retroceder 48
reunir **186**
revelar 118
reventar 162
revisar 118
revolver 238
rezar 60
ridiculizar 60
rizar 60
robar 118
rociar 88
rodar 56
rodear 118
rogar **188**
romper **190**
roncar 194
ronronear 118
rozar 60
ruborizarse 60
rugir 72
saber **192**
sacar **194**
sacudir 234
salir **196**
salpicar 194
saltar 118
saludar 118
salvar 118
sangrar 118
satisfacer **198**
sazonar 118
secar 194
secuestrar 118
seguir **200**
seleccionar 118
sembrar 162
sentar 162
sentir **202**
señalar 118
separar 118
ser **204**
serrar 162
servir 160
significar 194
silbar 118
sobrar 118
sobrevivir 234
soler **206**
solicitar 118
soltar **208**
solucionar 118
sonar **210**
sonreír 178
soñar 56
soplar 118
soportar 118
sorber 48
sorprender 48
sospechar 118
sostener 214
soterrar 118
subir 234
subrayar 118
subvencionar 118
suceder 48
sudar 118
sufrir 234
sugerir 202
sujetar 118
sumar 118
suministrar 118
superar 118
suplicar 194
suponer 168
suprimir 234
surgir 72
suspender 48
suspirar 118
sustituir 54
susurrar 118
tachar 118
taladrar 118
tallar 118
tambalearse 68
tantear 118
tapar 118
tapizar 60
tararear 118
tardar 118
tartamudear 118
tasar 118
tatuar 6
teclear 118
tejer 48
telefonear 118
televisar 118
temblar 162
temer **212**
tender 86
tener **214**
tensar 118
tentar 162
teñir 180
terciar 118
tergiversar 118
terminar 118
timar 118
tirar 118
tiritar 118
titubear 118
titularse 68
tocar **216**
tolerar 118
tomar 118
topar 118
torcer **218**
torear 118
torturar 118
toser 48
tostar 56
trabajar 118
traducir 50
traer **220**
tragar 156
traicionar 118
tramitar 118
tranquilizar 60
transformar 118
transmitir 234
transportar 118
trasladar 118
trasnochar 118
traspasar 118
trasplantar 118
tratar 118
trazar 60
trepar 118
trillar 118
trinchar 118
triturar 118
triunfar 118
tronar[1] 56
tronchar 118
tropezar 82
trotar 118
tumbar 118
turnarse 68
tutear 118
unir 234
untar 118
usar 118
utilizar 60
vaciar 88
vacilar 118
vacunar 118
vagar 156
valer **222**
valorar 118
variar 88
velar 118
vencer **224**
vendar 118
vender 48
vengar 156
venir **226**
ventilar 118
ver **228**
veranear 118
verificar 194
verter **230**
vestir **232**
viajar 118
vibrar 118
viciar 118
vigilar 118
vindicar 194
violar 118
visitar 118
vitorear 118
vituperar 118
vivificar 194
vivir **234**
volar 56
volcar **236**
volver **238**
vomitar 118
votar 118
zambullirse 112
zampar 118
zanjar 118
zarpar 118
zumbar 118
zurcir **240**
zurrar 118

Notes

[1] The verbs **anochecer**, **atardecer**, **granizar**, **helar**, **llover**, **nevar**, **nublarse** and **tronar** are used almost exclusively in the infinitive and third person singular forms.

[2] The **past participle** of the verb **pudrir** is **podrido**.